D0781852

ADOLESCENT RATIONALITY AND DEVELOPMENT

Cognition, Morality, and Identity

Third Edition

ADOLESCENT RATIONALITY AND DEVELOPMENT

Cognition, Morality, and Identity

Third Edition

David Moshman

University of Nebraska-Lincoln

Psychology Press
Taylor & Francis Group

New York   London

Psychology Press
Taylor & Francis Group
270 Madison Avenue
New York, NY 10016

Psychology Press
Taylor & Francis Group
27 Church Road
Hove, East Sussex BN3 2FA

© 2011 by Taylor and Francis Group, LLC
Psychology Press is an imprint of Taylor & Francis Group, an Informa business

Printed in the United States of America on acid-free paper
10 9 8 7 6 5 4 3 2 1

International Standard Book Number: 978-1-84872-860-8 (Hardback) 978-1-84872-861-5 (Paperback)

For permission to photocopy or use material electronically from this work, please access www.copyright.com (http://www.copyright.com/) or contact the Copyright Clearance Center, Inc. (CCC), 222 Rosewood Drive, Danvers, MA 01923, 978-750-8400. CCC is a not-for-profit organization that provides licenses and registration for a variety of users. For organizations that have been granted a photocopy license by the CCC, a separate system of payment has been arranged.

Trademark Notice: Product or corporate names may be trademarks or registered trademarks, and are used only for identification and explanation without intent to infringe.

Library of Congress Cataloging-in-Publication Data

Moshman, David.
    Adolescent rationality and development : cognition, morality, and identity / David Moshman. -- 3rd ed.
        p. cm.
    Rev. ed. of: Adolescent psychological development : rationality, morality, and identity. 2nd ed. 2005.
    Includes bibliographical references and index.
    ISBN 978-1-84872-860-8 (hbk. : alk. paper) -- ISBN 978-1-84872-861-5 (pbk. : alk. paper)
    1. Adolescent psychology--Textbooks. I. Moshman, David. Adolescent psychological development. II. Title.

BF724.M67 2011
155.5--dc22
                                      2010045913

Visit the Taylor & Francis Web site at
http://www.taylorandfrancis.com

and the Psychology Press Web site at
http://www.psypress.com

To Eric and Michael,
no longer adolescents, if they ever were,
and for my Sara,
always

Contents

PART II Moral Development

PART III Identity Formation

PART IV Development Beyond Childhood

Preface

The psychological literature on adolescence, already overwhelming when the first edition of this volume was published in 1999, continues to expand rapidly. Nobody can read it all, not even the authors and editors of the very largest textbooks and handbooks. It is less clear, however, that we are making progress in our understanding. Perhaps we are just accumulating more and more information about topics, contexts, and variables of current interest. The central thesis of this book is that a more coherent picture of adolescence can come from a renewed focus on rationality and development.

Laurence Steinberg and Amanda Morris (2001), reviewing work on adolescence published in the 1990s, began with an informal analysis of the contents of three top journals—*Child Development, Developmental Psychology*, and the *Journal of Research on Adolescence*—during that period. The most popular areas of inquiry, it turned out, were family context, problem behavior, and puberty, which together accounted for about two thirds of the literature. "Indeed," they pointed out, "if a visitor from another planet were to peruse the recent literature, he or she would likely conclude that teenagers' lives revolve around three things: parents, problems, and hormones" (pp. 84–85). Compared with previous work, research of the 1990s "was more contextual, inclusive, and cognizant of the interplay between genetic and environmental influences on development" (p. 101). That seemed a positive trend, but Steinberg and Morris wondered, as do I,

> what happened to research on the psychological development of the individual adolescent amidst all of this focus on context, diversity, and biology. The study of psychosocial development— the study of identity, autonomy, intimacy, and so forth—once a central focus of research on adolescence, waned considerably, as researchers turned their attention to contextual influences on behavior and functioning and to the study of individual differences. The study of cognitive development in adolescence has been moribund for some time now, replaced by studies of adolescent decision-making and judgment. ... No comprehensive theories of normative adolescent development have emerged to fill the voids created by the declining influence of Freud, Erikson, and

Piaget. ... As a consequence, although the field of adolescence research is certainly much bigger now than before, it is less coherent and, in a sense, less developmental. (pp. 101–102)

Nearly a decade later, the 1,400-page third edition of the two-volume *Handbook of Adolescent Psychology* (Lerner & Steinberg, 2009) devoted just 4 of its 39 chapters to core domains of adolescent psychological development: thinking, social cognition, moral cognition, and identity. The remaining 35 chapters addressed brains, puberty, gender, attachment, motivation, religion, and sexuality; interpersonal influences such as parents, peers, and romantic partners; institutional influences such as school, work, and media; and broader contexts such as neighborhoods, poverty, immigration, and globalization. A single chapter on "positive youth development" was followed by 6 chapters concerning risk, developmental disabilities, clinical interventions, internalizing problems, conduct disorders, aggression, delinquency, and substance use.

The huge and fractured literature of adolescence is a major problem for both students and scholars, not to mention interplanetary visitors. For students there is simply too much to learn, and the lack of coherence across topics and studies makes it difficult to achieve deeper levels of understanding. For scholars, the paucity of integrative visions forces research and theorizing to proceed along narrow paths, collecting and explaining data in ways specific to particular topics, tasks, contexts, and populations.

The central thesis of this book, as noted earlier, is that a more coherent picture of adolescence emerges from a renewed focus on rationality and development. The purpose of such a focus is not to return to some purported golden age of developmental theory. By reflecting carefully on what we mean by *development*, however, and examining the literature with this in mind, we can identify major developmental trends in rationality associated with adolescence. By focusing on such changes, we can move toward a rational constructivist conception of adolescent development that accommodates evidence regarding context and diversity without jettisoning the coherence of a developmental perspective.

Audience

I intended the second edition of this book—like the first—to be an advanced text, one that would be accessible to students, at least advanced undergraduates and graduate students, but that would also be useful to scholars, especially those interested in connections across standard topics and research programs in adolescence and in processes of developmental change. My aim was a book broad enough to serve as the foundation for a course in adolescence or adolescent development; brief enough to serve as a supplement for courses in cognitive, social, moral, or life span development; and deep enough to advance the theoretical understanding of developmental change in adolescence. I am pleased that the book continues to be praised by students and teachers and cited in scholarly books and journals. In preparing the third edition, I have been careful to keep both audiences in mind. The book does not assume any prior knowledge of psychology. Rather than try to cover everything about adolescence at an elementary level, however, it presents and builds on concepts in such a way as to reach core issues in the scholarly literature. The intent is to enable students to wrestle with the questions of concern to experts and to help experts see what concerns them from a larger perspective.

The Third Edition

The third edition is not just updated throughout (with a slightly modified title) but also substantially enriched and reorganized. Each of the book's four parts has been expanded from three chapters to four. Part I (Cognitive Development) provides expanded coverage of thinking and reasoning and a new chapter systematically addressing metacognition and epistemic cognition. Part II (Moral Development) provides a new chapter on principles and perspective taking and expanded coverage of controversies concerning the foundations of morality. Part III (Identity Formation) provides a new chapter on the relation of personal identity (as studied in developmental psychology) to social identity (as studied throughout the social sciences and humanities). Part IV (Development Beyond Childhood) concludes with a new chapter addressing current controversies concerning the rationality, maturity, and brains of adolescents. Throughout I have maintained and enhanced the focus of the first two editions on developmental processes. I have also provided more detail on key studies and methodologies, have boldfaced key terms, and have added a glossary.

I begin with an introduction to the concepts of adolescence, rationality, and development. Not all changes are developmental in the sense of advancing rationality, but profound developmental changes can be seen in three foundational literatures of adolescent development—cognitive development, moral development, and identity formation. The first three major parts of this volume address each of these three domains in turn. The fourth and final part provides a more general account of rationality and development in adolescence and beyond.

Whether you are a student or a scholar, I hope this overview and synthesis of the literature on adolescent rationality and development will provide a broad and useful perspective. If you are a visitor from another planet seeking to learn about terrestrial adolescents by perusing the literature, I hope this tiny piece of it can serve as a gateway to a developmental vision of the rest.

Acknowledgments

I am grateful to four reviewers for detailed and thoughtful reviews of the second edition that served me well throughout the preparation of this one: Kathleen M. Galotti, Carleton College; John C. Gibbs, The Ohio State University; Charles C. Helwig, University of Toronto; and Deanna Kuhn, Teachers College, Columbia University. I remain grateful to Dan Lapsley for an exceptionally thorough review of the manuscript for the first edition and also thank Augusto Blasi, Gus Carlo, Rick Lombardo, Laura Mussman, Bill Overton, Pina Tarricone, Katie Wane, several anonymous reviewers, and many other colleagues and students for helpful feedback and suggestions. I also thank Judi Amsel and Bill Webber for editorial support for the first two editions and especially Debra Riegert for all her help with this one.

David Moshman

Introduction

> Child psychology today is surprisingly free of interest in building general models of human development. The discipline is filled with hyperactive efforts to accumulate data, but attempts to make sense of the data, in terms of models of basic developmental processes, are relatively rare.
>
> —Jaan Valsiner
> *(1998, p. 189)*

Valsiner's (1998) observation continues to hold not only for child psychology but even more strongly for adolescent psychology. In this introduction I provide a framework for a developmental conceptualization of adolescence. Adolescents are rational agents making progress toward more advanced forms and levels of rationality in multiple domains. This is the basis, I propose, for understanding their development.

Adolescence

What is adolescence? Who counts as an adolescent? A common answer to the first question is that adolescence is the period between childhood and adulthood. The corresponding answer to the second is that an adolescent is someone who is no longer a child but not yet an adult. Chronologically, a common answer to the second question is that adolescents are, roughly, teenagers, ages 13 to 19. Putting these intuitive definitions together provides the easy inference that teenagers are no longer children but not yet adults. And from here it is a short step to the notion that (a) 13-year-olds have achieved a level of rationality and maturity beyond that of children but (b) even older teens have not yet achieved the rationality and maturity of adults in their 20s and beyond. This is perhaps the standard adult intuition about adolescents in modern societies.

When we consult research on cognitive, moral, and identity development, as we will throughout this volume, it turns out that the first part of the standard adult intuition is true but the second is false. Beginning at about age 11 or 12 years, young adolescents show forms of reasoning and levels of understanding not seen in children. Adolescents are qualitatively and categorically distinct from children. There is no empirical support, however, for a state of rationality or maturity common to most adults but rarely seen in adolescents. Even young adolescents often show forms and levels of rationality beyond the competence of many adults, and adults of all ages often fall short of rational standards met by many adolescents. Adolescents develop—in various domains and to varying degrees—but adults are not categorically distinct from adolescents in the same basic way that adolescents are categorically distinct from children.

With this in mind, it is not so surprising to find that in most societies for most of human history there was no such thing as adolescence, at least as we understand it (Epstein, 2007; Grotevant, 1998; Hine, 1999). The end of childhood marked the beginning of adulthood. Individuals in their early teens had completed whatever formal or informal education they were going to receive, were expected to fulfill adult roles, and were, for the most part, physically, cognitively, and socially capable of doing so. They were deemed adults, albeit young ones. The Jewish bar mitzvah, for example, has for centuries marked 13 years as the age when a boy becomes a man, with corresponding rights and responsibilities. Modern American Jews joke about a middle school student being an adult, but traditional societies were serious in their expectations of teens (see Chapter 16).

Even in modern Western cultures in which a prolonged adolescence is the norm, moreover, the beginning of adolescence is much more clear-cut than the end. Children undergo a variety of interrelated changes between ages 10 and 13. Physically, there are changes associated with puberty. Cognitively, as we will see in Chapters 1–3, there are fundamental changes in intellectual competence. Socially, there are a variety of changes associated with the transition to an increasingly peer-focused orientation. Educationally, preadolescents leave elementary school and face the demands of secondary education. Although developmental changes are gradual and occur at variable ages, it does seem that most children show sufficiently dramatic change between ages 10 and 13 that we can regard them as entering a new developmental stage—adolescence.

Determining when adolescence ends, on the other hand, is more problematic. Does it end with completing an expected level of education, beginning a steady job, getting married, or having children? Relying on such social milestones as criteria for adult-hood leads to the conclusion that adolescence in modern Western societies commonly lasts well past age 30, and many people never achieve adulthood. An alternative would be to apply psychological criteria of cognitive or emotional maturity. As we will see throughout this volume, however, many teenagers show forms or levels of rationality, morality, or identity that many older individuals have never achieved. A distinction between adolescents and adults, it turns out, is much more difficult to make than a distinction between adolescents and children.

This is not, in my view, merely a difficulty of terminology or definition. On the contrary, the difficulty in identifying a meaningful psychological basis for marking the end of adolescence reveals something fundamental about adolescents and their development. Given that adolescents are more clearly distinguishable from children than from adults (as we will see throughout this volume), I conclude that adolescence is best conceptualized not as the last stage of childhood, or even as an intermediate period between childhood and adulthood, but rather as the first phase of adulthood. This phase may be more distinct in modern Western societies than it has been traditionally, but that is a matter of history and culture, not a biological fact inherent in adolescence. Adolescence, then, may be defined as the period following childhood in which one is not yet accepted as an adult.

Development

Development is a process of change, but not all changes are **developmental** (Amsel & Renninger, 1997; Overton, 2006; Piaget, 1985; Sen, 1999; Valsiner, 1998; van Haaften, 1998, 2001; Werner, 1957). To examine and refine the concept of development, compare **development** with **learning**. A good example of a developmental change would be attaining sexual maturity in the course of reaching puberty. A good example of learning would be attaining the knowledge that one should stop on red and go on green. Each involves an important change in an individual. What differences between these lead us to see the former, but not the latter, as a developmental change? There are at least four worth noting: Developmental changes are (a) extended, (b) self-regulated, (c) qualitative, and (d) progressive.

First, developmental changes are long-term changes that extend over a substantial period of time. One difference between going through puberty and learning color rules is the time span. Puberty is achieved over a period of months or years. Learning when to stop or go, on the other hand, may occur in a matter of minutes, hours, or days. There is no sharp divide between short-term and long-term change. In general, however, **development** refers to a change process extended over a substantial period of time.

Second, developmental changes are directed or regulated from within. Another difference between going through puberty and learning color rules is that sexual maturation is an internally regulated process whereas learning to stop on red and go on green is more a function of environmental influence. Here again the difference may not be as sharp as it initially appears. Sexual maturation is affected by environmental factors such as nutrition; learning color rules involves internal mechanisms of perception and cognition. Nevertheless, to the extent that a process of change is **self-regulated** we are more likely to consider it developmental; to the extent that it is caused by external forces we are less likely to use this label.

Third, developmental changes are **qualitative** rather than merely quantitative. They are changes in kind, not just in amount. Attaining sexual maturity, to return to our example, makes one a different sort of organism; it is a qualitative change associated with the transition to puberty. Color rules, on the other hand, are among the many things we learn. Learning a particular rule represents a quantitative increase in the number of rules known, but it doesn't, in general, transform the organism. The term **development** generally refers to a qualitative transformation in some underlying structure rather than to quantitative or superficial changes (Boom, 2010; Valsiner, 1998; van Haaften, 1998, 2001).

Finally, development is **progressive**. At the very least it extends over time in some sort of systematic ongoing way. Prototypically, to develop is to make progress. Going through puberty and learning color rules differ in that the attainment of sexual maturity has a natural directionality whereas learning to stop on red does not. A society could decide, for example, that people should stop on green and go on red; in such a society that is what children would learn. An adult who moved from our society to one with different color rules would learn the new rules; an adult who moved from a different society to ours would learn our rules. Developmental change, by contrast, is progressive (Chandler, 1997; Piaget, 1985; Sen, 1999; Smith, 2009; Smith & Vonèche, 2006; van Haaften, 1998, 2001; Werner, 1957). What counts as progress, to be sure, may be a matter of dispute. Psychological maturity, as we shall see, is a more problematical concept than biological maturity; psychological progress is correspondingly difficult to identify. To the extent that a change is seen as progressive, however, it is more likely to be labeled developmental. To the extent that we see it as arbitrary, neutral, culturally relative, regressive, or pathological, by contrast, we are less likely to label it developmental.

We live in a world of change. To make sense of this, we need to distinguish different sorts of changes, including a category of changes that may be referred to as **development**. Although the distinction between developmental and nondevelopmental change is not sharp, it is nonetheless important. Change is developmental in those cases where it is extended, self-regulated, qualitative, and progressive.

Nature and Nurture

It is noteworthy that my example of developmental change in the previous section—attainment of puberty—was a biological one. In fact, the anatomical and physiological changes that take place in the maturation of immature organisms represent prototypical cases of developmental change. The maturation of immature organisms includes many examples of changes that (a) take place gradually over an extended period of time, (b) are largely directed by genetic and other internal factors, (c) involve qualitative changes in fundamental bodily structures and functions, and (d) represent progress toward maturity. In the realm of biology, no one doubts that development is a real and important phenomenon.

But what about psychological changes? It is clear that the **behavior** of organisms, as well as their anatomy and physiology, changes over time. With respect to human beings, there are major changes in perception, communication, thinking, personality, social relations, moral understanding, and so forth. Do such changes constitute development?

This is neither a frivolous question nor a matter of arbitrary terminology. On the contrary, responses to this question reflect basic assumptions about the nature of psychological change (Case, 1998; Overton, 2006; Valsiner, 1998). If one sees at least some psychological changes as emerging via extended, self-regulated progress toward qualitatively higher levels of psychological maturity, one is likely to be sympathetic to the notion of psychological development. Alternatively, if one sees only a variety of discrete changes caused by particular features of the environment, one is likely to stress the role of learning. Psychological development, in this latter view, is a vague notion based on a misleading biological metaphor.

The traditional basis for distinguishing development from learning is that development is guided from within by the genes whereas learning is caused by the external environment. If psychological changes are caused by the genes, then they are the result of internal processes that generate ongoing progress toward mature structures. If psychological changes are caused by the environment, however, then we can expect change to be more discrete and variable, a matter of learning whatever happens to come your way whenever you happen to encounter it.

And there it is: the infamous **nature–nurture issue** (Spelke & Newport, 1998). Psychologists on the nature side are called **nativists**. They believe psychological change is primarily directed by genes that move the individual toward psychological maturity. Psychologists on the nurture side are called **empiricists**. They believe psychological change is primarily directed by the environment and can proceed in a variety of directions depending on individual experience within particular homes, schools, communities, and cultures. Nativists are thus likely to construe psychological change developmentally whereas empiricists put more emphasis on learning.

Research on development has convinced all contemporary psychologists that it is unnecessary and unhelpful to choose between nativism and empiricism. At the very least, modern psychologists emphasize that both nature and nurture play important roles in psychological change. Moreover, there is substantial evidence that the influence of genes depends on the environment and the influence of the environment depends on genes. Thus nature and nurture interact in influencing the course of development.

Rational Constructivism

Interactionism explains development as the outcome of gene–environment interaction. In its stronger version, often known as **dynamic interactionism**, this involves ongoing interactions of organism and environment throughout the course of development. Many psychologists believe even this does not go far enough, however. Beyond dynamic interactionism lies **constructivism**, which maintains that people play an active role in their own development (Bickhard, 1995; Chiari & Nuzzo, 1996, 2010; Gestsdottir & Lerner, 2008; Müller, Carpendale, & Smith, 2009; Phillips, 1997; Piaget, 1985, 2001; Prawat, 1996).

Consider, for example, a child's increasing ability in math. An empiricist would suggest that whatever changes take place in the child's mathematical knowledge are the result of the mathematical concepts and techniques taught in the child's home, school, and/or other environments. A nativist would suggest that fundamental sorts of mathematical knowledge are genetically programmed to emerge over the course of children's development. An interactionist would suggest a compromise account in which mathematical knowledge emerges from the interaction of heredity and environment.

A constructivist would go a step beyond this, noting that children are actively involved in counting, arranging, grouping, dividing, and doing other such activities with objects. Their voluntary actions have been influenced by, but cannot be reduced to, previous interactions of genes and culture. Without denying the ongoing interaction of genetic and environmental influences, the constructivist would suggest that children actively construct their own mathematical knowledge through ongoing reflection on and coordination of their mathematical actions and interactions. Thus the child is seen as an active agent with a role that cannot be reduced to genes, environmental history, or even an interaction of both.

Constructivists conceive the construction of knowledge and reasoning as a self-regulated process that, over time, generates qualitatively distinct structures of knowledge and reasoning. Most constructivists—those in the tradition of Jean Piaget, whom I will later refer to as **rational constructivists**—believe that the new structures are often not just different but better than those they supersede, representing progress toward higher levels of understanding and rationality. Thus most constructivists believe there is such a thing as psychological development. In contrast to empiricists, they believe there are indeed long-term, self-regulated, qualitative, and progressive changes in the psychological realm. In contrast to nativists, however, constructivists see self-regulation as an active process of action, reflection, and coordination by the individual rather than as a process of genetically guided maturation.

Adolescent Development

Development was defined earlier as change that meets four criteria: It is extended, self-regulated, qualitative, and progressive. There can be no doubt that children develop. As we will see throughout this volume, there is clear evidence for developmental change in adolescence and beyond with respect to cognition, morality, and identity. But the evidence is also clear that adolescent development is very different from child development. Development beyond childhood is much less inevitable, predictable, and tied to age than child development. Child development would be difficult to stop even if we wanted to, whereas adolescent development may require active encouragement and support. Research on adolescent development thus has important, and perhaps unexpected, implications for educational and social policy.

PART I

COGNITIVE DEVELOPMENT

Cognitive development is the development of knowledge and inference. In adolescence and beyond this includes the development of advanced forms and levels of thinking, reasoning, and rationality. We begin with Piaget's conception of cognitive maturity as formal operations. From there we proceed to diverse aspects and conceptions of advanced cognition and development. As we will see, current research and theory are consistent with Piaget's conception of cognitive development as a rational process with rational outcomes but challenge his depiction of cognitive development as a single universal sequence of general structures leading to a highest, and thus final, stage.

Piaget's Theory of Formal Operations

> To be formal, deduction must detach itself from reality and take up its stand upon the plane of the purely possible.
>
> —**Jean Piaget**
> *(1928/1972b, p. 71)*

D evelopmental psychologists are quick to talk about matters such as emotional development, social development, personality development, and cognitive development. Because most people share the notion that children develop toward maturity, such terminology may be uncritically accepted. As discussed in the Introduction, however, psychological maturity is a more problematical notion than physical maturity. This raises questions about what we mean by **psychological development**.

Caution is in order, for example, regarding any claim that certain emotions are better than others. But what, then, is meant by emotional development? Similarly, on what basis are some social interactions, personalities, or thoughts deemed more advanced or mature than others? Are we deluding ourselves when we refer to social development, personality development, and cognitive development?

Although such questions are reasonable and important, I believe the issues they raise can be satisfactorily addressed. In this chapter, focusing on cognitive development, I present the theory of Jean Piaget, who believed that cognition is indeed a developmental phenomenon (Müller, Carpendale, & Smith, 2009). Piaget attempted to demonstrate that over the course of childhood and early adolescence, individuals actively construct qualitatively new structures of knowledge and reasoning and that the most fundamental such changes are progressive in the sense that later cognitive structures represent higher levels of rationality than earlier ones.

Piaget's Theory of Cognitive Development

Imagine a small pet store in which there are 10 animals for sale—6 dogs and 4 cats. If asked whether there are more dogs or cats in the store, you would immediately respond that there are more dogs. Suppose, however, you are asked whether there are more dogs or more cats in a pet store you have never seen on the next block. You would indicate that, without more information, you simply don't know.

Suppose now you are asked whether there are more dogs or more animals in the original store. This might seem a peculiar question. After clarifying that you have understood it correctly, however, you would respond that there are more animals. If asked whether there are more dogs or animals in the store on the next block, you would indicate that it has at least as many animals as dogs. You would not need any additional information about the other store to reach this conclusion: Knowing that dogs are animals, it follows as a matter of logical necessity that any pet store must have at least as many animals as dogs.

Imagine that a preschool child is brought into the original pet store and is asked the same questions. It might turn out that she is unfamiliar with dogs or cats or that she has trouble telling them apart. It is also possible that the numbers involved here exceed her counting skills. Alternatively, she might come from a cultural background where dogs and cats are not classified together as animals. For a variety of reasons of this sort, a child might fail to provide satisfactory answers to the questions you had been asked. This would provide little basis for questioning her rationality, however. We would simply note that for reasons relating to her individual or cultural background, she has not learned certain things that are eventually learned by all normal individuals in our culture.

Suppose, however, that the child is indeed familiar with dogs and cats, is able to distinguish and count them, and understands that all dogs and cats are animals. When asked whether there are more dogs or cats, she responds correctly that there are more dogs.

When asked about the store on the next block, she responds correctly that without going there to see, she cannot know whether it has more dogs or cats.

You then ask whether there are more **dogs** or **animals** in the store she is in, repeating the question to make sure she understands it. She responds that there are more dogs. You ask why, and she notes that there are six dogs and only four cats. When you ask about the store on the next block, she responds that without further information, she cannot know whether it has more dogs or animals. Just to be sure, you ask whether dogs are animals. "Of course," she says.

What is going on here? A plausible account is that the child does not understand the nature and logic of hierarchical classification. She knows that dogs are animals and that cats are animals, but she does not fully grasp that any given dog is simultaneously a member of the class of dogs and of the class of animals (see Figure 1.1). Thus she does not realize that in any situation, the class of animals *must* have at least as many members as the class of dogs. When asked to compare dogs with animals (two different levels in the class hierarchy), she ends up comparing dogs with cats (which are at the same level in the class hierarchy) and concludes there are more dogs. In other words, she is not ignorant of relevant facts about dogs, cats, and animals, and she is not deficient in particular arithmetic skills. What she apparently lacks is abstract conceptual knowledge about the nature of hierarchical classes.

Logical understandings of this sort were the main focus of interest for the renowned Swiss developmentalist Jean Piaget (1896–1980). In numerous studies over many decades, Piaget and his collaborators found that preschool children routinely show patterns of reasoning qualitatively different from those of older children and adults. Moreover, the later forms of reasoning and understanding were demonstrably more coherent and adaptive. Piaget did not deny that children learn new facts and skills as they grow older and that there is thus a quantitative growth of

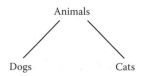

FIGURE 1.1 Hierarchical classification.

knowledge. He suggested, however, that qualitative shifts in the nature of reasoning are more fundamental. It is these that represent progress toward higher levels of rationality. What accounts for such changes, he wondered.

One possibility is that sophisticated cognitive structures are learned from one's environment. There is no evidence, however, that logical knowledge of the sort Piaget studied is taught to young children or that direct teaching of logical facts or procedures has much effect on their thinking. An empiricist view has difficulty accounting for the relatively early and universal attainment of basic logical conceptions.

Another possibility is that the rational basis for cognition is innate, emerging as a result of genetic programming. But there is no evidence that we inherit genes for logic and little reason to believe that genes containing the sorts of logical understandings just discussed could be generated by the process of evolution. A nativist view turns out to be no more plausible than an empiricist view.

Constructivism

On the basis of such considerations, Piaget suggested that rational cognition is constructed in the course of interaction with the environment (Campbell & Bickhard, 1986; Moshman, 1994, 1998; Müller et al., 2009). Although this does not rule out a substantial degree of genetic and environmental influence, it emphasizes the active role of the individual in creating his or her own knowledge.

One might wonder, however, why individual construction would enhance rationality. If we all construct our own cognitive structures, why doesn't each of us end up with a unique form of cognition, no more or less justifiable than anyone else's? Why does individual construction lead to higher levels, and universal forms, of rationality?

Equilibration

Piaget suggested that rationality, which he construed largely as a matter of **logical coherence**, resides in corresponding forms of **psychological equilibrium**. People relate to their environments by **assimilating** aspects of those environments to their cognitive structures. If their current structures are adequate, they can **accommodate to** the matter at hand. If this cannot be done, however, the individual may experience a state of **disequilibrium**. New cognitive structures must be constructed to resolve the problem and restore equilibrium. Piaget (1985) referred to this process as **equilibration**.

Consider, for example, the child in the pet store. When asked to compare dogs with cats, she assimilates this request to her cognitive schemes of grouping and counting. Accommodating to the specifics of the situation, she concludes that there are more dogs. When asked to compare dogs with animals, however, she makes the same assimilation. Grouping the dogs together leaves the cats, whereupon she compares dogs with cats and concludes that there are more dogs. Not realizing that she has failed to answer the intended question, she may remain in equilibrium.

Suppose, however, that you now ask her to divide the dogs from the animals. And perhaps you throw in a few questions encouraging her to explain and justify what she is doing. In the course of the resulting interchange, she may realize that the dogs fit in both categories. This may create a sense of disequilibrium, leading her to vaguely recognize a problem with her approach to the matter. Reflecting on the nature of her classification activities, she may construct a more logically coherent scheme of hierarchical classification that will enable her to make sense of the situation and restore equilibrium.

Notice that the new classification scheme is constructed in the course of interaction with the physical and social environment but is not internalized from that environment. Thus it is neither innate nor (in the usual sense) acquired.

Notice also that the new equilibrium derives from a more advanced cognitive structure that in some sense transcends the child's earlier ones. Equilibration, in other words, leads not just to **different** structures but to **better** ones. Thus Piaget's conception of construction via equilibration suggests that cognitive changes, rather than being arbitrary and idiosyncratic, show a natural tendency to move in the direction of greater rationality. Piagetian constructivism is a form of what I later refer to as **rational constructivism**.

Research since the 1970s has refuted a number of Piaget's specific interpretations and hypotheses and has raised serious questions about various aspects of his account of development (Karmiloff-Smith, 1992; Moshman, 1998). There is substantial agreement, however, with his most general claim: Children actively construct increasingly rational forms of cognition, thus it is meaningful to speak of **cognitive development**.

The question for adolescent psychology is whether such development continues into adolescence. Piaget's own view was that early adolescence marks the emergence of the final stage of cognitive development—**formal operations**.

Piaget's Theory of Formal Operations

The child of age 9 or 10, in Piaget's theory, has attained and consolidated a stage of cognition known as **concrete operations** (Inhelder & Piaget, 1964). The concrete thinker, according to Piaget, is a logical and systematic thinker who can transcend misleading appearances by coordinating multiple aspects of a situation. She or he understands the logic of classes, relations, and numbers and routinely makes proper inferences on the basis of coherent conceptual frameworks. Research since the 1960s has substantially confirmed this picture of early rationality, suggesting that, if anything, children show various forms of sophisticated reasoning and understanding even earlier than Piaget indicated (Case, 1998; DeLoache, Miller, & Pierroutsakos, 1998; Flavell, Green, & Flavell, 2002; Gelman & Williams, 1998; Karmiloff-Smith, 1992; Wellman & Gelman, 1998).

Piaget believed, however, that adolescents construct a cognitive structure that incorporates and extends concrete operations. He referred to this more advanced form of rationality as **formal operations** and suggested, on the basis of research by his colleague Bärbel Inhelder, that it begins to develop at approximately age 11 or 12 and is complete and consolidated by about age 14 or 15 (Inhelder & Piaget, 1958). Central to his conception of formal operations is the cognitive role of possibilities.

Reality as a Subset of Possibilities

Children begin considering possibilities at very early ages (Piaget, 1987). The imaginative play of the preschool child, for example, explores a variety of possible characters, roles, and social interactions. For children, however (in Piaget's view), possibilities are always relatively direct extensions of reality. The real world lies at the center of intellectual activity. Possibilities are conceived and evaluated in relation to that reality.

For the formal operational thinker, on the other hand, possibilities take on a life of their own. They are purposely and systematically formulated as a routine part of cognition. Reality is understood and evaluated as the realization of a particular possibility.

Consider, for example, gender role arrangements. In every culture, children learn what are deemed proper roles for males and females. In a culture where women in medicine are expected to be nurses, not physicians, for example, a young child might think about a girl becoming a surgeon but would evaluate this possibility with respect to the actual gender role arrangements of the culture and likely see it as amusing, bizarre, or inappropriate.

A formal operational thinker, on the other hand, would be able to imagine a wide variety of gender role arrangements. The actual arrangements of his or her society, then, would come to be seen as the realization of one of many possibilities. That reality could then be reconsidered and evaluated with respect to those other possibilities. At the level of formal operations, then, there is a radical reversal of perspective: Rather than considering possibilities with respect to reality, reality is considered with respect to possibilities. The formal thinker spontaneously and systematically generates possibilities and reconstrues realities in light of those possibilities.

Hypothetico-Deductive Reasoning

Closely related to the new use of possibilities is **hypothetico-deductive reasoning**. Such reasoning begins with an assertion that is purely hypothetical or even false. Consider, for example, the following two arguments (adapted from Moshman & Franks, 1986):

Elephants are bigger than mice.
Dogs are bigger than mice.
Therefore, elephants are bigger than dogs.

Mice are bigger than dogs.
Dogs are bigger than elephants.
Therefore, mice are bigger than elephants.

A preformal child is likely to consider the first to be more logical in that every statement within it is true. The second, by contrast, would be dismissed as illogical in that every statement within it is false. A formal thinker, on the other hand, would notice that the conclusion to the first argument, although true, does not follow from the premises given. By contrast, the conclusion to the second, albeit false, does follow from the premises given.

The formal thinker, in other words, is able to distinguish logic from truth and thus to formulate and evaluate arguments independent of the truth or falsity of their premises. Hypothetico-deductive reasoning, then, enables one to consider the logical implications of a set of premises whether or not one accepts those premises. Such reasoning plays a central role in the rigorous exploration of possibilities.

Second-Order Operations

Concrete operations, in Piaget's theory, are first-order operations: They are intended to apply logic directly to reality. Formal operations may be defined as operations *on* operations—that is, as **second-order operations**. Consider, for example, the following proportion:

$$\frac{10}{5} = \frac{4}{2}$$

To comprehend the logic of this proportion, one must understand that the relation of 10 to 5 (first number twice as great as second) is **equal to** the relation of 4 to 2 (again, first number twice as great as second). The focus is on a relation (of equality, in this case) between two relations. A proportion, in other words, is a relation between two relations, or a second-order relation.

Piaget worked out the logic of second-order operations in great detail. His account drew on abstract mathematical structures— the lattice and the Identity-Negation-Reciprocity-Correlative (INRC) Group—and an associated set of 16 binary operations involving logical relations such as conjunction, disjunction, implication, biconditionality, and incompatibility. Second-order operations, he argued, enable adolescents and adults to elaborate combinations and permutations of elements systematically, to identify correlations, and to manipulate variables independently so as to determine their individual effects.

Formal operations, then, involves a higher-order logical structure that enables insights and reasoning impossible at the concrete operations level. Thus the formal operational orientation toward hypothetical possibilities, far from being a turn from reality to fantasy, is associated with a rigorous and systematic logical structure. The construction of that structure in early adolescence, Piaget suggested, is the transition to cognitive maturity.

Research on Formal Operations

The original empirical basis for Piaget's theory of formal operations was psychological research by his associate Bärbel Inhelder on what came to be known as the Inhelder tasks, in which children and adolescents attempted to explain a variety of physical phenomena associated with balance scales, pendulums, and other sorts of apparatus. After the publication of this research in the classic work on formal operations (Inhelder & Piaget, 1958), researchers began attempting to replicate and extend Inhelder's findings. In addition, many researchers extended the study of formal operations to focus more directly on specific forms of advanced logical reasoning central to Piaget's theoretical account of Inhelder's tasks and results.

There are now hundreds of published studies intended to test or extend Piaget's theory of formal operations and hundreds more presenting data directly relevant to the theory. The results are complex, and their interpretation has generated substantial theoretical controversy (for reviews and analyses, see Amsel, in press; Blasi & Hoeffel, 1974; Bond, 2001; Byrnes, 1988a, 1988b; Campbell & Bickhard, 1986; Gray, 1990; Halford, 1989; Keating, 1980, 1988, 1990; Kuhn, 2008; Leiser, 1982; Moshman, 1998, 2009a; Müller, 1999; Neimark, 1975; Ricco, 1993, 2010; Smith, 1987). In general, the research shows that there are indeed important forms of reasoning of the sort Piaget identified as formal operational that are rarely seen before about age 11 but become increasingly common beyond that age. However, research does not support the original Piagetian claim that formal operational reasoning is consolidated by age 14 or 15 and used spontaneously and consistently beyond that age.

Consider, for example, a series of studies by Moshman and Franks (1986) and Morris (2000). In the original series of three experiments, Moshman and Franks (1986) presented fourth graders, seventh graders, and college students with a variety of valid and invalid arguments varying in form, content, truth of premises, and truth of conclusion. The intent was to see whether they could systematically distinguish valid arguments, in which the conclusion follows logically from the premises, from invalid arguments, in which it does not. This required hypothetico-deductive reasoning in that validity did not always correspond to truth. Recall, for example, the two arguments presented in the section on hypothetico-deductive reasoning:

Elephants are bigger than mice.
Dogs are bigger than mice.
Therefore, elephants are bigger than dogs.

Mice are bigger than dogs.
Dogs are bigger than elephants.
Therefore, mice are bigger than elephants.

The first of these arguments is invalid because the conclusion does not follow logically from the premises, despite the fact that the premises and conclusion are true. The second argument, in contrast, is valid because the conclusion follows logically from the premises, despite the fact that the premises and conclusion are false. To recognize the validity of the second argument requires hypothetico-deductive reasoning to determine what follows from premises known to be false.

Conditions were systematically varied with respect to whether students received an initial explanation of the concept of validity and whether they received regular feedback regarding the correctness of their responses. Fourth graders, as expected on the basis of the theory of formal operations, showed little or no understanding of the distinction between valid and invalid arguments regardless of whether they received explanations and/or feedback. College students generally did show such understanding regardless of condition, though many were inconsistent in applying that understanding.

Seventh graders turned out to be the group most affected by experimental condition. Without explanation or feedback, the performance of the seventh graders was highly variable, with some reasoning at the level of the fourth graders and others at the level of the best college students. With explanation or feedback, however, seventh graders' performance improved to the level of the college students.

These results are consistent with Piaget's claims about the initial appearance of formal operations but not with his view about its relatively rapid consolidation. Fourth graders, who were 9 and 10 years old, showed little or no ability to use hypothetico-deductive reasoning even in conditions carefully designed to facilitate this. Seventh graders (aged 12 and 13), on the other hand, often did apply such reasoning spontaneously; most were at least able to profit from explanation and feedback. Even college students, however, were far from consistent in their use of formal reasoning. Formal operational reasoning, it seems, does begin to develop about age 11, but the resulting formal competence is not consistently applied even by adults.

In a systematic extension of this research with 220 children in Grades 3 through 5 (ages 8 to 11), Anne Morris (2000) examined in more detail the capacities of children just below what Inhelder and Piaget (1958) proposed as the usual onset of formal operational reasoning about age 11 or 12. On the basis of a systematic analysis of how people comprehend and apply the concept of inferential validity, Morris devised experimental tasks that ingeniously directed children's attention to several key considerations. Children were pretested and posttested on validity tasks from Moshman and Franks (1986), with additional delayed posttesting in some cases. The experimental tasks, administered a month after the pretest, were varied systematically.

None of the children used validity of form as a basis for sorting arguments in the pretest, consistent with the findings of Moshman and Franks. On the posttest, however, many of the children, including some of the third graders, did indeed distinguish valid from invalid arguments on the basis of logical form and adequately explain the distinction. All of those who met this criterion, moreover, still showed substantial ability to distinguish valid from invalid arguments in a delayed posttest a month later. At least some children under age 11, it appears, have at least a nascent capacity for hypothetico-deductive reasoning.

But if the glass of early competence is partially full, it is also more than half empty. Even in the most effective experimental condition, a combined task that set up an elaborate fantasy context and repeatedly directed the child's attention to structural relationships, the percentages of students in Grades 3, 4, and 5 who adequately distinguished valid from invalid arguments at least once out of four opportunities were only 25%, 35%, and 35%, respectively. That is, even among the 10- and 11-year-olds who had just participated in a highly elaborate and sophisticated effort to assist them, a substantial majority still failed to distinguish valid from invalid arguments (see also Amsel, Trionfi, & Campbell, 2005).

These results are consistent with a constructivist view of the development of formal operations as an ongoing process of reflection and coordination that may proceed at somewhat different rates in different individuals. Some children as young as age 8 were able to construct and apply formal conceptions of inferential validity given the right kind of educational experiences, but even as late as fifth grade (ages 10–11), children did not spontaneously apply this concept, and most were unable to construct it. Formal operations does not simply emerge out of our genes at some predetermined age, but this does not mean that it can be taught or learned at any age.

Morris's (2000) interpretation of her results highlights the multifaceted complexity of both reasoning and development in the domain of logic:

> These findings suggest that distinguishing between logical and nonlogical arguments involves the coordinated application of various skills: treating the component sentences of an argument as an integrated whole, attending carefully to the detailed character of statements, attending to links between component statements as well as to the content of individual statements, comparing adjacent statements, setting aside background knowledge and using only premise information to make inferences, ignoring or actively inhibiting irrelevant personal information in processing a text, and selectively introducing information from long-term memory during the reasoning process. All of these must be coordinated with the application of metalogical understandings; an individual who applies these comprehension processes cannot distinguish between logical and nonlogical arguments if he or she has not constructed an understanding of the necessity of logical forms and the indeterminacy of nonlogical forms or fails to recognize the applicability of these concepts in a particular context. (p. 754)

One might expect from this account that the development of logical reasoning would be an ongoing process extending, at least in some cases, well beyond childhood and that logical performance would vary not only across individuals and ages but also across tasks and contexts. Research on logical reasoning in adolescence strongly supports this picture (Barrouillet, Markovits, & Quinn, 2001; Daniel & Klaczynski, 2006; De Neys & Everaerts,

2008; Efklides, Demetriou, & Metallidou, 1994; Franks, 1996, 1997; Klaczynski, Schuneman, & Daniel, 2004; Markovits, 2006; Markovits & Barrouillet, 2002; Markovits & Bouffard-Bouchard, 1992; Markovits & Nantel, 1989; Markovits & Vachon, 1989; Simoneau & Markovits, 2003; Venet & Markovits, 2001).

Consider, for example, the much studied "selection task" (Wason, 1968). You are asked to consider a set of four cards, each of which has a letter (vowel or consonant) on one side and a number (odd or even) on the other. The cards are as follows:

E   K   4   7

The following hypothesis is presented:

IF A CARD HAS A VOWEL ON ONE SIDE, THEN IT HAS AN EVEN NUMBER ON THE OTHER SIDE.

Your task is to test this hypothesis by turning over those cards—and only those cards—necessary to determine conclusively whether the hypothesis is true or false for this set of four cards. Which card(s) must be turned?

Most people choose to turn either just the E or the E and the 4. The card with a vowel showing (E) is turned to see if it has an even number on the other side, and, in some cases, the card with an even number showing (4) is turned to see if it has a vowel on the other side. The assumption is that finding a vowel combined with an even number supports the hypothesis, and seeking such a combination thus tests the hypothesis. Research on a variety of tasks supports the view that people have a strong orientation toward testing hypotheses by seeking data that would verify them (Evans, 1989; Friedrich, 1993; Klayman & Ha, 1987; Wason & Johnson-Laird, 1972).

Upon reflection, however, it is clear that this **verification strategy** is inadequate. The only combination that could falsify the hypothesis is a card with a vowel that does not have an even number on the other side. Thus we must seek cards that combine a vowel with an odd number. The correct response to the task, then, is to turn the E and the 7. The E must be turned because it would falsify the hypothesis if it had an odd number on the other side. The 7 must be turned because it would falsify the hypothesis if it had a vowel on the other side. The 4 need not be turned because, no matter what is on the other side, it cannot falsify the hypothesis.

A formal operational thinker might be expected to work out, via hypothetico-deductive reasoning, what predictions follow from the hypothesized relation between numbers and letters in the selection task. A formal thinker might also be expected to systematically consider all possibilities in regard to the unseen sides of the four cards and the consequences of each possibility for the hypothesis. Nevertheless, it has long been clear that most adults fail to apply a **falsification strategy** to standard versions of the selection task (Evans, 1989; Stanovich, 1999; Wason & Johnson-Laird, 1972).

The failure of most people to solve the selection task via application of a falsification strategy raised serious questions about whether even adults use formal operational reasoning. Research by Willis Overton (1990) and his associates, however, showed that adolescent and adult performance can be improved by various manipulations that make the task more meaningful, whereas children fail to profit from such variations. Adolescents and adults, they concluded, have the **competence** to engage in formal operational reasoning, but their (successful or unsuccessful) **performance** is a function of specific features of the task at hand. Children under age 11 or 12, in contrast, lack formal operational competencies and thus fail to apply formal operations regardless of task.

Müller, Overton, and Reene (2001) extended developmental research on the selection task by assessing two groups of students— 6th graders and 8th graders—on five versions of the selection task and then assessing them again a year later and a third time a year after that (when they were, respectively, 8th and 10th graders). As expected, performance improved across time, a pattern that held for both groups. Interestingly, the students who were initially 6th graders showed better reasoning at their third assessment (when they were in 8th grade) than the group initially in 8th grade showed at their first assessment (i.e., in 8th grade). Even without feedback, it appears, the experience of thinking about a series of selection tasks once each year in three consecutive years was sufficient to promote logical reasoning in early adolescence.

Research on the selection task thus supports other findings that formal operational competence appears, as Inhelder and Piaget (1958) suggested, at the transition to adolescence. As Piaget (1972a) later acknowledged, however, application of that competence to various tasks and situations, although somewhat increasing over the course of adolescence, remains difficult and inconsistent even in adulthood.

The Quest for Postformal Operations

In 1973, Klaus Riegel proposed a stage of **dialectical operations** that, he suggested, follows Piaget's stage of formal operations. This proposal was substantially elaborated by Michael Basseches (1980, 1984), who formulated a set of 24 **dialectical schemata**—distinct forms of **dialectical reasoning**. Dialectical reasoning, he proposed, draws on postformal understandings of structure, relations, context, perspective, contradiction, activity, change, and progress.

Suppose, for example, an individual who believes that knowledge is innate in the genes (nativism) encounters the view that knowledge is learned from one's environment (empiricism). It may appear that the two views contradict each other and that a choice must be made between them—they cannot both be right. A dialectical thinker, however, would consider the possibility that these two views can be synthesized to generate a perspective more defensible than either—in this case, perhaps, some sort of interactionist view. More generally, given an initial view (a **thesis**) and an apparent contradiction of that view (an **antithesis**), the dialectical thinker resists the tendency simply to choose between them. Instead she or he attempts to formulate a new perspective that transcends both (a **synthesis**).

The dialectical thinker recognizes, however, that the synthesis is not a final resolution but may itself be contradicted. For example, an interactionist perspective on knowledge (a synthesis of nativism and empiricism) may itself be challenged by the view that knowledge is constructed. Rather than choose between interactionism and constructivism, however, the dialectical thinker may attempt to synthesize the two. More generally, any synthesis can itself become a thesis contradicted by a new antithesis, leading to a higher-level synthesis. Appreciation of this **thesis–antithesis–synthesis cycle** may lead a dialectical thinker to actively seek out contradictions to promote the development of his or her understanding.

Although dialectical reasoning is not illogical, neither is it simply a matter of reasoning in accord with formal rules of logic. Rather, dialectical reasoning provides a rational approach to complex phenomena that cannot be assimilated to the logical structure of formal operations. One cannot prove logically

The Stage Beyond

Time was
      when first you'd burst beyond
                  the adolescent border
you'd proudly flex your operations of the second order
Your oh-so-formal thinking knew no formal inhibitions
To produce a proper proof you'd proposition propositions

But now your schemes are seeming
            to be scheming
                  in your dreaming
Metacognitive absurdity has every structure screaming
You're fenced against a Lattice
      by the groping of a Group
Your cognitorium is caught within a schizocognic loop:

Conjunction and disjunction
      merit binary ablations
           and who could give a hoot for implication's implications?
Biconditional relationships
      have failed to set you free
           yet you're incompatible with incompatibility
Combinations make you queasy
      permutations make you blue
You never confound variables and yet they confound you

$$\text{Correlation is} \underset{\displaystyle\text{statistical}}{\overset{\displaystyle\text{a meaningless}}{\diagdown\!\!\!\!\diagup}} \text{contortion}$$

$$\frac{\text{Your distrust of all proportions}}{\text{Has grown out of all proportion}} = \,?$$

        And though
beneath it all
            your INR still comes to C
you're strangling in your own combinatoriality

BUT DON'T DESPAIR!!
      Don't tear your hair!
           Don't let your mind grow numb!
        you've not yet reached the terminal disequilibrium
Just snap those cognivalent cogs
      predialectic bonds

(continued on next page)

and start constructing structures
of the stage that lies beyond:

A place where contradiction's knock
will never leave you vexed
where every dialectic ──────→
is a pointer toward the next
where paradox is paradigm!
(cognitions all in season)
where thoughts are all self-reinforced
and reason is the reason
You're asked to give colloquia from Paris to New Paltz
Say everything you've said
including this
is truly false
Or falsely true!
What difference for a transcendental hero
who drolly juggles even roots of numbers less than zero?
Then in a voice
that's choice to voice
a choice you once thought grave
you tell of light-wave particles
particulary waves
Such epistemic stunts!
—you laugh!!—
and now the most unnerving:
You trace how space
(inside black holes)
is infinitely curving!
But how is one to move beyond?
I often am beseeched
How is this stage of metastructuration to be reached?
A triune track to truth pertains
of which I'll gladly tell:
Assimilate
Accommodate
Equilibrate like hell

Reprinted from Moshman, D. (1979). The Stage Beyond. *Worm Runner's Digest*, 21, 107–108.

that a particular solution to the nature–nurture controversy is necessarily true, for example, but one may be able to demonstrate that a particular synthesis is better justified than either of the simpler views it transcends. The poem in the box reflects my efforts as a graduate student to understand the postulated transition from formal operations to a postformal stage of dialectical reasoning.

Just two years after Riegel proposed a postformal stage of dialectical operations, Patricia Arlin (1975) proposed an alternative conception of postformal cognition, suggesting that formal operations as conceived by Piaget is a **problem-solving stage** and that it is followed, at least in some individuals, by a **problem-finding stage**. Although subsequent research failed to support Arlin's conception of problem finding as a postformal stage of development (Cropper, Meck, & Ash, 1977), the quest for postformal stages was on. Within just a few years, there were at least a dozen theories of postformal cognition addressing, in diverse ways, what might lie beyond formal logic (for the definitive compilation from this era, see Commons, Richards, & Armon, 1984).

There continues to be considerable interest in postformal cognition. Some theories follow Riegel and Basseches in highlighting the dialectical nature of advanced reasoning. Others, extending Piaget's conception of formal operations as second-order operations, have proposed elaborate conceptions of operations of the third order and beyond, the results of successive reflections on and coordinations of formal and postformal structures. Michael Commons and Francis Richards (2003) developed a model of this sort that posits a succession of four stages beyond formal operations. **Systematic operations** forms systems out of formal operational relationships. **Metasystematic operations** constructs metasystems out of disparate systems. The **paradigmatic stage** synthesizes metasystems into paradigms, and the **cross-paradigmatic stage** synthesizes paradigms.

Commons and Richards (2003) estimated that only 20% of the U.S. population achieves even the first of these stages, however. Research on other postformal stages similarly suggests that these are forms of reasoning that, if they exist at all, are not achieved by most people. Although postformal reasoning continues to interest some theorists of adult development (Dawson-Tunik, 2004; Sinnott, 2003), most theorists of adolescence have been more concerned with nonlogical modes of reasoning and thinking that appear to develop alongside formal logic rather than on top of it, in tandem rather than in sequence.

Conclusion

Cognitive development, according to Piaget, is the construction of increasingly rigorous and encompassing forms of logic, culminating in the formal operational logic of the adolescent. Although research shows that adolescents and adults often fail to use formal operational reasoning, extensive evidence supports Piaget's postulation of forms of logical reasoning that are common among adolescents and adults but rarely seen much before age 11. One might wonder, however, whether adolescents and adults also construct and use forms of reasoning and rationality different from those postulated and investigated by Piaget. We turn now to this question.

CHAPTER 2

Inference, Thinking, and Reasoning

> You know my methods, Watson.
>
> —**Sherlock Holmes**
> *(Doyle, 1893/2000, p. 163)*

O ne way we identify developmental changes in cognition is that we see progress to higher levels of rationality. But do formal operations, rooted in a formal logic, encompass all of advanced rationality?

Rationality, in its oldest, broadest, and deepest sense, is a matter of having good reasons for one's beliefs and actions (Audi, 1997, 1998, 2001; Keefer, 1996; Moshman, 1990b, 1994; Nozick, 1993; Rescher, 1988; Searle, 2001; Sen, 2002; Siegel, 1988, 1997; Stanovich, 2008). Formal logic provides very good reasons for inferring particular conclusions from particular premises and is thus an important aspect of rationality. But we can be rational in interpreting complex evidence that does not logically require one particular conclusion or in choosing among alternatives in cases where none of the potential choices can be logically eliminated. Even in the absence of formal proof, we often have good enough reason to choose one belief or course of action over another. There is much more to rationality than formal logic (Bickhard & Campbell, 1996; Blasi & Hoeffel, 1974; Evans, 2002; King & Kitchener, 1994; Koslowski, 1996; Searle, 2001).

The Ubiquity of Inference

Cognition is inferential: It always goes beyond the data. We assimilate reality to active structures of knowledge and inference and accommodate those structures to the realities assimilated. This is how we know; we have no direct access to reality itself. However true to reality it may be, our factual knowledge is in part a function of our cognitive structures. Understanding, in turn, is more than recording facts. Even perception is now understood to go far beyond the data of our senses. And however real our memories seem, remembering is now recognized as an active reconstruction of the past. The language of assimilation and accommodation is Piagetian, but this conception of inference beyond the data as intrinsic to cognition has been widely accepted by cognitive and developmental psychologists since the 1970s.

Young children, it should be added, don't just go beyond the data. They make analogical, probabilistic, and deductive inferences. Their ability to act in accord with rules of inference would be impressive even if their rules were incorrect, but in fact preschool children routinely make logical and other normatively defensible inferences (Braine & O'Brien, 1998; Chen, Sanchez, & Campbell, 1997; Scholnick & Wing, 1995; Singer-Freeman, 2005; Singer-Freeman & Bauer, 2008). There is a rationality, it appears, intrinsic to our inferential systems.

Inferential systems can make inferences that are in accord with logical and other norms without being aware of their own rationality. But we can become aware of our rationality and advance it. The development of rationality is in large part a process of becoming aware of our inferences, evaluating them, and gaining control over them. Total awareness and control, however, not only is unachievable but would surely be maladaptive. Given the information processing limitations of the human mind, automatic inferences permit efficient functioning in complex environments (Moors & De Houwer, 2006). The development of thinking and reasoning, to which we now turn, supplements automatic systems of inference but does not replace them. Automatic inference remains, throughout life, a ubiquitous aspect of cognitive functioning.

Thinking as Purposeful Inference

Thinking may be defined as the deliberate application and coordination of one's inferences to serve one's purposes (Moshman, 1995a). There are multiple types of thinking serving multiple purposes. Research on the development of thinking (Kuhn, 2009) has concerned itself with the development of **problem solving** (DeLoache, Miller, & Pierroutsakos, 1998), **decision making** (Baron & Brown, 1991; Byrnes, 1998, 2005; Galotti, 2002; Jacobs & Klaczynski, 2005; Klaczynski, Byrnes, & Jacobs, 2001; Umeh, 2009), **judgment** (Jacobs & Klaczynski, 2005; Kahneman, 2003; Millstein & Halpern-Felsher, 2002), and **planning** (Galotti, 2005; Scholnick & Friedman, 1993).

Decision making has been an area of particular concern with regard to adolescents, in part because of its perceived link to risky behavior (Beyth-Marom, Austin, Fischhoff, Palmgren, & Jacobs-Quadrel, 1993; Michels, Kropp, Eyre, & Halpern-Felsher, 2005; Reyna, Adam, Poirier, LeCroy, & Brainerd, 2005; Reyna & Farley, 2006; Van Leijenhorst & Crone, 2010; see Chapter 16). Taking risks is not in itself irrational, however. Systematic evaluations of adolescent decision making with respect to the elaboration of options, consideration of pros and cons, and reasonable weighing of multiple dimensions show that adolescents at their best are capable of a level of deliberate decision making rarely seen in children (Moshman, 1993; Weithorn & Campbell, 1982). Of course adolescents fall far short of standards of perfect rationality, but so do adults, whose decision making does not differ notably from that of adolescents (Beyth-Marom et al., 1993). In a commentary on a set of chapters concerning decisions in context, Cynthia Berg (2005) noted that although adolescents fall short of perfect decision making, an emphasis on their shortcomings is highly misleading:

> As I read the chapters on adolescent decision making, I wondered how different adolescent decision making really is from adult decision making. Could not the same characterizations of adolescents (i.e., thoughtful and impulsive, deliberative and impetuous) characterize adults' decisions regarding whether to engage in potentially risky behaviors (e.g., investing in a volatile stock market, having an affair that may cause the dissolution of one's marriage, trying diet supplements to lose weight)? Both adolescent and adult decision making can be characterized by competence and incompetence, rationality and irrationality, depending on the specific domain of decision making and the activation of one's emotional, cognitive, and motivational systems. (p. 246)

Research on problem solving, judgment, and planning generates results generally consistent with what is seen in the decision-making literature. Rather than examine each of these, let me suggest four generalizations about the nature and development of thinking.

First, good thinking is not just the application of logic, though it does include good judgments about when and how logic is relevant. In daily life we routinely face problems for which there is no single logically correct solution and decisions that cannot be made by logically eliminating all but one of a set of options. Logic may play a role in making defensible judgments and formulating coherent plans, but there is rarely a uniquely correct judgment or plan mandated by formal rules. Thinking is not just a matter of logic.

In fact, thinking is very much a part of daily life, highly intertwined with emotions and social relations and highly influenced by task demands, environments, and cultural contexts. This is the second generalization. All people everywhere plan, judge, face problems, and make decisions, but how they go about these activities is highly variable.

Third, adolescents and adults often show forms or levels of thinking rarely seen in children. Even if formal operations is just one piece of advanced rationality, it allows adolescents and adults to generate and consider hypothetical possibilities in a systematic fashion that enables advanced forms of problem solving, decision making, judgment, and planning.

Finally, postchildhood developmental changes in thinking are not tied to age and do not culminate in a state of maturity. Although it seems likely that many individuals show progress beyond childhood in the quality of their problem solving, decision making, judgment, and planning (Cauffman & Woolard, 2005; Steinberg & Scott, 2003), the deployment and progress of thinking in adolescence and beyond is highly variable, depending on specific interests, activities, and circumstances (Fischer, Stein, & Heikkinen, 2009). No theorist or researcher has ever identified a form or level of thinking routine among adults that is rarely seen in adolescents. Adolescent thinking often develops but not through a fixed sequence and not toward a universal state of maturity.

Reasoning as Self-Constrained Thinking

Reasoning may be defined as epistemologically self-constrained thinking (Moshman, 1995a)—that is, thinking aimed at reaching justifiable conclusions. To reason is to think in such a way as to constrain your inferential processes on the basis of logical and other norms. The prototypical case of reasoning is **logical reasoning**, in which the norms are most clear and their justifiability is least in doubt. As we will see, **scientific reasoning** and **argumentation** are also epistemologically self-constrained, but their rationality is not simply a matter of following logical rules.

Logical Reasoning

Logical reasoning is reasoning in accord with logical norms. The prototypical case of logical reasoning is **deductive reasoning**, in which the norms consist of strict rules of deduction that respect the constraints of **logical necessity**. This includes **conditional reasoning**, which involves premises of the form *If p then q* that link an **antecedent** (*p*) to a **consequent** (*q*) in a conditional relation (*If ... then*).

The study of conditional reasoning has been a mainstay of cognitive and developmental psychology since the 1960s. The most basic conditional inference is **modus ponens**, which takes the form *If p then q; p; therefore, q* (major premise, minor premise, and conclusion, respectively). Another valid conditional inference is **modus tollens**, which takes the form *If p then q; not-q; therefore, not-p*. There are also two standard fallacies of conditional reasoning. **Denial of the antecedent** (DA) takes the form *If p then q; not-p; therefore, not-q* (the minor premise denies the antecedent of the major premise). **Affirmation of the consequent** (AC) takes the form *If p then q; q; therefore, p* (the minor premise affirms the consequent of the major premise). Both are fallacies because the conclusion does not necessarily follow from the premises.

Henry Markovits, Paul Klaczynski, and others have investigated conditional reasoning developmentally (Daniel & Klaczynski, 2006; De Neys & Everaerts, 2008; Klaczynski, Schuneman, & Daniel, 2004; Markovits, 2006; Markovits & Barrouillet, 2002). One major focus has been the influence of content. Consider, for example, the premises "If zig then zark. Zark." It seems natural to conclude "zig," thus succumbing to the AC fallacy. Suppose instead you face the premises "If I exercise then I lose weight. I lost weight." The conclusion "I exercised" again seems natural, but you may immediately remember that diet is an alternative basis for weight loss, so the weight loss cannot be attributed conclusively to exercise. Thus, having meaningful content that enables you to recall an alternative antecedent dissuades you from this unjustified conclusion. In other cases, however, meaningful content may interfere with good reasoning by distracting you from the underlying logic of an argument. If you disagree with a potential conclusion, and especially if you deem it highly objectionable, you may be less likely to see that it follows necessarily from premises you have accepted (see Chapter 13). Thus conditional reasoning is not always easier with meaningful content; rather it involves a complex interplay of content knowledge and formal logic.

Consider now a child given the premises "If zig then zark. Zig." Even a very young child is likely to conclude "zark." Does this modus ponens inference show conditional reasoning? It certainly is a proper conditional inference and a good reminder that we should not dismiss young children as illogical. But before we call this **reasoning**, we should note that the same child will also make the erroneous AC inference noted above. Automatically concluding zig from zark and vice versa is sometimes a proper inference and sometimes not, but it is not epistemologically self-constrained and thus does not constitute reasoning. You and I also make erroneous inferences, but upon reflection we understand in the abstract why arguments of the AC form are invalid.

Preschool children often make proper logical inferences, and adults often make fallacious ones. Nonetheless, adolescents and adults at their best can recognize that an inference is fallacious, whereas children, regardless of whether their inferences are justified, have limited ability to reflect on inference and justification (see the research on formal operations in Chapter 1). The developmental transition from childhood to adolescence is a matter not of learning correct inferences but of attaining greater awareness, understanding, and control of one's inferences (a matter of **metalogical understanding**; see Chapter 3).

Research on other forms of deductive reasoning is generally consistent with research on conditional reasoning (Ricco, 2010). Adolescents and adults show metalogical competencies not seen in children, but no one of any age relies on logic alone. Paul Klaczynski, Eric Amsel, and others (Amsel et al., 2008; Evans, 2002, 2007; Kahneman, 2003; Klaczynski, 2000, 2001, 2004, 2005, 2009; Stanovich, 1999; Stanovich & West, 2000) have shown that logical reasoning coexists with a variety of nonlogical inferences, as suggested by dual processing theories (discussed below).

Scientific Reasoning

The developmental study of scientific reasoning is rooted in Inhelder and Piaget's (1958) research and theory on formal operational reasoning (Chapter 1) but has evolved far beyond its roots in formal logic. Thus the study of scientific reasoning provides a good example of the role and limits of logic in advanced reasoning.

Suppose I believe children understand short sentences better than long sentences. I test my hypothesis by comparing a group of 10-year-old girls reading short sentences in a quiet room to a group of 8-year-old boys reading long sentences in a noisy room. I report that, as predicted, the short sentences are better understood. You would likely respond, politely I hope, that my research is flawed and fails to support my hypothesis.

What precisely is the problem? My evidence is indeed consistent with the hypothesis that short sentences are understood better. The problem is that the design of my research does not rule out a variety of alternative explanations for my results. Perhaps the two groups differ because 10-year-olds, in general, comprehend more than 8-year-olds. Perhaps they differ because girls, in general, are better readers than boys. Perhaps they differ because children, in general, learn more in quiet settings. Logically, the research is inconclusive because, without additional information, I have no way of knowing whether it is age, gender, setting, sentence length, or some combination of these that accounts for the difference between the two groups.

What should I have done to provide a genuine test of my hypothesis? I should have compared groups that were identical to each other with regard to age and gender and made sure that the reading took place in identical conditions. This insight is not based on substantive knowledge about the psychological processes involved in reading or on particular beliefs about age or gender differences or effects of setting. At issue is a purely formal insight about the logic of hypothesis testing: To determine the effect of a variable, one must manipulate that variable while holding all other variables constant.

In the classic presentation of the theory of formal operations, Inhelder and Piaget (1958) argued that the ability to isolate variables to determine their effects is an important aspect of formal operational logic and showed that this ability develops in early adolescence. Extensive research by Deanna Kuhn, Eric Amsel, Leona Schauble, and their associates provides a detailed picture of how children, adolescents, adults, and scientists coordinate theories and evidence (Amsel & Brock, 1996; Amsel, Goodman, Savoie, & Clark, 1996; Kuhn, 1989; Kuhn, Amsel, & O'Loughlin, 1988; Kuhn, Garcia-Mila, Zohar, & Andersen, 1995; Schauble, 1996). Consistent with other research on formal operational reasoning (Chapter 1), the results show some progress in at least some adolescents in understanding the logic of hypothesis testing, but appropriate isolation of variables and logically defensible inferences from data remain far from consistent even among adults.

Without denying the importance of isolating some variables in some circumstances, a variety of theorists have proposed that conformity to logically derived formal rules of scientific methodology is not sufficient for scientific reasoning (Kuhn, Iordanou, Pease, & Wirkala, 2008; Zimmerman, 2000). Not only must researchers avoid confounding potentially relevant variables, but they must select variables and interpret results on the basis of a domain-specific theoretical understanding of the phenomena under investigation. This typically requires judgments that are rational in the sense that good reasons can be provided but that are not mandated by formal logical or methodological rules. In the words of Leona Schauble (1996),

> Rationality entails more than mere logical validity. To decide which of several potential causes are plausible, people bring to bear both specific knowledge about the target domain and general knowledge based on experience about the mechanisms that usually link causes with effects. ... The goal of scientific reasoning is not primarily the formulation of inductive generalizations, but rather the construction of explanatory models. ... Explanatory models, in turn, are constrained in that their hypothesized causal mechanisms must be consistent with and sufficient to account for the known data. Thus prior knowledge guides observations, as surely as new observations lead to changes in knowledge. (p. 103)

Barbara Koslowski (1996) conducted an extensive program of research on adolescent scientific reasoning and, on the basis of her results and related considerations from the philosophy of science, reached a similar conclusion:

> I have argued that neither covariation alone nor theory alone constitute algorithms that guarantee the right answer in scientific reasoning. Theory and data are both crucial, and theory and data are interdependent. Sound scientific reasoning involves bootstrapping: considerations of theory or mechanism constrain data, and data in turn constrain, refine, and elaborate theory. (p. 86)

Scientific reasoning, then, is something richer and more complex than a logic of scientific inference, but it is nonetheless rational. In addition to the logic of hypothesis testing, there is, at least potentially, a rationality rooted in the domain-specific theories that guide the process of theorizing, promoting justifiable choices about what variables to investigate, what constitutes relevant evidence, what hypotheses to pursue, and so forth (see also Koslowski, Marasia, Chelenza, & Dublin, 2008).

Even young children, however, have and test domain-specific theories (Karmiloff-Smith, 1992; Kuhn, 2000; Wellman & Gelman, 1998). This has led many theorists to see children as fundamentally like scientists: Both children and scientists, they suggest, engage in the same sort of rational processes, differing mostly in that scientists have more experience and expertise. This conception of the **child as scientist** fits with Piaget's constructivist image of the child but underplays the sort of domain-general reasoning competencies associated with his stage of formal operations.

In a major critique of the child-as-scientist metaphor, Deanna Kuhn (1989) acknowledged that children, like scientists, have rich structures of domain-specific conceptual knowledge and continually test and refine this knowledge. But children, in contrast to scientists, fail to understand the distinction between theory and evidence and thus are unable to coordinate these in a conscious and deliberate manner:

> In scientific exploration activities, lack of differentiation and coordination of theory and evidence is likely to lead to uncontrolled domination of one over the other. Exploration may be so theory-bound that the subject has difficulty "seeing" the evidence, or so data-bound that the subject is confined to local interpretation of isolated results, without benefit of a theoretical representation that would allow the subject to make sense of the data. (Kuhn, 1989, p. 687)

Progress in scientific reasoning consists of progress in

> thinking about theories, rather than merely with them, and thinking about evidence, rather than merely being influenced by it. This development is thus metacognitive, as well as strategic. From a very early age, children modify their primitive theories in the face of evidence, but only through the development that has been the topic of this article does one attain control over the interaction of theory and evidence in one's own thinking. It is a development that occurs not once but many times over, as theories and evidence repeatedly come into contact with one another. It is also, however, a development that is incompletely realized in most people. (Kuhn, 1989, p. 688)

Scientific reasoning, then, has its roots in early childhood, but it continues to develop long beyond that (Klahr, 2000; Kuhn, 2000; Zimmerman, 2000). Adolescents and adults are far from perfect, but they do show forms or levels of scientific reasoning not seen in children. The development of scientific reasoning is largely a matter of increasing consciousness of and control over theories, evidence, and inferential processes.

Argumentation

Argumentation involves processes of reciprocal justification. Particular arguments can be logical, in the strict sense of formal and deductive, but argument, as Deanna Kuhn (2009) noted, lies squarely in "the realm of everyday, informal reasoning. If there were a single intellectual skill that would serve adolescents well in their lives … this would seem to be it" (p. 171). Beyond the value of skillful argument to individuals, moreover, argumentation is central to societal ideals such as rational jury deliberation (Warren, Kuhn, & Weinstock, 2010) and democratic governance (Habermas, 1990; Sen, 2009). Thus argumentation has been of longstanding interest to philosophers (Cohen, 2001), and Deanna Kuhn and other developmental psychologists have extensively studied its development (De Fuccio, Kuhn, Udell, & Callender, 2009; Felton, 2004; Iordanou, 2010; Kuhn, 1991, 2009; Kuhn, Goh, Iordanou, & Shaenfield, 2008; Kuhn, Shaw, & Felton, 1997; Kuhn & Udell, 2003; Leitao, 2000; Udell, 2007).

Argumentation begins with providing reasons to justify one's claims, positions, or actions, but ideally it goes far beyond this. It includes coordinating reasons and elaborating evidence to produce convincing arguments. It includes evaluating the arguments of others. In its most social aspect, argumentation involves refuting arguments with counterarguments and refuting counterarguments with rebuttals. At its highest levels it involves understanding that sometimes there is not a right and a wrong view, but neither are all views and arguments equally good; rather, some views and arguments may be better or worse than others (see the discussion of epistemic cognition and development in Chapter 3). It is possible, moreover, that some combination of views, or an alternative not yet considered, may end up being accepted by consensus as the best yet.

Consistent with other research on reasoning, research on argumentation shows that adolescents are capable of arguing at a level beyond that of children but that the skills of argument in people of all ages leave much to be desired. Research with individuals ranging from adolescence to adults beyond age 60 showed that education, but not age, correlated strongly with argument skill (Kuhn, 1991). Development of argumentation skills beyond early adolescence appears possible but not inevitable or universal. Extensive research by Deanna Kuhn and her associates has shown that interventions designed to promote and support argumentation can enhance developmental progress over a period of months (De Fuccio et al., 2009; Felton, 2004; Iordanou, 2010; Kuhn, Goh, et al., 2008; Kuhn et al., 1997; Kuhn & Udell, 2003; Udell, 2007).

Diversity in Thinking and Reasoning

Rationality for Piaget reaches its culmination in formal operations, which he took to be the universal state of cognitive maturity. As we have seen throughout this chapter, however, there are multiple types of thinking and forms of reasoning. If we are to understand the nature and development of rationality, we must understand its diversity. As we will now see, although claims of cognitive diversity have been made with regard to group differences, dual processing research shows that the primary locus of cognitive diversity is within individuals.

Group Differences

Richard Nisbett, Kaiping Peng, and their associates (Nisbett, Peng, Choi, & Norenzayan, 2001; Peng & Nisbett, 1999), on the

basis of their own research and a review of other studies, concluded that the primary locus of diversity is between cultures:

> The authors find East Asians to be *holistic*, attending to the entire
> field and assigning causality to it, making relatively little use of
> categories and formal logic, and relying on "dialectical" reason-
> ing, whereas Westerners are more *analytic*, paying attention pri-
> marily to the object and the categories to which it belongs and
> using rules, including formal logic, to understand its behavior.
> The 2 types of cognitive processes are embedded in different naive
> metaphysical systems and tacit epistemologies. (Nisbett et al.,
> 2001, p. 291)

Others agree there are group differences in thinking and reasoning but see the primary locus of such diversity in gender. In many
cases, forms of cognition seen by culture theorists as Western are
attributed by gender theorists to men; forms seen as non-Western
are attributed to women. Research consistently shows, however,
that diverse forms and aspects of thinking and reasoning are commonly seen among women and men in diverse cultural contexts
(Hyde, 2005). There are indeed individual differences in the use
of these processes, and some of these differences may be related
to culture or gender, but research does not support a categorical
distinction between cultural or gender groups in thinking or reasoning. No gender or cultural group has ever been shown to rely
on a particular kind of thinking or reasoning to the exclusion of
some other kind. On the contrary, human thinking and reasoning in men and women in all cultures involve the coordination of
multiple processes.

Nisbett et al. (2001) maintained that people use different
types of cognitive processes because their cultures represent distinct epistemologies (theories of knowledge; see Chapter 3). East
Asians, they claimed, use holistic and dialectical cognitive processes reflecting an East Asian epistemology, whereas Westerners
use analytic and logical processes reflecting a Western epistemology. Here again, switching the focus from culture to gender,
gender theorists have proposed gendered epistemologies, often
making similar distinctions. However, although the title of a
classic work referred specifically to "women's ways of knowing"
(Belenky, Clinchy, Goldberger, & Tarule, 1986), there is no
evidence in this book or, to my knowledge, anywhere else that
women have epistemologies distinct from those of men. Since

the 1990s, gender difference theorists have generally written of "gender-related" (rather than gender-exclusive) epistemologies (Baxter Magolda, 1992, 2002; Clinchy, 2002), but even this claim may be too strong. Systematic reviews of research on gender differences in epistemic cognition show such differences to be negligible or nonexistent (Brabeck & Shore, 2003; King & Kitchener, 1994, 2002). The question of cultural differences in epistemic cognition is more complex and less investigated. Whatever statistical differences there may be across cultures in the prevalence of various epistemic beliefs and orientations, however, it seems highly unlikely that the various cultures of the world will turn out to have distinct epistemologies of their own or that individual epistemologies will simply be a reflection of culture. On the contrary, as we will see in Chapter 3, major differences in epistemic cognition are a function of level of development and domain of reasoning, not gender or culture.

Dual Processing Theories

Dual processing researchers have made cognitive distinctions similar to those of culture and gender theorists but have provided substantial and convincing evidence that the locus of diversity lies within individuals—adolescents and adults, regardless of culture or gender, use both analytic (formal) and heuristic (contextual) processes (Amsel et al., 2008; Evans, 2002, 2007; Kahneman, 2003; Klaczynski, 2000, 2001, 2004, 2005, 2009; Stanovich, 1999; Stanovich & West, 2000). Others have suggested and provided evidence for even more complex forms of internal diversity in thinking and reasoning (Kuhn et al., 1995; Siegler, 1996). In the realm of advanced cognition, we are each a multitude.

To simplify, however, we process at no fewer than two levels. Dual processing theories are compatible with common conceptions of Piaget's theory of formal operations as a competence theory (Overton, 1990; see Chapter 1). Deliberate application of logical norms does not replace earlier modes of functioning but rather supplements them. Given Piaget's concern with development, it is reasonable that he focused especially on formal and analytic processes, which show important developmental change. Dual processing theories, as applied to development, help us see how such developmental changes interact with the heuristic and contextual processes that produce automatic inferences throughout our lives.

In summary, research on advanced cognition indicates that the major locus of diversity is *within* individuals rather than across individuals or groups. Interestingly, if this sort of diversity is universal, our focus on diversity has illuminated a universal aspect of human rationality: We all coordinate diverse processes, strategies, and perspectives.

Conclusion

Research shows that adolescents often make progress in their thinking and reasoning, thus enhancing the quality of their inferences. But what is developing in the development of reasoning? From the universality of internal cognitive diversity, another human universal likely follows: Given the demands of cognitive coordination, we all, to varying degrees, develop metacognitive understanding and control of our diverse inferential processes. Thus we turn now to the development of metacognition.

CHAPTER **3**

Metacognition and Epistemic Cognition

Part of reasoning rationally is reasoning *about* rationality.

— **Daniel Cohen's "Principle of Meta-Rationality"**
(2001, p. 78)

The human mind is a metamind.

— **Keith Lehrer**
(1990, pp. 1–2)

The first two chapters provided some sense of the scope of human rationality, ranging across the cognitive and developmental literatures on inference, thinking, and reasoning. The resulting picture of advanced rationality is complex and multifaceted. One common theme, however, is that advanced thinking and reasoning involve advanced forms of what psychologists call **metacognition**. I suggest in the present chapter that what lies at the core of advanced cognitive development is the development of metacognition. I focus especially on **epistemic cognition**, an aspect of metacognition central to the development of reasoning and rationality in adolescence and early adulthood.

Rationality as Metacognition

As we have seen, research since the 1970s has increasingly transcended the logico-mathematical framework of formal operations. The research suggests that there may be postformal stages of development, but it also indicates that the limitations of Piaget's account cannot be overcome through proposals for postformal stages. Rather, it appears that multiple varieties of reasoning and thinking develop alongside formal reasoning. Rationality consists in large part of appropriately applying and coordinating our various reasoning processes.

With such considerations in mind, developmental, cognitive, and educational theorists and researchers have increasingly emphasized the importance of metacognition—cognition about cognition (Flavell, Green, & Flavell, 1998; Klaczynski, 1997, 2000, 2004, 2005; Kuhn, 1999, 2000, 2005; Schraw, 1997; Schraw & Moshman, 1995; Stanovich, 2008; Tarricone, in press). Broadly construed, the development of metacognition includes "the achievement of increasing awareness, understanding, and control of one's own cognitive functions, as well as awareness and understanding of these functions as they occur in others" (Kuhn, 2000, p. 320). Although the term dates back only to the late 1970s, a metacognitive conception of adolescent cognition as **thinking about thinking** can already be seen in Inhelder and Piaget's 1958 presentation of the theory of formal operations.

Even young children show substantial metacognition. Between ages 3 and 5, for example, they come to understand that people can hold false beliefs and that in such cases people will act on the basis of their false beliefs rather than on the basis of (what the child knows to be) the truth (Doherty, 2009; Mitchell & Riggs, 2000; Wellman, Cross, & Watson, 2001). It is clear, however, that metacognitive knowledge and skills often continue to develop long beyond childhood (Schraw, 1997). Many theorists see metacognition, broadly construed, as central to rationality and therefore see the development of metacognition as central to advanced cognitive development (Campbell & Bickhard, 1986; Klaczynski, 2004, 2005; Kuhn, 1999, 2000, 2005, 2009; Kuhn & Franklin, 2006; Moshman, 1990a, 1998, 2004b, 2009c; see also Lehrer, 1990; Stanovich, 2008).

Figure 3.1 highlights relationships among a variety of concepts central to a **metacognitive conception of rationality**. As indicated, **rationality** is characteristic of a **rational agent**, an individual who uses **epistemic cognition** to engage in **reasoning**. Epistemic cognition, which we consider in detail in the next section, is a type of **metacognition** involving knowledge about the justifiability of knowledge. This includes conceptual knowledge

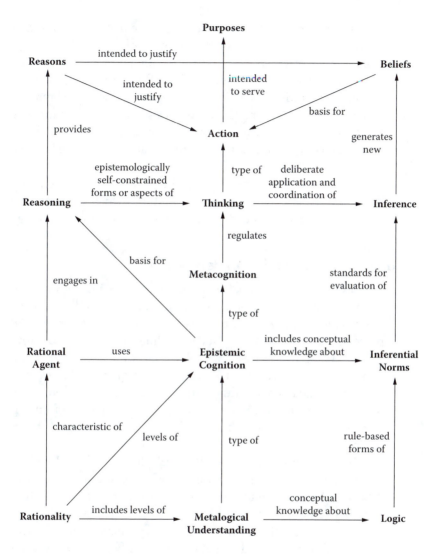

FIGURE 3.1 A metacognitive conception of rationality.

about **inferential norms**—that is, knowledge about standards for the evaluation of **inferences**.

Thinking, as already discussed, is the deliberate application and coordination of inferences to serve one's **purposes**. When thinkers constrain their inferences with the intent of conforming to what they deem to be appropriate inferential norms, they can be said to be reasoning. Reasoning, then, provides **reasons** for one's **beliefs** and **actions**.

Thinking, in this view, is a metacognitive phenomenon in that it involves the deliberate control of one's inferences. Reasoning, moreover, involves not just control of inferences but conceptual knowledge about their justifiability. Thus reasoning requires epistemic cognition, including conceptual knowledge about the nature and use of inferential norms. **Logic** is an important type of inferential norm. Thus knowledge about logic—**metalogical understanding**—constitutes an important type of epistemic cognition.

The core of cognitive development beyond childhood, then, may be the development of epistemic cognition, which enhances the epistemic self-constraints that transform thinking into reasoning.

Development of Metalogical Understanding

The development of rationality, as suggested in the previous section, is in large part the development of metacognition, including increasing awareness and control of one's various beliefs and inferential processes, and an emerging understanding of others as cognitive agents. As we will now see, a vital aspect of metacognitive development is the development of **epistemic cognition**—knowledge about the fundamental nature and justifiability of knowledge and inference. I begin in this section with the development of knowledge about logic and then turn in the next to research and theory on epistemic cognition in its most general sense.

When do children become logical? Although formal logic is central to Piaget's conception of formal operations, Piaget was clear that formal operations is not the beginning of logical inference but rather an advanced form of reasoning that involves the systematic application of deduction in hypothetical contexts (see Chapter 1). Inhelder and Piaget (1964) described a concrete operational logic of classes and relations that begins to be seen about age 7. Subsequent research has shown that preschool children routinely make inferences that are fully in accord with logical rules (Braine & O'Brien, 1998; Scholnick & Wing, 1995) and that even the behavior of infants shows an increasingly coordinated sensorimotor logic (Langer, 1980, 1986). If a ball is here or there and you cannot find it here, you look there.

A preschooler who looks for her ball at B when it does not turn up at A, however, is not even aware that she has made an inference, much less aware of the disjunction rule (*p or q; not p;*

therefore q) implicit in her inference. Preschoolers do not deliberately apply logical rules or understand when and why they should do so. Only beginning about age 6 do children recognize inferences as a potential source of knowledge (Pillow, 1999; Pillow, Hill, Boyce, & Stein, 2000; Rai & Mitchell, 2006; Sodian & Wimmer, 1987) or respond appropriately to even the most transparent logical necessities (Somerville, Hadkinson, & Greenberg, 1979) or blatant logical contradictions (Ruffman, 1999). Metalogical understanding then continues to develop (Miller, Custer, & Nassau, 2000; Moshman, 1990a, 2004b, 2009c; Piaget, 1987, 2001, 2006; Piéraut-Le Bonniec, 1980; Pillow, 2002; Pillow & Anderson, 2006; Smith, 1993), leading in early adolescence to the concept of inferential validity, which involves distinguishing the form of arguments from their content and making metalogical judgments about the validity of those logical forms (Moshman & Franks, 1986; see Chapter 1).

In a study of inference during reading, Bridget Franks (1996) presented fourth graders with stories involving premises that were true (consistent with their prior knowledge), neutral (unrelated to their prior knowledge), or false (inconsistent with their prior knowledge). Correct inferences were most likely for true content and least likely with false content. Seventh graders showed the same pattern, but the effects of content were not as great. College students, in contrast, reasoned equally well regardless of content. Franks interpreted the results as follows:

> With true content, no metalogic was required, because everything was consistent with what readers already know. With neutral content, empirical knowledge was of no use and could not be drawn on to help in the task, as can be done with true content. With neutral content, however, readers also do not need metalogic, because they are free to focus on the form of premises with no interference from their empirical knowledge. But with false content they do have interference, and so they must use metalogic—the awareness that one's empirical knowledge is a hindrance and must be disregarded in favor of exclusive focus on logical form. (p. 95)

In sum, the ability to apply and coordinate logical inferences to achieve one's purposes continues to develop for many years because of increasingly reflective epistemic cognition about the nature and use of logic. The central basis for the development of logical reasoning may be the development of metalogical understanding

(Moshman, 1990a, 1998, 2004b). To be rational about logic is to apply it consciously and deliberately with understanding of its uses and limitations. Rationality in the domain of formal logic is a metacognitive matter of understanding and controlling deductive inference.

Epistemic Cognition and Development

Metalogical understanding is an important aspect of epistemic cognition. What we know about formal logic, however, is only part of what we know about knowledge and inference and thus only part of our epistemic cognition. Children as young as 4 years understand that people lacking information may have, and act on the basis of, false beliefs (Doherty, 2009; Mitchell & Riggs, 2000; Wellman et al., 2001). Over the course of childhood, reflecting on and coordinating multiple subjectivities, they construct a **constructivist theory of mind**. By late childhood, children understand that they are active constructors of knowledge (Chandler, Hallett, & Sokol, 2002; Chandler & Proulx, 2010; Kuhn, 1999, 2000; Kuhn & Weinstock, 2002; Lalonde & Chandler, 2002).

But the epistemic cognition of children, observed Michael Chandler and his collaborators (2002), is strictly "retail," focused on particular beliefs and inferences. Children are aware of differing interpretations in particular cases but do not "see in ... localized and case-specific doubts the dangerous prospect that diversity of opinion is somehow intrinsic to the knowing process" (p. 162). Wholesale conceptions about the nature, limits, and justification of knowledge in the abstract often continue to develop long beyond childhood, though the extent of development is highly variable across individuals. If the early development of epistemic cognition in childhood is the development of rationality, continuing development in adolescence and beyond is the development of metarationality, understanding about what it means to be rational.

Although theories of advanced epistemic development vary in focus, detail, terminology, and age norms, there is substantial agreement on the general direction of development (Baxter Magolda, 1992, 2002; Belenky, Clinchy, Goldberger, & Tarule, 1986; Boyes & Chandler, 1992; Chandler, Boyes, & Ball, 1990; Chandler et al., 2002; Clinchy, 2002; Hofer & Pintrich, 1997, 2002; King & Kitchener, 1994, 2002; Kitchener, 2002; Kuhn, 1991, 1999, 2000, 2005, 2009; Kuhn, Cheney, & Weinstock,

2000; Kuhn & Franklin, 2006; Kuhn & Weinstock, 2002; Mansfield & Clinchy, 2002; Moshman, 2008, in press-a; Perry, 1970). Specifically, development proceeds from an **objectivist epistemology** to a **subjectivist epistemology** and ultimately, in some cases, to a **rationalist epistemology**. The objectivist believes there is an ultimate truth that is directly observable, provable, and/or known to the authorities. Denying this, the subjectivist believes truth is constructed from, and thus determined by, one's point of view. The rationalist, without any claim to absolute or final truth, believes ideas and viewpoints can be meaningfully evaluated, criticized, and justified.

Consider the following claims:

1. Whales are bigger than germs.
2. $5 + 3 = 8$.
3. Chocolate is better than vanilla.
4. Einstein's theory is better than Newton's.
5. Mozart's music is better than Madonna's.

Which of these claims are true, and how can such judgments be justified? An objectivist, who sees truth as unproblematic, would see the first two claims as prototypical examples of knowledge. It can readily be established that each of these claims is true and that alternative claims, such as *germs are bigger than whales* or *5 + 3 = 12*, are false. Claim 4 may be a more difficult matter because it involves technical knowledge, but an objectivist would maintain that this claim too is either true or false. If scientists determine that Einstein's theory is consistent with relevant evidence and Newton's theory is not, then Claim 4 is true. Claim 3 might be dismissed as a matter of opinion, not a matter of knowledge. Claim 5 might also be simply a matter of opinion, though perhaps an expert in music could establish its truth.

For the objectivist, then, truth and falsity are sharply distinct. True beliefs can be definitively distinguished from false beliefs on the basis of logic, evidence, and authority. Irreconcilable differences can exist only with regard to matters of opinion, which are sharply distinct from matters of fact and thus fall outside the domain of knowledge.

A subjectivist, in contrast, who sees truth as relative to one's point of view, would see Claim 3 as a prototypical example of the relativity of beliefs. No flavor is intrinsically better than any other; flavor preferences are literally a matter of taste. But isn't everything, at least metaphorically, a matter of taste? I may prefer Mozart's music to Madonna's (Claim 5), but you may prefer Madonna's music to Mozart's. I may find a musicologist who believes Mozart's music is superior to that of Madonna, but even this so-called expert, the subjectivist would argue, evaluates music from his or her own musical perspective, which is no better than anyone else's perspective. Similarly, it may be true that most contemporary physicists prefer Einstein's theory to Newton's (Claim 4), but there was a time when Newton's theory prevailed, and there may come a time when Einstein's theory falls into disfavor. Even in science, the subjectivist would point out, our "facts" are a function of our theoretical perspectives, and such perspectives are ultimately subjective, neither true nor false. Claims 1 and 2 may appear beyond dispute, but knowledge is rarely this simple. Even in these cases, moreover, the claims are true only within a shared network of concepts. If we think of an enormous cloud of pollution as a "germ," then germs can be larger than whales. If we reason in base 6, then "12" means 6 + 2 and is the sum of 5 and 3.

For the subjectivist, then, judgments of truth and falsity are always a function of one's perspective, and no perspective is better or worse than any other. Subjective perspectives are the primary reality and cannot be transcended through the use of logic or any other general system of absolute rules. Reasons are always relative to particular perspectives; justification is possible only within specific contexts. As one subject said, "I wouldn't say that one person is wrong and another person is right. Each person, I think, has their own truth" (King & Kitchener, 1994, p. 64). In the end, everything turns out to be simply a matter of opinion.

If everything is just a matter of opinion, then there is no need for justification but also no rational basis for belief or action, no reason to believe or do one thing rather than another. The cost of freedom from evaluation is the vertiginous terror of **epistemic doubt**—doubt that encompasses not just the truth or rightness of particular beliefs or actions but the very possibility of justified belief or action (Chandler, 1987; Chandler et al., 1990). Faced with an epistemic dead end, some subjectivists come to see that radical subjectivism as an epistemology undermines its own claim to justification (Siegel, 1987, 2004). If no view is justifiable, except from some perspective that is no better than any other perspective, then there is no reason to be a subjectivist, except from a subjectivist perspective, which is no better than any other perspective. Reflection on the self-refuting nature of radical subjectivism and on the interrelations of subjectivity and objectivity may enable the subjectivist to construct a rationalist epistemology, one that construes rationality as **metasubjective objectivity**—a fallible quest for truth through reflection on and coordination of subjectivities.

A rationalist might take Claim 4 as a prototypical example of knowledge. Einstein's theory may not be true in the same simple sense that whales are bigger than germs or 5 + 3 = 8, but preferring it to Newton's theory is not just a matter of taste, like preferring one flavor to another. In complex domains of knowledge, we may use justifiable criteria to evaluate various judgments and justifications. The criteria are not absolute—they are not beyond criticism—but neither are they arbitrary or specific to arbitrary perspectives. As a result, we may have good reason to prefer some beliefs to others even if we cannot prove any of those beliefs true or false. It may not be clear how musical preferences such as Claim 5 can be justified—if they can be justified at all—but this doesn't mean all knowledge is subjective any more than the existence of some relatively clear-cut truths—such as Claims 1 and 2—means that all knowledge is objective.

Research on advanced epistemic cognition has traditionally involved interviews focused on the justification of beliefs (Perry, 1970). Patricia King and Karen Kitchener (1994), for example, developed the *Reflective Judgment Interview*, in which the interviewer presents a series of issues, such as the safety of chemical additives in food, and then asks the interviewee about the origin and justification of his or her viewpoint. Regardless of methodology, research shows that many individuals make progress in epistemic cognition over the course of adolescence and early adulthood, but the relation of age to developmental level is not strong (Boyes & Chandler, 1992; Chandler et al., 1990, 2002; Hofer & Pintrich, 1997, 2002; King & Kitchener, 1994, 2002; Kuhn et al., 2000). Some adolescents have already made considerable progress toward sophisticated epistemic conceptions, whereas some adults have made very little. It appears that the development of epistemic cognition can continue during and beyond adolescence but that such development is not inevitable and universal.

Does epistemic cognition actually improve cognitive performance? Do people make better inferences if they have more sophisticated conceptual knowledge about the nature and use of inferential norms? Correlational research has shown that advanced epistemic cognition, including metalogical understanding, is indeed positively related to good thinking and reasoning (Hofer & Pintrich, 2002; Klaczynski, 2000; Kuhn, 1991, 2000; Markovits & Bouffard-Bouchard, 1992; Warren, Kuhn, & Weinstock, 2010). Paul Klaczynski (2000) found evidence to support the view that

> for some adolescents, beliefs regarding the nature, certainty, and acquisition of knowledge may be more influential than personal theories in evidence evaluation. Such beliefs are largely metacognitive because the course of one's own reasoning must be monitored and self-regulated to achieve various epistemic goals. Metacognitive dispositions related to intellectual self-regulation include reflectiveness, open-mindedness, and willingness to scrutinize one's knowledge, reevaluate one's opinions, postpone closure, and recognize that theories must sometimes be relinquished or revised to acquire knowledge [citations omitted]. These characteristics constitute a thinking style in which the goal of theory preservation is subordinated to the goal of knowledge acquisition. (p. 1350)

Deanna Kuhn and Susan Pearsall (1998) used a microgenetic methodology to provide more detailed evidence concerning the relation of epistemic cognition to strategic performance. A **microgenetic methodology** investigates developmental changes over relatively brief periods of time, usually by providing individuals with intensive experience on some set of tasks. In the present study, 47 fifth graders (ages 10–11) worked twice a week for 7 weeks (once individually and once with a peer) on tasks where they were asked to determine the causal role of a variety of variables. In one problem, for example, they had to determine how the speed of a boat was influenced by boat size, sail size, sail color, weight, and water depth.

Children improved over the course of the 7 weeks in both (a) the justifiability of their inferences and (b) their understanding about the purpose of the tasks and the use of various potential strategies for achieving this purpose. Progress toward better understanding about strategies and about the point of the task was strongly associated with a higher proportion of good inferences, although it did not guarantee such inferences. These results are consistent with the view that epistemic cognition enhances cognitive performance, especially on tasks that require the reflective application and coordination of inferential norms.

Epistemic Domains

An important aspect of epistemic development is distinguishing epistemic domains and understanding their epistemic differences (Chandler & Proulx, 2010). As we have seen, metalogical understanding includes knowledge about the necessity of deductive inferences. A valid inference from true premises yields a conclusion that is not just reasonable but true, and not just true but necessarily true, given those premises. Similarly, 2 + 2 = 4 is not just a better bit of arithmetic than 2 + 2 = 5; the former is correct, whereas the latter is not, and we cannot conceive it otherwise. Thus logic and mathematics constitute domains in which an objectivist epistemology is highly apt.

Science, in contrast, holds no hope of necessary truth, or even certain truth, but settles instead for provisional truths, what we know as of now until new evidence shows otherwise. In empirical, as distinct from logical, domains—involving evidence, not proof—we may come to recognize the limits of objectivity and later to understand the nature and limits of subjectivity as described in the standard three-stage model.

And then there is morality, which is seen by some as a matter of subjective taste or values. But morality can be understood as a matter of moral knowledge and moral rationality (see Chapter 5), raising questions of justifiability and thus of moral epistemology (Turiel, 2008). In fact, morality provides a particularly interesting and important example of a potential epistemic domain (Krettenauer, 2004; see Chapter 13).

Epistemic cognition, then, is a function not only of developmental level but also of epistemic domain. Variations in epistemic cognition across domains may in some cases reflect the difficulty of applying our best epistemic insights to complex or unfamiliar domains, but in others they may reflect genuine understanding of epistemic differences among various domains (Chandler & Proulx, 2010). Thus research on epistemic development must consider not only whether it proceeds at different rates in different domains (Kuhn et al., 2000) but also whether it takes a different course in different domains as developing individuals come to understand differing approaches to justification—such as logical proof versus empirical research versus principled reasoning.

Conclusion

We have seen throughout this chapter how the development of our inferential abilities, and especially of our thinking and reasoning, is made possible by progress in metacognition, especially epistemic cognition. We now consider, more directly, how rational agents enhance their own rationality.

CHAPTER 4

The Construction of Rationality

We can add to our knowledge of the world by accumulating information at a given level—by extensive observation from one standpoint. But we can raise our understanding to a new level only if we examine that relation between the world and ourselves which is responsible for our prior understanding, and form a new conception that includes a more detached understanding of ourselves, of the world, and of the interaction between them.

—Thomas Nagel
(1986, p. 5)

As seen in Chapter 3, developmental changes in rationality during adolescence are due in large part to progress in **meta-cognition**, our increasing knowledge about our own knowledge and inference, and especially to the development of **epistemic cognition**, knowledge about the justifiability of our beliefs and inferential processes. There remains the question of explaining the development of epistemic cognition. A nativist would suggest that epistemic cognition is genetically programmed to develop over a period of time extending into adolescence and beyond. An empiricist would suggest that advanced epistemic conceptions are learned in educational and/or other environments. An interactionist would suggest that genetic and environmental factors interactively determine the course of development.

There is little or no evidence, however, to suggest that epistemic cognition is genetically programmed or that it consists of some set of ideas and/or skills that can be learned from one's environment. Accepting the interactionist view that genetic and environmental

49

factors interact throughout development, a constructivist would go beyond this to suggest that individuals engage in an ongoing process of justifying their ideas, reflecting on their concepts of justification, and reconstructing those epistemic concepts as necessary. In this chapter, I first illustrate this constructive process with respect to several specific metalogical concepts. I then address the construction of rationality more generally, highlighting issues of subjectivity and objectivity, and the critical roles of reflection, coordination, and peer interaction.

The Construction of Metalogical Understanding

Alice, Ben, Carol, Dan, and Earl (the names are fictitious but the people are real) were college students participating in a study of collaborative reasoning on the Wason **selection task** (Moshman & Geil, 1998; see Chapter 1 for related research). They were presented with a picture of four cards, one showing the letter E, one showing the letter K, one showing the number 4, and one showing the number 7. They knew that each card had a letter on one side and a number on the other, though only one side of each card was visible.

Below the cards was the following hypothesis: If a card has a vowel on one side, then it has an even number on the other side.

What, the students were asked, is the most efficient way to determine conclusively whether the hypothesis is true or false for this set of four cards? Turning all four cards would surely settle the matter, but would it suffice to turn just three, or two, or even one? The students were asked to provide individual responses in writing and then to discuss their selections with each other and attempt to reach consensus.

The difficulty of the original selection task (the abstract version used by Moshman and Geil) is notorious in the literature on human reasoning; fewer than 10% of college students working individually typically solve it (Evans, 1989; Stanovich, 1999; Wason & Johnson-Laird, 1972). Why is the selection task so difficult? Probably because it involves much more than deducing a correct conclusion from premises, a matter of first-order logic. Rather, it requires sufficient metalogical understanding to coordinate one's logical inferences appropriately.

Specifically, comprehension of the selection task requires the coordination of at least four metalogical insights. First, any instance of the form *p and not-q* will falsify a hypothesis of the form *If p then q*. Second, no other instance can falsify such a hypothesis. Third, information that could falsify a hypothesis is relevant to testing it. Fourth, information that cannot falsify a hypothesis is irrelevant to testing it.

Thus, to test the hypothesis *If vowel then even*, one must be concerned with those cards, and only those cards, that could combine a vowel with an odd number. Such cards, and only such cards, could falsify the hypothesis. One must turn the vowel (E) because an odd number on the other side would falsify the hypothesis and must turn the odd number (7) because a vowel on the other side would falsify the hypothesis. The K and 4 cards, however, cannot falsify the hypothesis and thus need not be turned.

Consistent with earlier research, Moshman and Geil (1998) found that only 3 out of 32 college students who were individually presented with this task chose to turn just the E and 7 cards. In sharp contrast, although this combination of cards was not initially the majority—or even the modal—choice of individuals in any of the 20 groups in the study, it was ultimately the consensus choice for 15 of those groups.

The group presented here illustrates how a correct consensus based on genuine metalogical insight can be achieved through reflection and coordination even in a case where not a single student initially chose the correct combination of cards. Alice initially proposed to turn E, 4, and 7; the other four students each chose E and 4.

At the onset of discussion, the five students immediately agreed that E should be turned to check for an even number on the reverse side, that 4 should be turned to check for a vowel, and that the other two cards were irrelevant to the hypothesis. Alice noted that she had initially proposed turning E, 4, and 7 but dismissed her selection of 7 with a laugh, suggesting that she had somehow thought the 7 was even. As Alice, Ben, Carol, and Dan continued to discuss why E and 4, but not K and 7, were relevant to the hypothesis, however, Alice suddenly seemed to take her initial selection of 7 more seriously:

Alice: Maybe 7 has a vowel on the other side.
Ben: It could, but as far as this hypothesis here, it just doesn't matter.
Alice: But if it has …
Dan: It just says if it has a vowel on one side.

Alice: Yeah, but it says if it has a vowel on one side, then it has an even number on the other side.

Dan: So maybe we're wrong.

Carol: [surprised and excited] Oh, that's *true*!

Alice: 7 *could* have a vowel on the other side.

As everyone reflected on these complications, Ben proposed that turning the E and 4 would "test" the hypothesis and that finding an even number behind the E and a vowel behind the 4 would "support it, as opposed to proving it" but suggested "we couldn't prove it unless we turned over all of them." The discussion went off on a tangent regarding the mechanics of turning and keeping track of all four cards until Dan abruptly shifted the focus:

Dan: Do we need to turn over K?

Alice: I don't think so because …

Dan: We don't have to turn over K.

Alice: We're concerned with vowels.

Dan: It has a letter and a number, and we know that that one [the K] has a letter, and it's not a vowel.

Alice: Yeah.

Carol: But what if it has an even number on the other side?

Dan: It doesn't say anything about …

Alice: It doesn't say that if it's a consonant …

Dan: It just says if it has a vowel. It doesn't say if it has a consonant it can't have any of them.

Carol: That's true.

Dan: I don't think we have to turn over K.

There was a pause in the conversation until Carol, apparently convinced that turning K was unnecessary and now questioning the need to turn 4, added, "And it doesn't say that if it has an even number on one side it has a vowel on the other." After another pause, she added, "Really we don't need to turn over 4." She and Ben then elaborated as follows:

Carol: You don't have to turn over 4 because it [the hypothesis] says if it has a vowel on one side it has an even number on the other side.

Ben: It doesn't say if it has an even number on one side it has a vowel on the other.

Alice and Dan, however, continued to insist that the 4 must be turned. Carol tried to explain that the 4 "could have a consonant on the other side and it still wouldn't ..." but was cut off by Alice, who interjected, "Yeah, but we need to check it because it *is* an even number, so we have to find out if it *has* a vowel on the other side." "Yeah, I guess," said Carol.

Alice continued that, in addition to the 4, the E must be turned because "we have to find out if it's an even number," and the 7 must be turned because "we need to find out if it's a consonant or a vowel, because if it's a vowel then it's false." Ben and Carol expressed continuing reservations about the 4, however. Ben wondered about the implications of it having a consonant on the reverse side, leading Carol to observe that turning the 4 would prove the hypothesis if there were a vowel on the reverse side and "wouldn't do anything" if there were a consonant. "It would either prove it or it wouldn't do anything," she concluded. "The 7 and the E are the only ones that can disprove it."

There was a long pause, followed by this interchange:

Dan: OK, we have to turn over E for sure, right?

Carol: Yeah.

Dan: Because it has a vowel on one side, and we need to find out if it has an even number on the other. K we don't have to worry about, because it doesn't say anything about ...

Ben: ... consonants ...

Dan: ... having a consonant.

Alice: It doesn't say if it has a consonant it's odd, or whatever.

Dan: And 4 ...

Ben: I think we need to turn 4.

Dan: I think we have to turn over 4 because ...

Earl: It's the same as E, really.

Alice: It's the same as E, yeah, we know it's an even number, so we have to find out if it has ...

Dan: Well, maybe we don't. [He pauses, then proceeds slowly, with Carol nodding and murmuring assent.] If it has a consonant on one side, it doesn't matter if it has an odd or an even number. So it really doesn't matter if we look at 4. Does it? Do you see that?

Alice and Ben: [simultaneously] I see what you're saying.

Dan: It can tell us where that's right, but it can't tell us it's wrong.

Carol: Yeah.

Dan: And 7 I think we have to turn over 'cause we need to find out if that has a vowel.
Carol: Because it can prove right or wrong.
Dan: Because it can prove it wrong.

The group then confirmed that agreement had been reached and reflected on the process that had generated this consensus:

Ben: So, are we narrowing it down to E and 7 this time?
Dan: I think so.
Carol: I think it should be E and 7, now.
Dan: I do too.
Ben: That's pretty interesting to watch us all concur.
Alice: I wouldn't have come up with this if we hadn't, you know, talked about it.
Carol: I know. I was totally set on E and 4.
Ben: We *all* were.

After a brief additional discussion reviewing the irrelevance of 4 and the irreversibility of the hypothesis, each of the five students independently wrote on his or her final task sheet that only the E and 7 should be turned, and each provided a written explanation consistent with the group's final arguments. Reflection on matters of logic, it appears, may enhance metalogical understanding. It is note-worthy that such reflection, in the present case, involved the coor-dination of multiple perspectives in the course of peer interaction. We now consider, at a more general level, the relation of subjectivity and objectivity, and the associated roles of reflection, coordination, and peer interaction in the construction of rationality.

The Construction of Metasubjective Objectivity

We see in the preceding account of reasoning about the selection task how reflection and coordination in the context of peer inter-action can generate progress in metalogical understanding. This observation, it turns out, holds across many domains and levels of knowledge and reasoning. Research and theory in psychology, philosophy, and education converge on the conclusion that ratio-nality is actively constructed by increasingly rational agents via processes of **reflection** (Audi, 1997, 2001; Campbell & Bickhard, 1986; Dewey, 1910/1997b; Felton, 2004; Karmiloff-Smith, 1992;

Kuhn & Lao, 1998; Moshman, 1994; Nagel, 1986; Piaget, 2001; Rawls, 1971, 2001), **coordination** (Fischer & Bidell, 2006; Helwig, 1995b; Piaget, 1985; Werner, 1957), and **peer interaction** (Akatsuko, 1997; Carpendale, 2000; Chinn & Anderson, 1998; DeLisi & Golbeck, 1999; Dimant & Bearison, 1991; Fuchs, Fuchs, Hamlett, & Karns, 1998; Habermas, 1990; Kruger, 1992, 1993; Lipman, 1991; Moshman, 1995b; Piaget, 1932/1965, 1995; Rogoff, 1998; Slade, 1995; Youniss & Damon, 1992).

Consider two children facing each other across a room (see Figure 4.1). Nora North is standing with her back to the north wall. Looking south, she sees a bench, a table, and three chairs across the table. She notices that there is a sofa against the left wall and a painting on the right. Directly ahead, beyond the chairs, she sees Simon South.

Standing with his back to the south wall, Simon South sees three chairs, a table, and a bench on the other side. He notices that there is a painting on the left wall and a sofa on the right. Directly ahead he sees Nora North, who suggests they sit down in the chairs behind the table. Simon responds that the chairs are in front of the table. It is the bench, he explains, that is behind the table.

Nora reexamines the room but is unconvinced. The table, she points out, is in the middle of the room, with the bench in front of it, the chairs arranged behind it, a sofa to the left, and a painting to the right. Simon responds that, on the contrary, the bench is behind the table, the chairs in front of it, the sofa to the right, and the painting to the left.

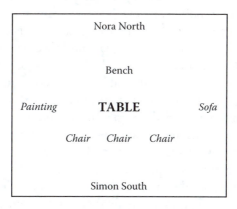

FIGURE 4.1 Nora North meets Simon South.

Suppose Nora and Simon now trade places several times and discuss their new observations with each other. Over the course of this interaction, they may come to a mutual understanding that the chairs are behind the table from a northern point of view but in front of it from a southern point of view. Correspondingly, the bench is in front of the table from a northern point of view but behind it from a southern point of view. Furthermore, the sofa and painting are to the left and right, respectively, from a northern point of view but to the right and left, respectively, from a southern point of view.

Suppose that, in time, Nora and Simon come to understand that the bench is north of the table, the chairs south of it, the sofa to the east, and the painting to the west. This new understanding may be considered more objective than either of their earlier perspectives. The claim that the bench is north of the table is true regardless of where one stands in the room. In contrast to a claim that is true from only one point of view, the new claim is, in a deeper sense, a claim about the room itself.

Note, however, that this new understanding is not just a matter of discovering more about the contents of the room through additional observations, such as finding a hidden compartment in the bench or marbles under the couch. Nora and Simon have not simply learned more about the contents of the room. How can greater objectivity result from a process that does not involve the acquisition of new information about what is in the room?

The answer, it appears, is that the increase in objectivity has come about through processes of reflection, coordination, and peer interaction. Reflecting on the difference between northern and southern points of view, Nora and Simon have coconstructed a reflective awareness of their original perspectives. This shared understanding is both individual and collective. Nora now understands that what earlier seemed to her to be objective perceptions (the chairs are behind the table, etc.) were actually relative to a (northern) point of view that, until now, she didn't know she had. Simon has achieved the same understanding with regard to his own perceptions and perspective. By coordinating northern and southern viewpoints, Nora and Simon have together generated a more objective conception of the room.

To be sure, the new understanding does not constitute an objective conception in any final or absolute sense. The directions north, south, east, and west are relative to the north pole of the earth and thus do not transcend all subjectivity. Nevertheless, reflection on and coordination of their original subjectivities have enabled Nora and Simon to construct a metasubjective objectivity. Their new subjectivity transcends their earlier subjectivities in a manner that constitutes a higher—albeit not final—level of objectivity. **Rationality,** then, is usefully construed as **metasubjective objectivity** (Moshman, 1994).

Rationality, in this view, is intrinsically subjective. A **rational agent** is, by definition, a subject with a point of view. This does not, however, entail a relativistic rejection of inferential norms or of objectivity as a meaningful and worthy value. Rather, rationality entails a metasubjective form of objectivity in which thinking is regulated by reflective knowledge about one's subjectivity, including knowledge about how subjectivity can be constrained, and why it should be constrained, via the use of logic and other inferential norms. Objectivity, in this view, is not an attainable state but a goal that can be approached through systematic reflection on and reconstruction of one's subjectivity (Campbell & Bickhard, 1986; Moshman, 1994, 1995b; Nagel, 1986; Piaget, 1985, 2001; Siegel, 2004).

Recall Nora and Simon first confronting each other across the room. Nora sees the bench as being on the near side of the table, the chairs as being on the far side of the table, the sofa to the left, and the painting to the right. Simon, in contrast, sees the bench as being on the far side of the table, the chairs on the near side, the sofa to the right, and the painting to the left. Not recognizing that these divergent perceptions are a function of different points of view, each finds the other's observations incomprehensible.

The problem is not just that they fail to take each other's point of view. Nora sees the room from a northern perspective that she doesn't know she has. She is ignorant not only of Simon's point of view but equally of her own. Simon, correspondingly, is perplexed by their differing observations because he is unaware that either he or Nora has a perspective.

As Nora and Simon discuss their observations in the course of moving around the room, however, Nora may come to see that what earlier appeared to be an objective observation of the contents of the room reflected a northern perspective that she didn't know she had and that was not shared by Simon. Similarly, Simon may become aware not only of Nora's perspective but of his own. As a result they may construct a higher-level understanding that

encompasses the possibility of multiple perspectives and the relation of divergent perceptions to those divergent perspectives.
Their increasing understanding of their own subjectivity constitutes developmental progress in rationality.

What accounts for such development? As we have seen, three
aspects of this situation are crucial. First, development involves a
process of **reflection**. Nora is not just learning more about what
is in the room but reflecting on a perspective she already had. As
a result of her reflections, she becomes aware of this perspective
and can thus recognize and compensate for its influence on her
observations.

Second, development involves a process of **coordination**. Nora
is improving her understanding of the interrelations of multiple
perspectives. She comes to understand, for example, that what is
on the near side of the table from a northern point of view is on
the far side from a southern point of view, and vice versa. Such
coordinations are facilitated by an increasingly reflective awareness of the various perspectives. The new coordinations, in turn,
can become objects of further reflection.

Finally, development typically occurs in a context of **peer interaction**, involving individuals who are roughly equal in knowledge,
power, and authority. If Nora had construed Simon as older or
smarter than herself, she might have accepted his observations as
better than hers. Alternatively, if she had perceived Simon as inferior in some relevant respect, she might simply have rejected his
observations. The fact that neither Nora nor Simon could resolve
the apparent conflict in their observations by accepting one set
of observations and rejecting the other provided the context for
reflection and coordination that made development possible.

Suppose, now, that you are seated on the sofa and want to
help the children. If you simply tell them that they have different
points of view, they will not know what you are talking about.
They do not know that they have any viewpoints at all, which is
precisely the problem.

You could, however, tell them that they each have a point of
view, that what appears to each to be on the near side of the table
appears from the other point of view to be on the far side, that
what seems to be to the left is to the right from the other point of
view, and so forth. If you can motivate Nora and Simon to attend
to and accept your rules of translation, they might both do well on
a subsequent test in which they are asked questions about how the

other would describe aspects of the room. What is right to me, Simon might have learned, is left to Nora. Generalizing beyond the present particulars, Simon and Nora might even apply their new insights and abilities to analogous contexts.

With regard to a purely objectivist conception of rationality, we might say Nora and Simon are more rational as a result of your teaching. That is, when asked to translate from one viewpoint into the other, they are more likely to provide correct answers.

Recall, however, the conception of rationality as metasubjective objectivity. You understand that some translations are correct and others incorrect because you understand the interrelations of Nora's and Simon's viewpoints. Of course you can understand this only from some perspective of your own, but that perspective is a metaperspective that includes awareness of various perspectives. Your metaperspective coordinates and reflects on Nora's point of view, in which the painting is to the right; Simon's point of view, in which the painting is to the left; and your own first-order viewpoint, in which the painting is straight across the room. Nora, in contrast to you, does not understand your viewpoint, or Simon's, or her own, and Simon is equally oblivious to the existence of viewpoints.

You are thus at a level of rationality that enables you to teach Nora and Simon correct responses on tests of translation, but this will not necessarily make them more rational. Unless Nora and Simon reflect on and coordinate their viewpoints and thus construct a metaperspective, they are still functioning at their original levels of rationality. You may have taught them some useful facts and skills, but they have not become more rational.

Rationality develops via processes of reflection, coordination, and peer interaction, not by learning facts and skills from someone who is already more rational. This does not mean, however, that you can do nothing to help Nora and Simon develop. At the very least, you may be able to facilitate their development by encouraging them to interact and reflect. Directly pointing out various systematic relationships—such as *what's near to you is far to him*—may play a positive role by providing additional bases for reflection and discussion. New terms and concepts you introduce—such as north, south, east, and west—may provide linguistic and intellectual scaffolding for the construction of new conceptual structures (Bickhard, 1995). Ultimately, however, Nora and Simon must construct their own rationality.

Reflection, Coordination, and Peer Interaction

As Nora and Simon engage in reflection, coordination, and peer interaction, notice that progress toward objectivity involves the reflective coordination of multiple subjective perspectives on the room. Coordination and reflection are best viewed not as distinct processes but as dual aspects of the construction of rationality. Reflection on one's own perspective enables one to understand other perspectives and thus to coordinate them with one's own; such coordination, in turn, fosters deeper reflection on the various perspectives and their interrelations and thus a more objective understanding of the underlying reality that is construed so differently from the various points of view.

Notice also that the constructive process in the present hypothetical example, as in the earlier case of group reasoning about the selection task, takes place in the course of peer interaction. Social interaction is a context where one is particularly likely to face challenges to one's perspective and to encounter alternative perspectives.

In explaining the effects of social experiences, it is helpful to distinguish symmetric from asymmetric social interactions. **Asymmetric social interactions** involve individuals who differ in knowledge, authority, and/or power. In such interactions, the lower-status individual may learn what the higher-status individual teaches without much impact on the rationality of either.

Symmetric social interactions, in contrast, involve individuals who are—and perceive themselves to be—comparable in knowledge, authority, and power. In such interactions, neither individual can impose his or her perspective on the other, and neither is inclined simply to accept the other's perspective as intrinsically superior to his or her own. Symmetric social interactions are thus especially likely to encourage individuals to reflect on their own perspectives and to coordinate multiple viewpoints. Because peer interactions are more likely than adult–child or teacher–student interactions to approximate the ideal of symmetric social interaction, they likely play a critical role in fostering the autonomous processes of reflection and coordination that generate progress toward higher levels of objectivity.

Objectivity, in this view, is a guiding ideal, not an achievable goal. We cannot transcend all subjectivity and thus attain a final and absolute knowledge of the world. Reflection on a particular subjective perspective, however, may enable the construction of a metasubjective perspective that enhances our objectivity and that may later serve as the object of further reflection in an ongoing developmental process (Campbell & Bickhard, 1986; Nagel, 1986).

Rationality, then, resides in **metasubjective objectivity** (Moshman, 1994). Even if we can never achieve what philosopher Thomas Nagel (1986) called "the view from nowhere," reflection, coordination, and peer interaction enable us to transcend particular subjective perspectives and thus make progress toward higher levels of objectivity and rationality. Thus rationality may be fostered by posing interesting problems; encouraging reflection, coordination, and peer interaction; and maintaining an environment in which students are free to express and discuss their ideas and to seek additional information (see Chapter 15).

Conclusion

Research and theory reviewed in these first four chapters indicate that (a) adolescents commonly make progress toward higher levels of rationality, (b) rationality is metacognitive in nature, and (c) rationality is actively constructed via reflection and coordination, often in the context of peer interaction. As a result of developmental changes during the transition to adolescence, adolescents routinely show types of thinking, forms of reasoning, and levels of understanding rarely seen in children. Advanced rationality takes multiple forms, however, and its development is not strongly tied to age. Cognitive development beyond childhood is less certain than we might have liked, but its potential is richer and greater than we thought.

Part II

MORAL DEVELOPMENT

Is morality nothing more than whatever values and rules of behavior we happen to acquire from the specific culture in which we happen to be raised? If so, then morality is learned but cannot be said to develop. If there is a rational basis for morality, however, then there may be a basis for identifying moral progress in a general sense. This is the guiding assumption in the study of moral development.

CHAPTER 5

Kohlberg's Theory of Moral Development

> Everyone is aware of the kinship between logical and ethical norms. Logic is the morality of thought just as morality is the logic of action.
>
> **—Jean Piaget**
> *(1932/1965, p. 398)*

E ven within a seemingly homogeneous culture, there are serious disagreements about what is morally right and what is morally wrong. Across cultures, disagreements about morality may be profound. Before considering moral development we need to address what is meant by **morality** and what basis there is for believing there *is* such a thing. Consider an example.

Female Circumcision: A Case Study in Culture and Morality

Female circumcision, also known as **female genital mutilation**, is practiced in more than 40 countries, mostly in Africa and the Middle East. It is intended to discourage promiscuity and maintain virginity until marriage. One form, known as **excision** or **clitoridectomy**, involves the removal of part or all of the clitoris and often some surrounding tissue. Another version is **infibulation**, in which

> virtually all of the external female genitalia are removed. With this type of circumcision, a dramatic excision is performed—removing

the entire clitoris and labia minora—and in addition, much or most of the labia majora is cut or scraped away. The remaining raw edges of the labia majora are then sewn together with acacia tree thorns, and held in place with catgut or sewing thread. The entire area is closed up by this process leaving only a tiny opening, roughly the size of a match stick to allow for the passing of urine and menstrual fluid. The girl's legs then are tied together—ankles, knees, and thighs—and she is immobilized for an extended period, varying from fifteen to forty days, while the wound heals. (Slack, 1988, pp. 441–442)

This is usually done without anesthetic, using instruments such as "kitchen knives, old razor blades, broken glass, and sharp stones" (p. 442), on girls between ages 3 and 8. In addition to intense pain and extreme psychological trauma, severe and lifelong medical complications are routine among the millions who survive the procedure. For many, the process is fatal (Wainryb, 2006).

My immediate reaction, which is probably typical of those who share my cultural background, is revulsion at such a grotesque combination of sexism and child abuse. There are evil things in the world, and this is one of them.

A moral relativist, however, would suggest that I have no rational basis for this reaction. Female circumcision is a tradition that goes back thousands of years and plays a central role in a way of life that I have never lived and do not understand. It is typically done by local midwives or older women who believe they are performing a valuable service. It is perceived by mothers as essential to the social prospects of their daughters and as a key element in the moral order that defines their lives. For me to denounce it on the basis the moral values of my own culture, a relativist would argue, is simply ethnocentric. Each culture determines its own morality; what is moral is what is deemed moral within a given culture.

My response, then, is seen as understandable, given my own cultural background, but completely illegitimate. In the numerous cultures where female circumcision is the standard practice, any effort to prevent a girl from being circumcised would be immoral—that is, contrary to the culture's standards regarding the proper way to live.

From a moral relativist perspective, there is little basis for any notion of moral development distinct from social learning. Morality is cultural conformity; one learns to be moral by

FIGURE 5.1 Moral relativism. (From *Z Magazine*, p. 30, November, 1997. With permission.)

internalizing the values of one's culture. The direction of moral change, then, is a function of culture. There is no internal force moving one toward greater morality (see Figure 5.1).

Moral Rationality

The moral rightness or wrongness of actions, as relativists have demonstrated, cannot be evaluated without consideration of the cultural context of those actions. Moral relativists are also correct to note that cross-cultural moral evaluations often consist of evaluating actions in one culture against the values of another and that such evaluations are ethnocentric. If we can formulate general moral standards that transcend any particular culture, however, such standards may provide a basis for transcultural moral evaluation. The task of formulating such standards is daunting; what seem to be universal standards are usually more ethnocentric than we realize. Nevertheless, we should not rule out the possibility that universal standards can be formulated, justified, and applied.

With respect to female circumcision, for example, Alison Slack (1988) noted that the Universal Declaration of Human Rights, adopted by the United Nations General Assembly in December 1948, states, "Everyone has the right to life, liberty, and the security of person" and that "no one shall be subjected to torture or to cruel, inhuman or degrading treatment." Are these indeed general norms of morality? Does female circumcision violate them? Whatever one's response to these specific questions, it does seem plausible that there could be justifiable moral claims, with regard to fundamental human rights, that transcend any particular culture (Morsink, 2009; Moshman, 1995b, 2005; O'Neill, 2004; Perry, 1997; Sen, 1999, 2002, 2009; Shestack, 1998; Tilley, 2000).

Consider another example. Suppose there are four children and eight identical pieces of candy. How should the candy be distributed? An initial response would be that, to be fair, each child should get two pieces.

Additional information might yield a different conclusion. Suppose the candy is a reward for work performed, and two children did substantially more work than the other two. Perhaps the hard workers should get three pieces each and the others get only one piece. Notice, however, that this does not undermine the basic principle of fairness that initially suggested an even distribution. We are simply reminded that there may be multiple factors to consider.

Suppose now that two of the children are boys and two are girls. The natural reaction of someone from my cultural background would be that this should make no difference. Someone from a culture where boys are explicitly favored, however, might argue that the boys should receive more of the candy. A moral relativist would suggest that in such a culture the boys should indeed receive more candy. For me to object would be simply an ethnocentric assertion of my own culturally specific commitment to gender equality.

A rationalist perspective on morality, by contrast, would suggest that an assertion of cultural tradition is not enough to override the basic fairness of an even division. Unless the moral relevance of gender, in this context, can be demonstrated, it should not be taken into account. This is not to say that the principle of gender equality is an absolute basis for morality that all must accept. The point is that such a principle may be justifiable on the basis of considerations of human rights that are not specific to any culture. To the extent that such a principle is justified, deviations from it require adequate justification. Cultural tradition may be a legitimate consideration but is not automatically the last word.

Piaget's Theory of Moral Development

Rationalists, unlike relativists, distinguish morality from cultural conformity. Given that all children are raised within cultures, however, where do transcendent moral principles come from? In one of his early works, Piaget (1932/1965) addressed precisely this issue. He argued that genuine morality is not imposed by parents or other agents of culture but rather constructed in the context of **peer interaction** (see also Piaget, 1995).

Suppose, for example, the four children with the eight pieces of candy are left to decide for themselves how to distribute the candy. Some of the children may want it all for themselves. It would quickly become obvious to each child, however, that most of the children probably want most or all of the candy and that it is not logically possible for this to be achieved. This realization may result in disagreement and/or hostility. One child may grab all the candy and run off. Who ends up getting the most candy may ultimately depend on who is strongest, fastest, or most devious.

Even without adult intervention, however, it is possible that in the course of discussion the children may realize that any proposed solution in which any child gets less candy than any other child is perceived as unacceptable by the child who gets less. Correspondingly, an equal division of the candy, although not giving any child as much as she or he might like, avoids giving any child a valid basis for complaint. In the course of multiple such interactions, all the children may come to recognize the inherent fairness of no one getting more or less than anyone else—at least not without reason. Thus, the children may construct a social equilibrium based on mutual respect. This may include moral insights on the part of each child into considerations of justice and equality.

But would it not be more efficient for an adult simply to tell the children to divide the candy equally? In the short run, an externally imposed rule to this effect might indeed avoid hostility or violence. Piaget believed, however, that such a rule would be perceived by a child as simply one of the many rules that must be followed because they come from those with power or authority. Genuine morality, he argued, cannot result from being constrained by adults to behave in certain ways. Rather, morality consists of norms of cooperation and mutual respect that can be constructed only in the course of interaction with peers—that is, those with whom one interacts on a basis of social equality.

Morality, then, is not a matter of culturally specific rules learned from parents and other agents of society. Rather, in Piaget's (1932/1965) conception, morality has a rational basis and develops through an internally directed process of constructing increasingly sophisticated understandings about the inherent logic of social relations. Moral development comes about as children, in their interactions with other children, increasingly grasp "the permanent laws of rational cooperation" (p. 72).

Despite Piaget's work, mid-20th-century psychology, at least in the United States, tended to accept relativist notions of morality as social conformity. In particular, social learning theories attempted to account for age-related increases in such conformity as a matter of imitating adults and being reinforced for socially approved behavior. In the 1950s, however, Lawrence Kohlberg (1927–1987), a graduate student at the University of Chicago, turned to Piaget's work as a foundation for a more developmental theory rooted in a more cognitive account of morality. He shared Piaget's conception of morality as rationally based and actively constructed. Whereas Piaget emphasized childhood, however, Kohlberg's theory posits that moral development often continues through adolescence and well into adulthood.

Kohlberg's Theory of Moral Development

Kohlberg (1981, 1984) proposed that morality develops through a sequence of qualitatively distinct stages (Boom, 2010), each representing a higher level of moral rationality (Arnold, 2000). The stages are defined abstractly based on the form of reasoning involved. Consistent with the Piagetian tradition, Kohlberg maintained that morality is neither innate nor learned. Rather, its development involves active construction of a succession of cognitive structures, each able to resolve conflicts and contradictions produced by previous ways of thinking about moral issues.

Assessment of moral development is based on how individuals reason about moral dilemmas rather than on specific moral beliefs or conclusions. Such assessment involves a standard set of dilemmas and interview questions and evaluation of responses on the basis of a detailed scoring manual. Since the 1950s, Kohlberg, his associates, and subsequent researchers have tested and refined the theory through research involving thousands of children, adolescents, and adults. The evidence has confirmed that males and females of all ages from diverse cultural and religious backgrounds can be classified into Kohlberg's stages and develop through those stages in the order postulated (Boom, Wouters, & Keller, 2007; Boyes & Walker, 1988; Dawson, 2002; Gibbs, 2010; Gibbs, Basinger, Grime, & Snarey, 2007; Kohlberg, 1984; Lapsley, 1996; Snarey, 1985; Walker, 1989; Walker, Gustafson, & Hennig, 2001; Walker & Hennig, 1997). The six stages follow.

Stage 1: Heteronomous Morality

For the young child, according to Kohlberg, morality is construed as **heteronomous** rather than **autonomous**. That is, it is construed to be a matter of following externally imposed rules. Neither the rules themselves nor the expectation of obedience is deemed to require justification. Rather, the child has an intuitive sense that immoral actions are punished because they are immoral and are immoral because they are punished. What is moral, in other words, is what does not get punished.

Central to this moral orientation is a sense that goodness and badness are inherent in acts and that knowledge of what acts are good and what acts are bad is held by parental and other authorities whose role is to pass such knowledge on to children. Asked why it is wrong to tell on someone, a child may say, "Because it's tattling." Tattling is seen as inherently wrong because the child has been told by an authority that it is wrong. No further analysis or justification is contemplated.

Stage 2: Individualism and Exchange

Over the course of their cognitive development, children increasingly recognize the existence of social perspectives other than their own and become increasingly capable of understanding and coordinating a variety of such perspectives. Recognizing that others have interests different from—and often conflicting with—their own, Stage 2 children show a substantial degree of enlightened self-interest. They understand that to get what they want, they must acknowledge and respond to the needs of others.

Stage 2 morality, then, involves some degree of respect for the rights of others to pursue their own interests. As a Stage 2 moralist, however, I would be concerned not for your welfare but for my own. I recognize that if I interfere with you, you are likely to interfere with me. A willingness to make fair deals and equal exchanges benefits us both.

Stage 2 may be regarded as a higher level of moral insight in that it enables me to justify and refine Stage 1 moral rules on the basis of a need to mediate conflicting social perspectives. I don't tattle on you because I wouldn't want you to tattle on me. The morality, however, is strictly "tit for tat." Kohlbergian research suggests that Stage 2 moral reasoning is predominant by age 10, though Stage 1 thinking remains common at this age, and some Stage 3 reasoning can already be seen in some individuals.

Stage 3: Mutual Expectations

Further social-cognitive development involves increasingly sophisticated perspective taking. Whereas the Stage 2 individual can see situations from the perspective of another individual, the Stage 3 individual can understand social interactions from the perspective of the relationship between or among the individuals involved. Thus, there is a greater understanding of social roles and expectations.

As a Stage 3 moralist, I do not see you in terms of how I may get you to serve my purposes rather than interfering with them. I view our relationship—based on mutual trust and loyalty—as important for its own sake. I feel morally obligated to live up to the expectations of those close to me and to fulfill my various roles. I want to be a good friend, son or daughter, sibling, or parent, for example, because I genuinely care about others and want them to see me as a good person.

Stage 3 reasoning transcends that of Stage 2 in that it places Stage 2 considerations within a broader framework. The (Stage 2) consideration of multiple perspectives continues but now takes place from the (Stage 3) standpoint of social relationships. Kohlbergian research indicates that Stage 3 moral reasoning, which can be seen in some individuals as early as age 10, becomes increasingly predominant over the course of adolescence. Stage 2 reasoning shows a corresponding decline, and Stage 1 reasoning disappears.

Stage 4: Social System

Stage 4 represents a still broader social perspective where moral determinations are made from the perspective of society as a whole. Rather than accept moral conventions on the basis of one's direct interactions with others, such conventions are now understood and refined based on an abstract understanding of social institutions. The social system defines appropriate roles, rules, and relationships. Personal relationships remain important but are reconsidered from whatever legal, religious, or other perspective is deemed central to the social system. Preserving that system is one's fundamental moral obligation.

Stage 4 justifies and refines the Stage 3 concern for relationships by rooting this concern in a newly constructed abstract conception of one's society. Cross-cultural research suggests that individuals whose lives are focused within traditional cultures are less likely to construct moral understandings beyond Stage 3 than are individuals active in societies with more complex governments, legal systems, and other such institutions. Consistent with the Piagetian conception of **development via equilibration**, Kohlbergians argue that progress beyond Stage 3 is facilitated by experience with social institutions that cannot be understood on the basis of Stage 3 conceptions of face-to-face relationships. The point is not that such societies *teach* Stage 4 morality but rather that they make its construction helpful. In societies such as the United States, Kohlbergian research indicates that Stage 4 reasoning becomes increasingly common over the course of adolescence and is the predominant mode of moral understanding for most adults, although Stage 3 reasoning remains common, and even Stage 2 reasoning can be found in adolescents and adults.

Stage 5: Social Contract

Stage 5 involves a further shift of perspective. Rather than construe moral issues exclusively from the perspective of the social system, Stage 5 involves the evaluation of social systems from a **prior-to-society perspective**. Society, at this very abstract moral level, is viewed as a rational contract for mutual benefit. Laws must be determined through fair procedures and with respect for individual rights. Thus, laws and entire social systems can now be morally evaluated on the basis of **postconventional moral principles**.

Kohlbergian research suggests that Stage 5 moral reasoning is most likely to develop in complex societies where there is a clash of cultures. Conventional moral reasoning, even at the sophisticated level of Stage 4, cannot mediate conflicting social systems. The individual is thus motivated to construct postconventional reasoning that transcends any particular culture and permits cross-cultural analyses. Even in societies where such reasoning develops, however, it is virtually never seen before adulthood and remains rare at any age.

Stage 6: Universal Ethical Principles

Kohlberg believed that certain self-conscious moral systems (e.g., those of Habermas, 1990, or Rawls, 1971, 2001) might be construed as Stage 6 morality in that they provide for the metaethical evaluation, reconstruction, and justification of Stage 5 ethical principles. Outside the abstruse realm of moral philosophy, and related areas such as law and theology, there is no evidence of human reasoning at this level.

Research on Kohlberg's Theory

As noted earlier, there is a great deal of support for Kohlberg's theory. Cross-sectional studies, in which individuals of different ages are compared, have shown that individuals of all ages can be classified on the basis of Kohlberg's system and that, as predicted, higher stages are positively associated with age (Kohlberg, 1984). Longitudinal studies, in which individuals are assessed several times over a period of years, have supported the claim that each stage is a prerequisite for the next so that progress occurs one stage at a time (Walker, 1989) via predictable patterns of transition and consolidation (Walker et al., 2001). Comprehension studies have demonstrated the influence of Kohlbergian moral schemas on the comprehension of moral narratives (Narvaez, 1998; Rest, Narvaez, Bebeau, & Thoma, 1999). Preference studies have shown that people evaluate examples of moral reasoning, at least up to their own level, in a manner consistent with the postulated hierarchical structure of Kohlberg's stages (Boom, Brugman, & van der Heijden, 2001). Experimental studies have shown that individuals who benefit from environmental input do not simply imitate the reasoning they are exposed to but rather move toward the stage just beyond their present one (Walker, 1982). And correlational studies have shown that "adolescents who are more advanced in their moral reasoning appear to be not only more moral in their behavior, but also better adjusted and higher in social competence" (Eisenberg, Morris, McDaniel, & Spinrad, 2009, p. 236; see also Stams et al., 2006).

It is particularly noteworthy, moreover, that Kohlbergian research has shown the generality of the theory across cultures (Boom et al., 2007; Boyes & Walker, 1988; Gibbs, 2010; Gibbs et al., 2007; Snarey, 1985). A classic review by John Snarey (1985) synthesized research from 45 studies in 27 countries using the standard Kohlbergian moral judgment interview. A follow-up review by John Gibbs and colleagues (2007), beginning with Snarey's database, added 75 additional studies from 23 countries using a neo-Kohlbergian measure of sociomoral reflection based on Kohlberg's first four stages. The overall database, representing 42 countries from around the world, included groups diverse in religion, language, education, socioeconomic status, and urban setting versus rural setting. Nevertheless, the results supported the applicability and sequentiality of Kohlberg's stages. In particular, regarding the transition to adolescence, Gibbs et al. (2007) found,

> In the years from late childhood into early adolescence, a qualitative shift from instrumental (Stage 2) to mutualistic (Stage 3) moral judgment was robust enough to manifest across different methods of assessment and diverse cultures. This shift has been characterized as a transition from concrete to ideal or "do as you would be done by" moral reciprocity by Piaget (1932/1965), from the preconventional to the conventional level by Kohlberg (1984) and Snarey (1985), and from the immature to the mature level of standard development by Gibbs [2010]. The shift typically occurs somewhat earlier for females and much later (if at all) for delinquents, findings that may relate to differential social perspective-taking opportunities. (p. 489)

This does not show, however, that Kohlberg's theory provides a correct and comprehensive account of moral development. Numerous studies have shown that children as young as 3 or 4 years old, contrary to Kohlbergian expectation, already distinguish morality from social convention (Killen, 1991; Nucci, 2001; Smetana, 2006; Turiel, 2002, 2006a). At the more advanced end of the scale, it has been suggested that we need a more pluralistic conception of Stage 5 (Snarey, 1985), if indeed we include it as part of standard moral development at all (Gibbs, 2010, sees Stage 5 and Stage 6 concerns as "existential"). It is also clear that Kohlberg's cognitive theory does not adequately consider the role of emotion and empathy in moral development (Gibbs, 2010; Hoffman, 2000; Kristjánsson, 2009). Because of its focus on what develops, moreover, it fails to address the specifics of moral functioning in context and underestimates the impact of situational factors on behavior (Arnold, 2000; Brugman, 2010; de Wolff & Brugman, 2010; Kim & Sankey, 2009; Krebs & Denton, 2005; Lapsley, 1996; Reed, 2009; Rest, 1983, 1984; Rest et al., 1999; Walker & Hennig, 1997). And Kohlberg's focus on justice leaves unanswered questions about the moral nature and roles of care and virtue.

Conclusion

Kohlberg's theory of advanced moral development, like Piaget's theory of formal operations, constitutes a major contribution to the literature. Recall, however, that broad considerations of rationality led theorists and researchers beyond Piaget's focus on logic. Similarly, as we shall now see, many believe there is much more to morality than is dreamt of in Kohlberg's philosophy.

CHAPTER **6**

Justice, Care, and Virtue

Through the glorious ideal of a universal realm of ends-in-themselves (rational beings) a lively interest in the moral law can be awakened in us. To that realm we can belong as members only when we carefully conduct ourselves according to maxims of freedom as if they were laws of nature.

—**Immanuel Kant**
(1785/1959, p. 82)

We must not only state this general account but also apply it to the particular cases. For among accounts concerning actions, though the general ones are common to more cases, the specific ones are truer, since actions are about particular cases, and our account must accord with these.

—**Aristotle**
(1985, p. 46)

By 1970, Kohlberg's theory was the preeminent approach to the study of moral development, especially with regard to adolescence and early adulthood. Research on adolescent morality has flourished since that time, and diverse theoretical views have been proposed (Arnold, 2000; Bergman, 2002, 2004; Blasi, 1984; Carlo, 2006; Eisenberg, Fabes, & Spinrad, 2006; Gibbs, 2010; Gilligan, 1982; Lapsley, 1996; Moshman, 1995b, 2005; Nucci, 2001; Turiel, 2002, 2006a, 2006b, 2008). Many of the theoretical differences involve fundamental questions about the nature of morality. What do people mean by morality? What do theorists mean by morality? When we study moral development, what exactly are we studying the development of?

Conceptions of the Moral Domain

What should the study of morality study? Certainly, research on morality might include research on violent behavior and associated beliefs about when violence is or is not justified. Likewise, we can agree that moral development researchers should not focus their attention on adolescents' spelling problems, sense of fashion, or ability to carry a tune, which are generally not regarded as moral issues.

But what about studies of adolescent drug use, sexual behavior, friendships, community activities, empathy, or character? Whether a given study is viewed as relevant to morality depends not only on what is studied and what results emerge but also on how the moral domain is construed. Research on morality always reflects the researcher's assumptions about what issues are moral issues. Such assumptions are often taken for granted, especially when they are widely shared. Since the 1970s, however, moral development theorists have increasingly recognized the importance of being explicit about the conceptions of the moral domain that have guided, or should guide, research on moral development.

Four distinct conceptions of the moral domain can be identified in the moral development literature. One of these, presented in Chapter 5, is Kohlberg's conception of morality as justice and respect for rights. A second conception construes morality as no less fundamentally a matter of care and compassion. A third conception highlights questions of character and virtue. A fourth posits five moral foundations. After considering, in the present chapter, these alternatives to Kohlberg's conception of the moral domain, I turn in Chapter 7 to the role of principles and perspective taking in adolescent moral development and to claims of cultural diversity in morality and its development. Then, in Chapter 8, in an effort to synthesize current theories and reconcile diverse empirical findings, I present a conception of moral development that is potentially more pluralist than Kohlberg's but retains his emphasis on the rational construction of moral rationality.

Prosocial Conceptions of Morality as Care

Carol Gilligan (1982), among many others, argued that Kohlberg's theory is based on an overly narrow conception of the moral domain. Specifically, she saw Kohlberg's theory as based on a conception of morality as justice. His stages, she argued, are best construed as stages in the development of the concept of justice. But morality, in Gilligan's view, is more than justice. Thus, she attempted to expand the scope of theory and research on moral development by postulating a morality of care.

What is the difference, in Gilligan's analysis, between **justice** and **care**? Justice focuses on rights, whereas care focuses on responsibility to others. Justice glories in individual autonomy, whereas care values relationships. Justice aims to avoid improper interference, whereas care seeks to help. Justice emphasizes the application of abstract rules and principles, whereas care emphasizes sensitivity to social context. Justice stresses strict equality and fairness, whereas care stresses compassion. The development of morality as justice, then, moves toward individuation and abstraction, whereas the development of morality as care moves toward connection, inclusion, and contextual sensitivity.

The most controversial feature of Gilligan's (1982) theory is her claim that an orientation toward justice is male whereas care represents the female voice. She suggested that Kohlberg's focus on morality as justice reflected the fact that the philosophers who influenced his theory, and the research participants who provided his initial data, were all male.

Gilligan's own data, however, were largely anecdotal. More systematic overviews of the vast literature on gender differences in moral development have not supported her categorical claims regarding male and female moralities (Brabeck & Shore, 2003; Dawson, 2002; Jaffee & Hyde, 2000; Walker, 1984, 1991, 2006). Both males and females reason in terms of both justice and care. The actual reasoning in any particular case has much more to do with the nature of the dilemma than with the gender of the thinker (Helwig, 1995a, 1997, 1998; Jadack, Hyde, Moore, & Keller, 1995; Juujärvi, 2005; Pratt, Skoe, & Arnold, 2004; Smetana, Killen, & Turiel, 1991; Turiel, 2006a; Wainryb, 1995; Walker, 1989; Wark & Krebs, 1996, 1997). Even when gender shows statistically significant correlations with measures of moral reasoning and behavior, these associations are generally modest (at best) in magnitude and show complex and inconsistent patterns (Carlo, 2006; Carlo, Koller, Eisenberg, Da Silva, & Frohlich, 1996; Eisenberg et al., 2006; Eisenberg, Morris, McDaniel, & Spinrad, 2009; Turiel, 2006a; Walker, 2006; Walker & Pitts, 1998). Whatever specific influences gender may have, moreover, are likely to vary across diverse cultural contexts (Turiel, 2002, 2006a). Most psychologists are thus dubious of any notion that moral orientations be labeled **male** or **female** or associated with particular genders.

Nevertheless, even if there is nothing specifically female or feminine about morality as care, a care-oriented conception of morality may highlight important aspects of the moral domain that Kohlberg initially overlooked. Kohlberg himself came to see benevolence and justice as dual aspects of an underlying respect for persons (Kohlberg, Boyd, & Levine, 1990; see also Strike, 1999). There is, moreover, a long tradition of research on prosocial reasoning and behavior in children (Eisenberg et al., 2006), adolescents (Eisenberg, Carlo, Murphy, & Van Court, 1995; Eisenberg, Cumberland, Guthrie, Murphy, & Shepard, 2005; Eisenberg et al., 2009; Eisenberg, Zhou, & Koller, 2001), and adults (Colby & Damon, 1992; Eisenberg et al., 2002).

In an ambitious longitudinal investigation of prosocial moral development, Nancy Eisenberg and her associates (Eisenberg et al., 1995, 2002, 2005, 2009) assessed prosocial reasoning and related characteristics in a group of individuals on 12 occasions from the time they were 4 and 5 years old until, most recently, they were 25 and 26. Although progress in prosocial reasoning continued into adolescence, developmental changes beyond childhood were less clear and robust than those seen in children. Adolescents showing the most advanced prosocial reasoning tended to be those who were best in understanding the perspectives of others. This association of advanced morality with advanced perspective taking is consistent with other research on prosocial development (Carlo, 2006; Eisenberg et al., 2001, 2009) as well as with Kohlbergian theory and research (Carpendale, 2000; Gibbs, 2010; Kohlberg, 1984; Moshman, 2005; see also Chapter 7).

The theoretical relationship of care to justice has been a matter of ongoing dispute. Some theorists have proposed that Gilligan's theory is superior to Kohlberg's in its recognition of a moral self that is fundamentally and inextricably embedded in social relationships (Day & Tappan, 1996). Research indicates, however, that, over the course of development, children and adolescents become increasingly able to reflect on their social relationships from an impersonal perspective (Martin, Sokol, & Elfers, 2008; Selman, 1980) and that such development is positively related to moral development (Gibbs, 2010; Kohlberg, 1984). Most developmentalists see care and compassion as complementary to a concern for justice and individual rights, thus acknowledging the value of Kohlberg's theory as a theory of justice development but favoring a somewhat broader conception of morality (Carlo, 2006; Carlo et al., 1996; Eisenberg, 1996; Eisenberg et al., 1995, 2006; Turiel, 2006a; Walker & Hennig, 1997; Walker & Pitts, 1998).

Eudaimonist Conceptions of Morality as Virtue

Adding prosocial considerations of care, compassion, and relationships to Kohlbergian considerations of justice and human rights broadens our conception of the moral domain. Robert Campbell and John Christopher (1996a, 1996b), however, believed there is still more to morality. They suggested that contemporary research on moral behavior and development, although apparently diverse, is overly influenced by the moral philosophy of Immanuel Kant (1724–1804). Kant's pervasive influence, they suggested, has resulted in an overemphasis on formal principles of justice (in the case of Kohlberg and neo-Kohlbergians such as Elliot Turiel) and an overemphasis on concern for others (in the case of theorists such as Gilligan and Eisenberg).

Although Campbell and Christopher (1996b) suggested a number of alternative moral conceptions—including Confucianism, Tibetan Buddhism, and orthodox Hinduism—their primary focus is **eudaimonism**, a moral philosophy that dates back to the ancient Greek philosopher Aristotle (1985; Hursthouse, 1999). Eudaimonism highlights the moral relevance of character, virtue, and human flourishing, broadly interpreted to include personal values outside the Kantian moral realm of justice and concern for others:

> From the eudaimonic standpoint, rights to person and property are but a subset of moral standards and a consequence of deeper moral principles. Private moral standards, such as honesty with

oneself, integrity, and pursuit of one's specific excellence, are central to the moral field ... as is practical wisdom, or skill in balancing and choosing among competing goods. (Campbell & Christopher, 1996b, p. 17)

Moving beyond Kant, in Campbell and Christopher's (1996b) view, is critical to the study of moral development:

When we no longer accept a Kantian model of the study of moral development, many possibilities open up. Is moral development simply a department of cognitive development, as Kohlberg wanted to believe? Or must those who study it deal with goals, values, emotions, personalities, and habits of action? Are the issues around which people develop their moral orientations to be restricted to our relationships with other people, to questions of rights and justice, or to questions of caring for others? Or must we deal with self-conceptions, self-understanding, and the ideals and aims that individuals set for themselves? (p. 35)

In separate replies, Eisenberg (1996) and Helwig, Turiel, and Nucci (1996) argued that contemporary research on moral development reflects a variety of philosophical and psychological influences, including eudaimonist concerns, and is not nearly so Kantian as Campbell and Christopher believe. They remained unconvinced that Kantian blinders have unduly limited the study of moral development.

Helwig et al. (1996), moreover, added that a eudaimonist perspective raises problems of its own. Following Kant (1785/1959), Piaget (1932/1965), Rawls (1971), and others, Kohlberg attempted to establish a rational basis for morality by limiting the moral domain to matters of justice and postulating principles that respect the fundamental rights of all persons in all societies. Although the rational basis for any given set of principles may be disputable, there is at least the possibility that such an approach could lead to a justifiable morality. In expanding the scope of morality to include broad considerations of personality, one includes in the moral domain a variety of personal goals and values that vary widely across individuals and cultures. Campbell and Christopher considered this a good thing, but Helwig, Turiel, and Nucci were not so sure. To what specific virtues are we referring? What sets of virtues constitute good character? Won't judgments of virtue and character vary across individuals and cultures? Although

Campbell and Christopher explicitly rejected moral relativism, and apparently sought a rational basis for morality, it is not clear how a eudaimonist approach avoids relativism or establishes rationality.

Consider, for example, the virtues of diligence, loyalty, responsibility, and courage. It seems difficult to deny the goodness of these virtues. But are they moral virtues? The September 11 hijackers apparently rated high on all four of these character traits; they could not otherwise have accomplished what they did. But that doesn't make their actions moral. Personal and social virtues such as these help individuals and groups achieve their goals regardless of the morality of those goals. Nonmoral virtues play major roles in our lives, but they can serve a variety of purposes, not all of them consistent with considerations of care and justice.

Morality, Kohlberg (1970) famously insisted, is not a "bag of virtues" (p. 63). Eudaimonism remains a serious approach to ethics (Hursthouse, 1999) and identity theory (see Chapter 12), but many philosophers have shared Kohlberg's (1981) skepticism that it can serve as a moral theory. In the early part of the past century, John Dewey (1916/1997a) warned that virtue is not a matter of cultivating "a few nameable and exclusive traits" (p. 358). In the present century, Kwame Anthony Appiah (2008) argued convincingly that eudaimonism is about the good life, which is a matter much larger than morality. Thus virtue is not on a par with justice and care. Virtue is a matter of personality, not action, a matter of character, which includes fair and compassionate behavior but much more as well (see the related discussion of moral identity in Chapter 13).

Even if eudaimonism fails to provide a sufficient basis for a moral philosophy, however, it seems clear that some individuals, at some developmental levels, in some cultures, apply eudaimonist conceptions to at least some issues that they deem, on eudaimonist grounds, to be moral in nature (Walker & Hennig, 1997; Walker & Pitts, 1998). At the very least, Robert Campbell, John Christopher, and Aristotle are three such individuals. A comprehensive theory of moral development must be able to account for this. More generally, a comprehensive theory of moral development may construe some conceptions of the moral domain to be more justifiable than others, but the theory must attempt to explain the development of all such conceptions, even those it deems inadequate.

Moral Foundations

Since the turn of the century, discussion of the scope of the moral domain has focused in large part on a highly controversial proposal by Jonathan Haidt and associates (Graham, Haidt, & Nosek, 2009; Haidt & Graham, 2007) that morality has five potential foundations: harm/care, fairness/reciprocity, ingroup/loyalty, authority/respect, and purity/sanctity. The "five foundations" theory is "nativist" (Haidt & Graham, 2007, p. 106) in that each of the five foundations is deemed to be rooted in the evolutionary heritage of the human species. It is *neo*nativist, rather than nativist in the more rigid traditional sense, in that cultures are deemed to vary in their relative emphasis on the various foundations, resulting in cultural diversity in morality rather than a single innate morality. The theory is antirationalist in that behavior and judgment are deemed to result from automatic intuitions and emotions rooted in the evolutionary history of our species and the cultural context in which we learned the specific moral emphases of those around us (see also Haidt, 2001). Thus each of the postulated five foundations is described in terms of its postulated evolutionary basis, associated emotions, and related cultural virtues.

Harm/care is rooted in the evolution of empathic abilities, originally with regard to one's own offspring. This sensitivity to suffering, cruelty, and harm is "culturally codified in virtues such as kindness and compassion, and also in corresponding vices such as cruelty and aggression" (Haidt & Graham, 2007, p. 104).

Fairness/reciprocity is rooted in the long evolutionary history of primate cooperation and reciprocal altruism and associated emotions of anger, guilt, and gratitude. Cultural virtues of fairness and justice correspond to this foundation.

Ingroup/loyalty is rooted in our evolutionary heritage of "strong social emotions related to recognizing, trusting, and cooperating with members of one's co-residing ingroup while being wary and distrustful of members of other groups" (p. 105). Corresponding cultural virtues are loyalty, patriotism, and heroism.

Authority/respect is rooted in the social hierarchy of ingroups. Cultural virtues related to authority are magnanimity, fatherliness, and wisdom; the associated feelings are respect, awe, and admiration; the corresponding virtues of subordination are duty, obedience, and unilateral respect.

The fifth and final foundation, purity/sanctity, is rooted in disgust, a uniquely human emotion that, according to the theory, emerged during the evolutionary transition to an increasingly meat-based diet.

> In many cultures, disgust ... supports a set of virtues and vices linked to bodily activities in general, and religious activities in particular. Those who seem ruled by carnal passions (lust, gluttony, greed, and anger) are seen as debased, impure, and less than human, while those who live so that the soul is in charge of the body (chaste, spiritually minded, pious) are seen as elevated and sanctified. (p. 106)

In relation to moral conceptions discussed earlier, it should be clear that the first two foundations, harm/care and fairness/reciprocity, correspond to care and justice moralities, respectively. Despite some disagreement as to the relationship and relative importance of these two moral conceptions, most theorists regard the two together as constituting the moral domain. Along with eudaimonist approaches to morality, five foundations theory sees the moral domain as extending far beyond care and justice to include a variety of additional virtues. Unlike eudaimonist approaches, however, five foundations theory specifies precisely three additional sets of virtues and roots these not in personal excellence but rather in the evolution of the species.

Although five foundations theory leaves open the possibility of multiple combinations of the five foundations, it focuses on two major options: a strict conception of the moral domain consisting only of the first two foundations and a broad conception of the moral domain encompassing all five. Liberals in Western cultures, it is claimed, tend toward the strict conception; Western conservatives, along with most of the world's cultures, tend toward the broad conception (Graham et al., 2009; Haidt & Graham, 2007). As we will see in the next chapter, dichotomous conceptions of Western versus other cultures fail to account for extensive evidence concerning the complexity of cultural and individual diversity. Five foundations theory is further complicated by its questionable association of political conservatism with non-Western culture.

The deeper philosophical question, however, is whether the broader conception of the moral domain is more or less justifiable than the narrower conception or whether individuals or cultures are free to have their own conceptions. We already considered questions of this sort in the previous chapter and the present one; we will return to them again in Chapter 8. I will conclude that the first two foundations are deemed part of the moral domain by virtually all individuals, cultures, and theorists because they represent the core of any justifiable morality.

Conclusion

Few dispute the goodness of justice, care, and virtue. Whether all of these constitute *moral* goodness, however, is not so clear. At the very least morality includes justice. Most believe it includes care as well, and some believe it also includes additional virtues. Relatedly, morality surely includes determining what is fair, doing what is morally required, and not doing what is morally wrong. Most believe it includes prosocial behavior that goes beyond moral obligation, and some believe it has less to do with reasoning or behavior of any sort than with being the right kind of person.

Regardless of which of Haidt's five foundations are genuinely moral, all five profoundly influence our behavior. Considerations of ingroup loyalty, respect for authority, and disgust for impurity affect our behavior regardless of whether we deem these to be moral considerations and regardless of whether we have adequate reason to do so. Although morality requires rational cognition (Gibbs, 2010; Kohlberg, 1981, 1984; Moshman, 1995b; Piaget, 1932/1965; Sen, 2009; Turiel, 2006b, 2008), a full account of morality must encompass

- intuition (Haidt, 2001; Haidt & Graham, 2007),
- emotion (Gibbs, 2010; Haidt, 2001; Haidt & Graham, 2007; Hoffman, 2000; Smetana & Killen, 2008; Turiel, 2008),
- neural functioning (Smetana & Killen, 2008),
- identity (Bergman, 2002, 2004; Blasi, 1984; Hardy & Carlo, 2005, in press; Hart, 2005; see Chapter 13),
- social and cultural contexts (Haidt, 2001; Haidt & Graham, 2007; Helwig, 2006a, 2006b; Shweder et al., 2006; Shweder, Mahapatra, & Miller, 1987; Tappan, 1997, 2006; Turiel, 2002, 2006a, 2006b, 2008; Wainryb, 2006), and
- real-time processing of social information (Arsenio & Lemerise, 2004).

However strict our definition of the moral domain, morally relevant behavior connects with all aspects of psychological functioning (Kim & Sankey, 2009; Narvaez, 2010; Reed, 2009). To theorize about moral functioning is an ambitious project.

Our focus, however, is not moral functioning. Rather, our focus is moral development. Of course we cannot ignore the circumstances of behavior, but a focus on development directs our attention toward whatever it is that develops. With respect to adolescent moral development, many theorists have highlighted principled moral reasoning, many have highlighted advanced forms of perspective taking, and most see both as crucial to advanced morality.

CHAPTER 7

Principles and Perspective Taking

> Once we view a democratic society as a fair system of social cooperation between citizens regarded as free and equal, what principles are most appropriate to it?
>
> —**John Rawls**
> *(2001, p. 39)*

> Everyone wants to live like a person.
>
> —**Grace Paley**
> *(1984, p. 5), quoting her mother*

In Chapter 6 we considered diverse conceptions of morality. Now we turn more directly to questions of development. What develops in adolescent moral development? Research and theory suggest three answers: principled reasoning, perspective taking, and moral identity. Discussion of the latter will be deferred until Chapter 13, after consideration of identity formation in Chapters 9–12. In this chapter we consider the first two responses to the question of what develops morally in adolescence (and beyond): advanced morality as principled morality and advanced morality as advanced levels of perspective taking and empathy. These aspects of advanced morality are, as we shall see, closely interrelated. I conclude the chapter with a return to questions of culture, diversity, progress, and universality.

Advanced Morality as Principled Morality

Morality is in large part a matter of perception, intuition, emotion, and habit for children, adolescents, and adults at all developmental levels (Arnold, 2000; Cushman, Young, & Hauser, 2006; Gibbs, 2010; Graham, Haidt, & Nosek, 2009; Haidt, 2001; Haidt & Graham, 2007; Hoffman, 2000; Krebs & Denton, 2005; Lapsley, 1996; Narvaez, 2010; Nucci, 2001, 2009; Pizarro & Bloom, 2003; Reed, 2009; Rest, 1983, 1984; Rest, Narvaez, Bebeau, & Thoma, 1999; Walker, 2000; Walker & Hennig, 1997). Our dispositions, reactions, and behavior, moreover, accommodate to changing environments over the course of our lives. Such changes are not necessarily developmental, however, even though they extend over a period of time. Developmental changes are also self-regulated, qualitative, and progressive. Moral development, then, means progress toward more advanced forms of morality. Theorists of moral development acknowledge, to varying degrees, the role of multiple factors and changing circumstances in moral functioning but focus, appropriately, on moral progress and thus on advanced forms of morality.

For Kohlberg (1981, 1984; see Chapter 5), as for many others in the Kantian tradition, advanced morality is principled morality. Morality, in his view, develops from the premoral social cognition of childhood (Stages 1 and 2) to the conventional morality of most adolescents and adults (Stages 3 and 4) to the principled morality attained by some adults in some sociocultural contexts (Stage 5). In his view, the most advanced forms of morality involve "prior-to-society" principles that can assess the conventional morality of specific social systems. Principled morality is, in Kohlberg's scheme, postconventional. Thus Kohlberg provided a very stringent criterion for principled morality.

James Rest and colleagues (Rest et al., 1999; Thoma, 2006) maintained a Kohlbergian conception of principled reasoning as postconventional reasoning in their "neo-Kohlbergian" theory. Focusing on advanced development, they proposed a succession of three moral schemas that they labeled **personal interest** (corresponding to Kohlberg's Stages 2 and 3), **maintaining norms** (Kohlberg's Stage 4), and **postconventional** (Kohlberg's Stage 5). The theory is based on extensive research with the Defining Issues Test (DIT), which solicits responses to Kohlbergian dilemmas in a multiple-choice rather than an interview format. Rather than requiring people to produce moral reasoning, as in a Kohlbergian interview, the DIT only requires them to choose among a variety of potential considerations and arguments. This makes it easier to demonstrate one's optimal competence, the leading edge of one's moral understanding, even if one is far from spontaneous and consistent in applying such competence. Consistent with the use of the term "schema" rather than "stage," DIT research shows that people (a) usually use multiple schemas rather than fit into a single stage and (b) show gradual progress toward postconventionality rather than step up from one stage to the next. In contrast to traditional Kohlbergian findings that postconventional moral reasoning is rare, DIT research across a variety of cultural contexts shows postconventional moral understanding to be common among adolescents and adults.

Rest et al. (1999) suggested that a full account of moral development must address both **macromorality** and **micromorality**. Macromorality concerns general questions of social justice of the sort addressed by John Rawls (1971, 2001), Amartya Sen (2009), and other philosophers of political morality (Sandel, 2009). Micromorality is the interpersonal morality of everyday life. Kohlberg's primary concern was with the former. In particular, the prior-to-society perspective that underlies Kohlberg's conception of postconventional morality is concerned most directly with the morality of actual and potential social systems rather than with personal relations among individuals. In Rest et al.'s (1999) words,

> Typically in adolescence there is the dawning awareness that there is something beyond the personal, face-to-face level of everyday dealings with people—that there is a "system" in society, a macro level of morality. Kohlberg's theory illuminates the first solution (conventional moral thinking) to the problem of macro-morality (how to organize cooperation among strangers and competitors in a state system); and then describes how the second solution (postconventional thinking) evolves. At the same time, Kohlberg's theory does not illuminate the phenomena of micromorality. (p. 15)

Though Rest et al. (1999) found more principled reasoning than Kohlberg (1984), their conception of principled reasoning remains tied to Kohlberg's conception of postconventional reasoning, a matter of macromorality. In Moshman (1995b) I drew on a metacognitive perspective in an effort to provide a conception of principled moral reasoning stringent enough to be an advanced attainment associated with adolescence but not so stringent as to require a postconventional stance on matters of state to qualify as principled. Principles, I suggested, are metarules

that not only guide behavior but guide and justify the formulation and application of rules. For example, reflection on the rules
"don't hit," "don't kick," and "don't bite" may enable abstraction of
a more general ethical (i.e., meta-moral) principle such as "don't
hurt others." Because such a principle is more abstract, it does
not provide as clear a guide to behavior as do specific concrete
rules. It does have the advantage, however, of providing a basis for
the application and justification of such rules and assisting in the
formulation and evaluation of potential new rules, such as "don't
scratch." (p. 272)

Although moral principles are implicit in the moral inferences
and behavior of young children, children's morality is not truly
principled until those principles become sufficiently explicit to be
deployed deliberately and systematically.

The transition to [principled morality] typically begins in adolescence, with reflection on the previously tacit or isolated ethical principles one has formulated, learned, or encountered. Articulation,
coordination, and reformulation of one's ethical principles may
yield an increasingly integrated sense of one's ethical system,
including (a) the relations among one's various principles, and (b)
their applications to rules and behavior. Moreover, explicit understanding of ethical principles as a basis for moral rules and behavior yields a better understanding of one's moral disagreements with
others, involving consideration of the conflicting principles that
may underlie such disagreements. Reflection on, and social inter-
coordination of, conflicting principles and ethical systems may
ultimately lead to metaethical insights (intuitive at first) about the
justification of ethical principles and systems. (p. 273)

What is needed, it appears, are new ways to assess principled
moral reasoning that recognize principles as something more than
rules but something less than postconventional philosophies. In
studies of children, adolescents, and adults in diverse cultural
contexts, Charles Helwig and associates investigated principled
reasoning about matters of free speech, religious liberty, decision-
making processes, forms of government, and the rights of children, adolescents, and students. Such reasoning was assessed by
presenting dilemmas, posing questions, and requesting reasons
(Helwig, 1995a, 1995b, 1997, 1998, 2006a, 2006b; Helwig,
Arnold, Tan, & Boyd, 2003, 2007; Helwig, Yang, Tan, Liu, &
Shao, in press; Lahat, Helwig, Yang, Tan, & Liu, 2009; see also

Verkuyten & Slooter, 2008). The results show that adolescents, at their best, function at a more principled level than children. Some individuals may make progress in adolescence and beyond toward metaprinciples, which justify principles, but developmental change in principled reasoning beyond early adolescence is subtle and individual. As in other areas of reasoning, moreover, adolescents and adults routinely fall short of their best moral reasoning (Uhlmann, Pizarro, Tannenbaum, & Ditto, 2009; see the discussion of false moral identity in Chapter 13).

Even when we are at our best, moreover, the application of principles to cases may not be simple and cannot guarantee correct moral conclusions. The principles we have constructed may be wrong, and even if they are correct, they are hardly likely to be ultimate and comprehensive. Even if our principles are correct, we may not know which principle applies in a given case. Even if we know what principle to apply, we may not be sure what behaviors it requires, encourages, discourages, or forbids. Even if individual principles provided clear guidance, there are often several applicable principles, which may not point in the same direction, and it may not be clear how they can or should be coordinated. And then there is the question of coordinating our moral options and obligations with social norms and personal commitments (Nucci, 2001, 2009; Turiel, 2002, 2006a).

But principles do serve at least four fundamental purposes. First, they can justify rules that do provide clear moral guidance in specific contexts. Second, they can serve as a heuristic for taking all perspectives into account in cases where it is not possible to consider every actual and potential perspective individually. Third, strict formal principles may direct our attention beyond those with whom we naturally empathize and may counteract the self-serving biases that render us less sympathetic to persons or viewpoints we find objectionable. And finally, principles can be made public and thus serve as a basis for explanation, discussion, and shared decisions and commitments. Whatever else it may be, advanced morality must be principled.

Advanced Morality as Advanced Perspective Taking

In addition to being principled, advanced morality is in large part advanced perspective taking. Perspective taking can be defined as seeing from perspectives (orientations, viewpoints, etc.) other than one's own (recall Nora North and Simon South from Chapter 4). At higher levels, it involves increasingly complex coordinations of multiple perspectives. Robert Selman (1980) provided the classic account of the development of perspective taking, postulating a series of stages corresponding roughly to Kohlberg's stages of moral development. Selman's stage of **third-party perspective taking**, corresponding to Kohlberg's Stage 3 (Mutual Expectations), goes beyond seeing oneself from someone's else's point of view; it involves seeing one's relation to the other, including the intersubjective reciprocity of perspectives, from a third-party metaperspective. Adolescents and adults often fail to reflect adequately on their relationships, but they are generally capable of third-party perspective taking, whereas children are not. Selman posited a higher stage involving the perspective of the social order (corresponding to Kohlberg's Stage 4), and others have proposed still more advanced forms of "metareflective sociality" (Martin, Sokol, & Elfers, 2008), but development of advanced levels of perspective taking is not tied to age, and their attainment appears to be far from universal.

One of the major developments in the study of moral development since the turn of the century is a masterful theoretical synthesis by John Gibbs (2010), who saw perspective taking as central to morality. Perspective taking for Gibbs is both cognitive and emotional. Drawing on the cognitive views of Piaget (1932/1965) and Kohlberg (1981, 1984), Gibbs saw developmental progress in perspective-taking ability as central to moral development. Drawing also on the work of Martin Hoffman (2000), however, he recognized empathy as the emotional aspect of perspective taking (see also Eisenberg, 2005). Advanced morality, argued Gibbs, requires advanced perspective taking, which is both cognitive and emotional.

Jeremy Carpendale (2000) concurred regarding the centrality of perspective taking in moral development. The coordination of multiple perspectives, in his view, is central to advanced moral reasoning. Carpendale, moreover, suggested that perspective taking is distinct from principled reasoning and questioned what he saw as Kohlberg's conception of moral reasoning as a straightforward matter of applying principles to cases.

As Carpendale (2000) acknowledged, however, Kohlberg himself saw perspective taking as central to the process of moral reasoning, as did Piaget before him. The moral ideal for Piaget was reciprocity. The moral ideal for Kohlberg was the sort of idealized perspective taking he called "moral musical chairs" (1984, p. 636). Development through Kohlberg's stages can be construed as progress through increasingly inclusive and abstract perspectives, ranging from considering the perspective of the other (Stage 2), to considering individuals (including oneself in relation to another) from the perspective of their shared relationship (Stage 3), to considering human relations from the perspective of the overarching social system (Stage 4), to considering actual and potential social systems from a "prior-to-society" perspective (Stage 5).

Kohlberg (1981, 1984) saw no conflict between his dual conceptions of advanced morality as principled reasoning and advanced perspective taking. It is, in fact, implicit in his Kantian conception of moral principles as universalizable that ideal principles are precisely those that take all perspectives into account. Correspondingly, the proposition that ideal perspective taking constitutes the moral point of view can itself be taken as a principle—or perhaps better as a metaprinciple from which principles can be derived. In the end, it seems to me, we need not and cannot choose between principles and perspective taking as the ultimate basis for morality. When we apply universalizable principles to cases, we are implicitly taking the viewpoint of all actual and potential parties to the case, and when we try to systematically coordinate all actual and potential perspectives, we do so on the basis of a principled conception of morality.

Martin Hoffman (2000) saw empathy as the primary basis for morality and worked out a comprehensive theory of moral development centered on the development of empathy. Empathy is, roughly, feeling what the other feels. Hoffman suggested, however, that the anger one feels upon seeing someone attacked can be deemed empathic anger regardless of whether the victim responds to the aggression with anger. Rather than requiring a precise match of feelings, Hoffman (2000) defined a response as empathic if it involves "psychological processes that make a person have feelings that are more congruent with another's situation than with his own situation" (p. 30). Empathy, then, is the emotional side of perspective taking. Hoffman's emphasis on empathy, however, did not preclude strong attention to cognitive perspective taking, which he saw as vital to morality and its development but inadequate as a source of moral motivation. He also saw moral principles as important in providing structure and consistency in moral judgment but less fundamental than empathy as a basis for moral behavior. Principles, he argued, may expand our empathic reactions to those not present, but without empathy the principles would have no force. Gibbs (2010), drawing on Piaget, Kohlberg, and Hoffman, proposed that cognition and emotion are both foundational to morality.

Morality and Culture

Thus far in our consideration of moral development, I have presented multiple conceptions of the moral domain—morality as justice, care, virtue, and more—and two aspects of advanced morality—principled reasoning and perspective taking. I have also distinguished cognitive from emotional bases of moral behavior. Once we go beyond Kohlberg's universal stages in the development of conceptions of justice and his corresponding conception of postconventional moral principles as the outcome of advanced development, we are faced with the potential for moral diversity. The reality of diversity, however, is an empirical matter. A common assumption is that moral diversity results from cultural diversity. Perhaps some cultures stress justice, whereas others stress care, and still others stress virtue. Perhaps some encourage adherence to principles, whereas others foster advanced perspective taking. Perhaps some cultures stress cognitive processes of reasoning and judgment, whereas others encourage empathy and other emotional considerations. Perhaps, then, adolescents in different cultures are in the process of developing qualitatively different ways of conceptualizing and responding to moral issues. But perhaps not. The existence of moral diversity is not in doubt, but culture is not necessarily a primary basis for such diversity. The question, we should keep in mind, is an empirical one.

There is no doubt that people differ in their moral judgments and justifications, including their conceptions about what issues concern morality at all. For example, some people consider abortion to be morally wrong in most or all circumstances, some believe abortion is the moral choice in some circumstances, and some consider abortion a personal choice, outside the realm of morality, in most or all circumstances (Turiel, Hildebrandt, & Wainryb, 1991). Richard Shweder and others have provided substantial evidence that moral judgments and justifications vary across culture.

Cultural differences, moreover, include disagreement about what issues are moral issues, distinct from matters of social convention or personal choice (Graham et al., 2009; Haidt & Graham, 2007; Haidt, Koller, & Dias, 1993; Shweder, Mahapatra, & Miller, 1987; recall the discussion of Haidt's five foundations theory in Chapter 6).

On the basis of such cultural differences, Mark Tappan (1997, 2006) proposed, "Morality is not a naturally occurring universal concept, but is dependent on words, language, and forms of discourse that are socioculturally specific" (1997, p. 93). Elaborating on this, he suggested,

> Moral development does not occur in the same way, following the same sequence, for all persons around the globe, but rather it is specific to unique social, cultural, and historical contexts. Moreover, these unique sociocultural settings may well occur within the confines of a larger society—like the contemporary U.S.—defined, as such, by those who share similar experiences, values, or social, political, and/or economic assumptions. Thus, from this perspective, gender, racial, cultural, or socioeconomic differences in moral development, and in the forms of moral functioning/activity exhibited by members of different sociocultural groups, are to be expected, and they must be treated as differences, not deviations, by researchers and theoreticians alike. (1997, p. 95)

Elliot Turiel and other social cognitive domain theorists, however, have argued convincingly against the cultural determination of morality. In contrast to those who construe cultures as homogeneous entities that inculcate qualitatively distinct moral orientations, Turiel and his associates provided strong evidence for the internal heterogeneity of individual cultures and moral universality across cultures (Conry-Murray, 2009; Helwig, 2006a, 2006b; Helwig et al., 2003, 2007, in press; Killen & Wainryb, 2000; Lahat et al., 2009; Neff & Helwig, 2002; Nucci, 2001; Smetana & Villalobos, 2009; Turiel, 1996, 2002, 2006a, 2006b, 2008; Turiel, Killen, & Helwig, 1987; Wainryb, 1995, 2006; Wainryb & Turiel, 1995; see also Appiah, 2005; Nussbaum, 2008; Sen, 2006; Wikan, 2008).

Cecilia Wainryb (1995), for example, studied judgments about social conflicts in 351 Israeli children, girls and boys, in Grades 3, 5, 7, 9, and 11, with mean ages (in years and months) of 8-10,

10-9, 12-11, 14-11, and 16-8, respectively. Approximately half the children at each age were Druze Arabs from two exclusively Druze villages in northern Israel; they attended Druze schools. The Druze society is traditional and hierarchical, with a patriarchal family structure, fixed roles, and strong sanctions for violating duties and traditions. The other children in each age group were Jews from a secular, Westernized population and attended Jewish schools.

Each child in Wainryb's (1995) study was asked to make a judgment regarding what would be the right choice in each of a series of social conflicts pitting (a) justice against authority, (b) justice against interpersonal considerations, (c) personal against interpersonal considerations, or (d) personal considerations against authority. Examples of these conflicts follow:

> *Justice versus Authority (J-A):* Hannan and his father were shopping, and they saw that a young boy inadvertently dropped a 10-shekel bill. Hannan told his father that they should return the money to the boy (J). His father told him to hide the money in his pocket and keep it (A).
>
> *Justice versus Interpersonal (J-I):* On a field trip, Kobby realized that the school did not provide enough soft drinks for all the children. Kobby had to choose between taking two drinks for his two younger brothers who were very thirsty (I) or alerting the teachers so that drinks could be distributed equally among all children (J).
>
> *Personal versus Interpersonal (P-I):* Dalya was invited to a party, and she was looking forward to going there with her friends (P). Her young sister sprained her ankle and asked Dalya to stay home with her and keep her company (I).
>
> *Personal versus Authority (P-A):* Anat loves music and wants to participate in an after-school music class (P). Her father does not like music; he tells her not to participate in the music class and to take another class instead (A) (pp. 393–394).

Results showed a strong orientation toward considerations of justice at all ages and in both cultures. With respect to the justice–authority conflicts, the justice alternative was preferred by 96% of the participants, with no significant differences across ages or cultures. With respect to the justice–interpersonal conflicts, the justice alternative was preferred by 83%. Again there was no cultural difference. The preference for justice increased significantly with age, from 75% to 92%. These results support the view that justice constitutes a core form of moral understanding that is constructed from an early age by children from diverse cultural backgrounds.

The two conflicts that did not involve issues of justice yielded quite different results: a complex pattern of differences among individuals, across cultures, and across age groups. With respect to personal–interpersonal conflicts, 60% selected the personal option, and 40% selected the interpersonal option. Preference for the personal option increased from 44% in Grade 3 to 73% in Grade 11. Although the difference in personal choices between Jewish and Druze children (65% vs. 56%) was statistically significant, it was small compared to the individual differences within each culture and the age trend toward more personal choices that held for both.

The only substantial cultural difference in Wainryb's study was the stronger preference for the personal option over the authority option among Jewish children (79% personal) than among Druze children (49% personal). Although this expected difference is consistent with the more hierarchical nature of the Druze culture, it is noteworthy that the Druze children, far from being uniformly respectful of authority, were almost evenly divided between the two options. Overall, personal choices increased from 35% in Grade 3 to 87% in Grade 11. Although personal choices were more common among Jewish children than Druze children at each age, the same developmental trend held for both cultures.

Overall, Wainryb (1995) summarized the results as follows:

> Within each group, heterogeneity in judgments was found both between subjects and within subjects. Although Druze children appeared more oriented toward obedience to authority, this tendency was not overriding across contexts: Considerations of obedience clearly did not take precedence over matters of justice, and concerns with personal choice were often given priority over interpersonal considerations. Among Jewish children, who appeared more oriented toward personal choice, personal considerations indeed outweighed questions of obedience to authority but did not systematically override interpersonal responsibilities. (pp. 397–398)

Research on social reasoning with adolescents from three regions of mainland China yielded similar results (Helwig et al., 2003).

Participants evaluated consensus, majority rule, and authority as bases for decisions in peer, family, and school contexts. Although judgments and explanations were sensitive to specific contexts, concepts of rights and individual autonomy were salient, and there was strong support for decision making based on majority rule.

> Overall, these findings present a picture of Chinese adolescents' social reasoning that is not consistent with global construals of Chinese psychology and culture as oriented toward collectivism, filial piety, and rigid adherence to authority [citations omitted]. References to collectivist concerns, such as maintaining social harmony, or simple appeals to adult authority, represented only a small proportion of justification responses. (Helwig et al., 2003, p. 796)

More generally, research on social cognition suggests that differences among individuals and social contexts within cultures are greater than differences between cultures:

> Broad and overarching conceptualizations or identifications of the social environment, such as those implied in the concept of culture, overlook important aspects of diversity in development. The research shows that individuals in traditional, hierarchical cultures (supposedly duty-oriented and sociocentric) do judge in accord with roles, duties, and traditions in the social system. At the same time, they are cognizant of consensual issues of conventionality, draw boundaries on the jurisdiction of authority commands, and are aware of personal choice, entitlements, and rights as components of social interactions. (Wainryb & Turiel, 1995, p. 308)

Individual cultures are less monolithic than they may appear to an external observer; differences among them are not so profound as to rule out universal principles of justice. In fact,

> since our society is multicultural, composed of individuals with diverse and conflicting notions of the good life, and since there is increasing interaction with other societies, perhaps with very different values and beliefs about the human good, principles of mutual respect and justice are likely to be called upon for resolution of conflicts that may ensue. (Helwig, Turiel, & Nucci, 1996, p. 101)

Can there be mutual respect across cultures? Does justice have a core of common meaning across diverse social contexts? Would it be possible for representatives of divergent cultures to agree on a set of moral principles? International human rights law provides clear evidence that such agreements are indeed possible. As just one example, the Universal Declaration of Human Rights, approved by the United Nations in 1948, contains principles of liberty, equality, privacy, due process, and social welfare that were accepted by representatives of societies around the world as valid across all cultures. Over the ensuing decades, the Universal Declaration became the foundation of an international network of human rights covenants, documents, agencies, organizations, and activities (Alves, 2000; Morsink, 2009; Perry, 1997; Shestack, 1998).

Conclusion

The universality of human rights returns us to Kohlbergian conceptions of morality as rational and universal. Even if human rights are widely accepted, however, their precise formulation, application, and justification remain controversial (Brems, 1997). Female circumcision (see Chapter 5) is but one of many unresolved issues. Even if moral principles are universal, their application to diverse social contexts may create diverse moral conceptions. We are left, then, with a fundamental question: Can a developmental theory accommodate moral diversity without lapsing into moral relativism?

CHAPTER 8

The Construction of Morality

I understand it, and I believe it.

—**Mildred Loving**
(Dominus, 2008)

As we saw in Chapters 6 and 7, there are multiple conceptions of the nature of morality and multiple aspects of advanced morality. Individuals may differ to some degree in their primary conceptualizations and modes of reasoning, and such differences may be subtly associated with gender and culture. For the most part, however, moral diversity appears to exist within each individual, rather than across individuals or groups. That is, most adolescents and adults have multiple conceptualizations of morality, appeal to multiple moral principles, and actively engage in moral perspective taking—cognitive and emotional. In straightforward cases, situational factors may determine our response. Observing someone in pain, for example, we may respond with empathy and compassion, whereas hearing about inequitable treatment of people we don't know may arouse a more abstract commitment to principles of justice. In complex cases, divergent conceptualizations of the moral issue and conflicting principles, perspectives, and empathic reactions may make resolution difficult and uncertain. Yet it may be precisely the consideration of such difficult cases that promotes moral development.

Mildred Loving

Mildred met Richard Loving in the early 1950s when he came to hear her brothers play music at her home in the tiny town of

Central Point, Virginia (Dominus, 2008). They fell in love and subsequently got married, out of state, in 1958. Upon returning to Virginia they were arrested and jailed for being in violation of the state law against interracial marriage because, as she wrote in a letter to the American Civil Liberties Union, Richard was "White" and she was "part negro, and part indian." The ACLU took the case to court, and the U.S. Supreme Court ultimately ruled that the freedom to marry is a fundamental right that cannot be abridged on the basis of race. It was not sufficient that Virginia allowed non-Whites to marry each other. Two people who wished to marry must be permitted to do so regardless of whether they were the same or different race. The case, *Loving v. Virginia* (1967), literally pitted love against the state of Virginia, and love won out. And having won the right to be married in Virginia, Mildred and Richard Loving returned to private life, declining honors and numerous requests for interviews and public appearances.

Then, in 2007, long after Richard Loving had died in a car accident, a gay rights group called Faith in America, planning to recognize and celebrate the 40th anniversary of *Loving v. Virginia*, tried to persuade Mildred Loving to make a statement in favor of same-sex marriage at the celebration. Loving, who regularly attended church, met with representatives of Faith in America at her home and listened sympathetically but remained noncommittal. Having never given the matter much thought, she could tell them only "I just don't know." But she agreed to keep in touch, and she talked to her neighbors and her children. And finally, responding to a phone call from a representative of the group, she agreed to have them read a statement of support in her name. "Are you sure you understand what you're saying?" asked the representative. "You understand that you're putting your name behind the idea that two men or two women should have the right to marry each other?" "I understand it," said Loving, "and I believe it" (Dominus, 2008).

How did Mildred Loving come to support the right of two people of the same sex to marry? Our data are limited to what Dominus (2008) reported, but it seems clear that, far from succumbing to social pressures of one sort or another, she thought long and hard about the issue, actively consulted with others, and reached a conclusion she deemed justified. No doubt she looked at the issue from a variety of perspectives. Perhaps she felt once again what it was like for there to be laws against being married to the person you love. Perhaps the traditional belief of her culture that marriage must be between a man and a woman led her to consider whether sex was different from race with regard to marriage. Consenting adults, she believed, should be permitted to marry regardless of whether they are the same or different race. Is there any reason sex should be different? Apparently, Loving neither encountered nor thought of any distinction she found convincing and thus concluded that people should also be permitted to marry regardless of whether they are the same or different sex. In the end, empathic perspective taking and principled reasoning likely reinforced each other in generating a strong conviction.

Moral Reasoning and Moral Development

Mildred Loving's conclusion that same-sex marriage should be permitted was clearly, at least in part, the result of moral reasoning; her ability to engage in such reasoning was obviously the outcome of development. But can moral reasoning lead to further moral development? Even if Loving's conclusion about same-sex marriage is correct, adding a new belief to one's current beliefs does not constitute development. Not every act of moral reasoning necessarily has developmental consequences. But if, in some cases, active engagement in moral reasoning leads to more consistent application of defensible moral principles or an increase in advanced perspective taking, this might indeed be a developmental advance.

Especially at advanced levels, moral reasoning is in large part the reflective coordination of multiple social and moral perspectives (Carpendale, 2000). To construe moral reasoning as a process of coordination is to suggest that it typically involves not a choice between two or more perspectives but rather an effort to find a resolution that is satisfactory from multiple points of view. To suggest that this coordination is reflective is to propose that it does not occur automatically but rather involves a deliberate effort to construct a justifiable resolution. This is not to deny that we regularly make intuitive moral inferences, beginning at very early ages (Cushman, Young, & Hauser, 2006; Haidt, 2001; Walker, 2000). Consistent with the metacognitive conception of reasoning and rationality proposed in Chapters 2 and 3, however, the term **moral reasoning** should be reserved for those cases of moral inference that involve deliberate efforts to reach justifiable conclusions.

Although reflective coordinations may take place within an individual, they may also take place in the context of social interactions. It is useful in this regard to distinguish symmetric from asymmetric social interactions, as suggested in Chapters 4 and 5. **Asymmetric social interactions**, in which the interacting individuals differ in status, authority, and/or power, may privilege the moral perspectives of some individuals over others. **Symmetric social interactions**, in contrast, in which no individual has the power to impose his or her will on another, are more likely to involve genuine coordination and reflection (Habermas, 1990). Thus, peer interactions, which are more likely to approximate the ideal of symmetric social interaction, may be a setting in which genuine moral reasoning is most likely to occur (Kruger, 1992, 1993; Moshman, 1995b; Piaget, 1932/1965; Youniss & Damon, 1992).

Engaging in moral reasoning, moreover, may result not just in specific rational judgments but also in development toward increasingly principled reasoning and higher-order perspective taking. Thus, at higher levels of development it becomes increasingly difficult to distinguish reasoning from development. Both involve processes of reflection and coordination, often in the context of peer interaction. To the extent that moral reasoning generates long-term progress in moral rationality, it may be usefully construed as a process of moral development.

A Pluralist Conception of Moral Development

Orlando Lourenço (1996) identified **rationality** and **universality** among the core commitments of Kohlberg's theory of moral development. That is, Kohlberg believed that moral principles can be rationally justified without appealing to values specific to particular individuals or cultures and that such principles thus apply to all individuals and cultures. Although Turiel and other social cognitive domain theorists do not subscribe to Kohlberg's developmental stages, they share his guiding vision of a rational and universal morality. Theorists like Day and Tappan (1996; Tappan, 1997, 2006), however, suggested that what is moral varies so fundamentally across cultures that morality cannot be justified on any basis that transcends particular cultures.

In the theoretical controversies about moral development, rationality seems more basic than universality to the formulation of a defensible theory. As a constructivist, Kohlberg held that morality is constructed rather than determined by genes, culture, or the interaction of both. Following Piaget, he saw the construction of morality not as the arbitrary formulation of idiosyncratic moral preferences but rather as a rational process generating justifiable results (Arnold, 2000). I refer to this view, which I share, as **rational constructivism**.

Kohlberg also proposed that rational construction generates a universal sequence of stages. I refer to this as **universalist rational constructivism**. In contrast, without denying the existence of moral universals, and without claiming that every moral conception is equally justified, I propose that diverse moralities may be rationally justifiable. Call this **pluralist rational constructivism** (Moshman, 1995b; see also Neff & Helwig, 2002; Sen, 2009).

Pluralist rational constructivism, like universalist rational constructivism, is a **metatheory**, not a **theory**. A theory of moral development would provide a specific account of how morality develops and could be tested against data concerning the development of morality. A metatheory, in contrast, is a proposal about the basic assumptions that would undergird a plausible theory. Kohlberg's theory is an example of a theory within the metatheoretical framework of universalist rational constructivism. With respect to moral development, pluralist rational constructivism proposes five metatheoretical assumptions as a basis for theory and research.

First, rationality is fundamentally a matter of metacognition rather than a matter of logic (see Chapter 3). Moral rationality, then, involves reflection about the nature and justification of one's moral intuitions rather than the conformity of one's intuitive social inferences to some sort of moral logic. The equation of moral rationality with moral logic leads naturally to the idea that there is a universal moral logic that constitutes advanced morality for all individuals, contexts, and cultures. A conception of moral rationality as metacognitive reflection, in contrast, leaves open the possibility that the construction of morality may proceed in more than one justifiable direction.

Second, pluralist rational constructivism neither denies the possibility of moral universals nor assumes their existence. The issue of universality is a theoretical and empirical matter to be addressed on the basis of evidence and argument rather than an assumption built into the basic framework of research (Saltzstein, 1997).

The third metatheoretical assumption of pluralist rational construction, which follows from the second, is that research on moral development should seek evidence for both diversity and universality. To the extent that such evidence is found, theories of moral development must acknowledge and explain both differences and universals with respect to individual and cultural conceptions of the moral domain, including developmental changes in this regard. A comprehensive theory of moral development must account for all people in all cultures, including those who, at some levels of development, hold what the theory deems to be inadequate conceptions about the nature of morality.

Fourth, pluralist rational constructivism distinguishes symmetric from asymmetric social interactions. The fundamentally social nature of morality is often taken to suggest that because morality can develop only in the context of social interactions, it is therefore relative to culture. A distinction between symmetric and asymmetric social interactions, however, generates a useful distinction between the properties inherent to social interchange and those specific to particular cultures. Asymmetric social interactions involve authorities who transmit individual and cultural values. Such interactions may be a source of moral diversity. Symmetric social interaction, in contrast, is an idealized realm of dialogue, discourse, cooperation, and mutual respect among individuals who are, and perceive themselves to be, equal in knowledge, authority, and power (Habermas, 1990). Symmetric social interactions may especially encourage autonomous reflection on social relations among the interacting agents and thus be a context for the construction of a morality that is simultaneously social and rational. Symmetric social interactions may even have properties that are common across cultures and thus serve as a basis for the construction of moral universals. Peer interaction among children and adolescents may approximate the ideal of symmetric social interaction and thus play a special role in moral development (Kruger, 1992, 1993; Moshman, 1995b; Piaget, 1932/1965; Walker, Hennig, & Krettenauer, 2000; Youniss & Damon, 1992).

Finally, reflection on rules generates principles that explain and justify those rules and that may lead to the reconstruction of such rules. With respect to morality, moral rules may be learned from authorities and strongly reflect the values of particular cultures.

The direction of moral development may vary to some extent depending on the particular rules that constitute the starting point for reflection. To the extent that moral reflection takes place in the context of peer interaction, however, it may yield coconstructed moral principles that are not only rationally justifiable but, in some cases, universal across cultures.

Pluralist rational constructivism, then, provides more room for moral diversity than does Kohlberg's theory but avoids undermining the very concept of morality by lapsing into radical contextualism and relativism:

> For the universalist, differences among cultures are superficial compared to underlying commonalities in the direction and steps of moral development. The central point of cross-cultural research, then, is to show that individuals in all cultures proceed through the same stages in the same order. Some individuals may proceed further than others and differences across cultures may occur in this respect, but the primary focus of research is to show that individuals do not skip stages, that there are no reversals in the order of stages, and that there exist no forms of moral reasoning that do not fit one of the stages.
>
> For the pluralist, in contrast, cross-cultural research offers an opportunity to discover new structures of moral reasoning and understanding. The pluralist is wary of universalist efforts to force divergent moralities into the Procrustean bed of a specific theoretical sequence of stages. At the same time, the pluralist rejects the causal determinist view that people simply learn whatever their cultures teach. The pluralist also rejects the corresponding relativist view that comparisons across cultures can have no rational basis. The challenge is to distinguish levels of moral rationality without limiting the moral domain in advance to some small number of hierarchically ordered moral structures. (Moshman, 1995b, p. 276)

With this in mind, consider once again Jonathan Haidt's five foundations theory (Graham, Haidt, & Nosek, 2009; Haidt & Graham, 2007; see Chapter 6). Haidt added ingroup/loyalty, authority/respect, and purity/sanctity to the standard moral foundations of harm/care and fairness/reciprocity. We must immediately distinguish two potential claims. First, there is the psychological claim that all five considerations profoundly influence human moral functioning. Second, there is the moral claim that all five considerations are fully and equally moral.

The psychological claim is undoubtedly true. The moral claim, however, requires scrutiny.

Consider ingroup/loyalty and authority/respect, for example, with regard to the 1994 genocide in Rwanda. Rwanda was governed for centuries by the minority Tutsi, who exploited the majority Hutu. European colonial powers dominated—through Tutsi intermediaries—from the 1890s to the early 1960s, after which Rwanda became an independent country under Hutu majority control. The Hutu Power movement of the early 1990s, which crossed political parties and controlled major elements of the government and media, saw itself as representing the Hutu nation of Rwanda. Moderate (anti-Power) Hutu argued that the Tutsi were Rwandans too and should participate equally in a democratic Rwanda. But with an army of Tutsi exiles attacking from Uganda, Hutu Power broadcast traditional propaganda that the Tutsi were an alien race from the north who had taken Rwanda centuries before the Europeans and wanted it back.

When the president's plane was shot out of the air in April 1994, the 100-day genocide began. Hutu motivated by Hutu Power ideology and propaganda, following orders from local authorities and exhortations from national authorities, killed more than half a million Tutsi. In the early days of the genocide, they also killed thousands of anti-Power Hutu who were deemed to have betrayed their group. The ingroup/loyalty and authority/respect foundations may help explain the sense of the Hutu killers that they were doing what had to be done to save Rwanda from the Tutsi and their Hutu collaborators. But does this mean their actions, motivated by ingroup/loyalty and authority/respect, were moral? Were the actions of the Hutu killers as moral as the actions of moderate Hutu who defended Tutsi on the basis of harm/care and fairness/reciprocity? More generally, are those who follow orders to commit genocide on behalf of their group as moral as those who defend its victims?

Consider purity/sanctity, deemed to be rooted in disgust. Some people are disgusted by the idea of two individuals of different races having sex or getting married. Some are disgusted by the idea of two individuals of the same sex having sex or getting married. Some are disgusted by female genital mutilation. Some are disgusted by torture. Any of these considerations might be a basis for someone's judgment and might even be seen by that person as a moral basis. But does our subjective reaction of disgust make something objectively immoral? The evolutionary basis of disgust is postulated to be meat eating, an arbitrary basis for morality. A morally informed sense of disgust may motivate and guide rational judgments about how people ought to act and be treated, but it is the rational judgment, not the feeling of disgust, that determines what is moral.

Harm/care and fairness/reciprocity, I suggest, are virtually universal across individuals, cultures, and theorists because they represent the core of any justifiable morality. The other three foundations represent additional values and virtues that may be seen as moral by some individuals and cultures in some circumstances. But there is no reason to assume that any conception of the moral domain is as good as any other. All moral claims, including metaethical claims about the nature and scope of the moral domain, are subject to critical scrutiny. Some conceptions of morality may turn out to be more coherent and justifiable than others, and some may turn out to be indefensible.

In summary, overlaps in the views of diverse persons, cultures, and theorists suggest that matters of fairness, reciprocity, rights, justice, harm, care, and welfare—in brief, justice and care—constitute a universal domain of rational social action and understanding. All things considered, there is good reason to call this morality and to study its development.

Conclusion

Kohlberg's primary focus, reflecting a Kantian moral philosophy, was on strict obligations and prohibitions dictated by universalizable principles of justice. Most psychologists favor a broader conception of morality encompassing behavior deemed obligatory, desirable, undesirable, or forbidden on the basis of considerations of others' rights or welfare. A comprehensive account of moral development, however, must acknowledge that some individuals at some developmental levels in some societies may construe the moral domain as extending, without sharp demarcation, into broad considerations of virtue, honor, duty, obedience, care, compassion, benevolence, courage, character, responsibility, integrity, fidelity, solidarity, purity, sanctity, and so forth (Campbell & Christopher, 1996b; Carlo, 2006; Haidt & Graham, 2007; Haidt, Koller, & Dias, 1993; Hart, 1998; Lapsley, 1996; Moshman, 1995b; Walker & Hennig, 1997; Walker & Pitts, 1998).

Kohlbergian theory and research provide a strong basis for believing that the construction of advanced moral conceptions continues, at least in some individuals, through adolescence and well into adulthood. Although Kohlberg's theory gives us considerable insight into the development of increasingly principled conceptions of justice, we should keep in mind that there may be equally important aspects of morality—such as care, compassion, responsibility, character, virtue, intuition, and emotion—that the theory does not address adequately.

With respect to the process of developmental change, peer interaction emerges as a developmental context fundamental to most theoretical views, including both those emphasizing the social nature of morality and those emphasizing the autonomous nature of the rational moral agent. Peer interaction is clearly social, rather than individual, and yet potentially a context for rational reflection, rather than indoctrination. Thus, an emphasis on peer interaction enables us to see how morality comes about in interaction with others but is not simply internalized from others. Peer interaction, distinct from both cultural indoctrination and individual reflection, enables construction of a morality that is simultaneously social and rational.

Consistent with our focus on development, the present account of morality has highlighted progress toward higher levels of moral rationality and thus has emphasized moral reasoning and understanding. A full account of adolescent morality would need to address the complex interrelations of intuition, emotion, motivation, and habitual behavior in multiple social contexts (Carlo, 2006; Carlo, Koller, Eisenberg, Da Silva, & Frohlich, 1996; Cushman et al., 2006; Gibbs, 2010; Graham et al., 2009; Grotevant, 1998; Haidt, 2001; Haidt & Graham, 2007; Haidt et al., 1993; Nucci, 2001; Pizarro & Bloom, 2003; Turiel, 2002, 2006a; Uhlmann, Pizarro, Tannenbaum, & Ditto, 2009; Walker, 2000). Transformations and variations in moral reactions, feelings, motives, and actions, however, must have a rational basis to be designated progressive and thus to be identified as developmental.

Recalling the metacognitive conception of rationality proposed in Chapter 3, a focus on the rational nature of moral development suggests that we analyze moral changes from the point of view of the moral agent, considering his or her reasons for moral transformation. This may involve analysis of moral-cognitive structures (e.g., Kohlbergian stages), but it also requires us to consider people's metacognitive attitudes toward their own moralities, relationships, and societies. Ideal moral agents not only have various moral competencies but construe the social world and their relation to it with a "critical consciousness"—a disposition "to disembed from their cultural, social, and political environment, and engage in a responsible critical moral dialogue with it, making active efforts to construct their own place in social reality and to develop internal consistency in their ways of being" (Mustakova-Possardt, 1998, p. 13).

The concept of critical consciousness raises questions of moral motivation: Why do some people routinely construe social issues in moral terms, make moral judgments about such issues, and act on the basis of such judgments, whereas others, though equally capable of advanced moral reasoning, are less inclined to apply such reasoning in their daily lives? One intriguing possibility, noted by Augusto Blasi and others (see Chapter 13), is that moral action depends on how central morality is to one's sense of self (Arnold, 2000; Bergman, 2002, 2004; Blasi, 1984; Colby & Damon, 1992; Frimer & Walker, 2009; Hardy & Carlo, 2005, in press; Hart, 2005; Hart & Fegley, 1995; Lapsley, 1996; Moshman, 2005; Mustakova-Possardt, 1998; Walker & Hennig, 1997; Walker & Pitts, 1998). If morality is not important to you, then you are less likely to apply moral reasoning in your daily life and to act on the basis of moral judgments. If being moral is central to your deepest sense of who you are, however, then you are more likely to construe issues in moral terms, to reflect deeply on what you ought to do, and to do what you deem morally correct; the alternative is to betray yourself and suffer the self-imposed emotional consequences of your lack of integrity. Thus, at the level of behavioral choice and associated feelings, questions of morality direct us to questions of identity.

PART III

IDENTITY FORMATION

S elf-conceptions change across the life span, and some of these changes are developmental. Adolescents and adults, operating at levels of rationality not seen in childhood, often construct reflective self-conceptions of a sort that have come to be referred to as "identities." Erik Erikson was among the first to use the term "identity" in this way and to provide a theory of how identities develop.

CHAPTER **9**

Erikson's Theory of Identity Formation

Caterpillar: "Who are *you?* … Explain yourself!"
Alice: "I can't explain *myself,* I'm afraid, sir, because I'm not
    myself, you see."
Caterpillar: "I don't see."

—Lewis Carroll
(1865/1949, p. 60)

From early childhood we wonder and worry about ourselves. Young children typically see themselves as defined by their names, homes, families, physical characteristics, abilities, and so forth. As development progresses, however, individuals are increasingly likely to define themselves with respect to personality, ideology, and other such abstract characteristics (Garcia, Hart, & Johnson-Ray, 1997; Harter, 2006; Nucci, 1996). Moreover, as they move through adolescence, many increasingly see identity as something they can and must create for themselves. For adolescents, identity is both a matter of determining who one is and a matter of deciding who one will be.

Identity is generally seen as related to the self, with the understanding that neither term is easy to define and that the relationship of the two concepts is far from clear (Ashmore & Jussim, 1997; Côté, 2009). Psychological theorizing on consciousness of the self dates back at least to William James, who devoted a 111-page chapter to this topic in his classic *The Principles of*

Psychology (1890/1950). Psychological theory and research specifically focused on adolescent identity formation is more recent and generally seen as originating with the work of Erik Erikson (1902–1994). In this chapter, I summarize Erikson's (1950/1963, 1968) theory of personality development, including his highly influential conception of identity, and present James Marcia's (1966) reformulation of the identity concept. Then, in subsequent chapters, I consider how theory and research on identity formation have evolved since the 1970s.

Erikson's Theory of Personality Development

The centrality of identity formation in adolescence is a key insight in Erik Erikson's (1968) theory of personality development. Although Erikson's theory was highly influenced by Sigmund Freud's (1923/1960) psychoanalytic theory of personality development, Erikson differed from Freud in three crucial respects.

First, in contrast to Freud's emphasis on biology and sexuality, Erikson also highlighted the role of social and cultural contexts in development. In his classic *Childhood and Society* (1950/1963), for example, he addressed child development in two Native American (American Indian) tribes—the Oglala Sioux of the Midwest and the Yurok of the Pacific coast—as an interaction of biological forces (Freud's general psychosexual stages) and social forces (the specific cultural histories and circumstances of these particular tribes). Erikson proposed eight stages of development, described shortly, that incorporate biological and sexual considerations from Freud yet are generally construed as **psychosocial** rather than **psychosexual**.

Second, whereas Freud emphasized the role of unconscious and irrational forces, Erikson believed that conscious interpretations and adaptive choices also play important roles in development. Although Freud acknowledged a role for the **ego**, or self, as a mediator of biological drives (represented by the **id**) and cultural constraints (internalized as the **superego** or conscience), he typically presented the ego as engaged in a desperate effort to manage psychological forces largely beyond its control. Without denying the partial validity of that picture, Erikson presented a more positive conception of the ego as a conscious, rational coordinator of the personality. Erikson's version of psychoanalytic theory thus provides more room than does Freud's for Piagetian and Kohlbergian conceptions of the person as a rational and moral agent.

Finally, whereas Freud believed the personality is largely formed in early childhood, Erikson believed that personality development continues throughout the life span. In this regard, he postulated eight developmental stages: four associated with childhood, one with adolescence, and three with adulthood.

Each of Erikson's stages is presented as a crisis or turning point in development. The first stage, associated with infancy, involves developing, or failing to develop, a basic sense of trust in the world. The second, associated with toddlerhood, involves development of a sense of oneself as an autonomous agent. The third, associated with the preschool years, involves development of a sense of initiative and ambition. The fourth, associated with the elementary school years, involves development of a sense of industry and competence.

To the extent that childhood goes well, in Erikson's scheme, the adolescent approaches identity formation, the fifth stage, with a sense of self as an autonomous, active, and competent agent in a relatively secure world. To the extent that there are developmental problems in one or more of the first four stages, the adolescent may be hindered by feelings of **mistrust** (a lack of **trust**), **shame** and **doubt** (the alternatives to **autonomy**), **guilt** (the alternative to **initiative**), and/or **inferiority** and **futility** (the alternatives to **industry**). Identity formation is a challenging process even under the best circumstances; problems in earlier development may render it even more difficult and decrease the likelihood of positive outcomes.

Erikson posited three additional stages associated with adulthood. The central task of early adulthood, in his view, is development of a capacity for intimate relationships. Middle adulthood focuses on the development of generativity, a commitment to future generations. Finally, later adulthood is concerned with formation of a sense of integrity with respect to one's life. Negative outcomes in adulthood involve feelings of **isolation** (as opposed to **intimacy**), **stagnation** (as opposed to **generativity**), and **despair** or **disgust** (as opposed to **integrity**). Although nothing can guarantee positive developmental outcomes in adulthood, Erikson believed the formation of a strong identity in adolescence helps set the individual on the right course.

Erikson noted the important correspondences of the adult stages to the child stages with respect to relationships across the generations. In particular, positive outcomes in the early stages require generative adults who are concerned with, and supportive of, their own children, children in general, and/or the future of their society. At a more abstract level of analysis, Erikson (1950/1963) noted,

> Webster's Dictionary is kind enough to help us complete this outline in a circular fashion. Trust (the first of our ego values) is here defined as "the assured reliance on another's integrity," the last of our values. I suspect that Webster had business in mind rather than babies, credit rather than faith. But the formulation stands. And it seems possible to further paraphrase the relation of adult integrity and infantile trust by saying that healthy children will not fear life if their elders have integrity enough not to fear death. (p. 269)

Erikson's Theory of Adolescent Identity Formation

Having discussed the nature of identity in many publications, Erikson acknowledged, in *Identity: Youth and Crisis* (1968), the difficulty of specifying exactly what an identity is:

> So far I have tried out the term identity almost deliberately—I like to think—in many different connotations. At one time it seemed to refer to a conscious sense of individual uniqueness, at another to an unconscious striving for a continuity of experience, and at a third, as a solidarity with a group's ideals. In some respects the term appeared to be colloquial and naive, a mere manner of speaking, while in others it was related to existing concepts in psychoanalysis and sociology. And on more than one occasion the word slipped in more like a habit that seems to make things appear familiar than as a clarification. (p. 208)

Augusto Blasi and Kimberly Glodis (1995) summarized Erikson's multifaceted conception of identity as consisting of the following 12 elements and their various interrelations:

> (a) Identity is an explicit or implicit answer to the question, Who am I?; (b) that consists of achieving a new unity among the elements of one's past and one's expectations for the future, (c) such that it gives origin to a fundamental sense of sameness and

continuity. (d) The answer to the identity question is arrived at by realistically appraising oneself and one's past; (e) by considering one's culture, particularly its ideology, and the expectations that society has for oneself, (f) while, at the same time, questioning the validity of both culture and society and the appropriateness of the perceptions that others have of oneself. (g) This process of integration and questioning should occur around certain fundamental areas, such as one's future occupation, sexuality, and religious and political ideas. (h) It should lead to a flexible but durable commitment in these areas, (i) that guarantees, from an objective perspective, one's productive integration into society, and (j) subjectively, a basic sense of loyalty and fidelity, (k) as well as deep, subconscious feelings of rootedness and well-being, self-esteem, confidence, and sense of purpose. (l) The sensitive period for the development of identity are the adolescent years, even though its outline may become more precise and acquire age specific expressions throughout one's life. (pp. 405–406)

More briefly, Erikson's view was that adolescent exploration of alternatives ideally results in a sense of individuality, a role in society, an experience of continuity across time, and a commitment to ideals. By the standards of modern academic psychology, Erikson's formulation of this theory was vague and unsystematic, and his evidence for it was largely anecdotal. Nevertheless, a great deal of research has followed up on Erikson's conception of identity formation as central to adolescence. Much of the credit for this goes to the influential work of James Marcia (1966), who transformed Erikson's observations and reflections into a clear, testable theory (Kroger, 1993; Kroger & Marcia, in press; Marcia, Waterman, Matteson, Archer, & Orlofsky, 1993).

Marcia's Theory of Identity Formation

Central to Marcia's (1966) approach is the concept of **identity commitments**. Mature identity, in his view, is a matter of having strong, self-conscious, and self-chosen commitments in matters such as vocation, sexuality, religion, and political ideology.

Marcia suggested that individuals entering adolescence typically fall in one of two categories. The **identity-diffused** individual has no strong commitments and is not seeking any. Such individuals are satisfied to live day by day and simply see where life takes them. The **foreclosed** individual, by contrast, does have clear commitments. Those commitments have been internalized from parents or other agents of culture; they are not self-chosen, in that no alternatives have been seriously considered.

It is possible for an individual in either of these identity statuses to move into the other. As adolescence proceeds, a diffused individual may accept the ideas of those she or he is close to with regard to matters of vocation, sexuality, religion, or politics. If these commitments become sufficiently strong, without being purposely chosen from a set of genuine alternatives, the individual now has a foreclosed identity. Alternatively, a foreclosed individual may become increasingly dubious of his or her commitments yet have little or no interest in replacing these commitments with others. Such a decrease in concern with identity commitments would constitute a transition to identity diffusion.

It is possible, however, for an individual who is either foreclosed or identity-diffused to move into an **identity crisis**, which Marcia (1966) referred to as a state of **moratorium**. For the foreclosed individual, this would consist of questioning the specific commitments one has learned, seriously considering alternative possibilities, and seeking to construct new commitments of one's own. For the diffused individual, although there are no current commitments to be displaced, the transition to moratorium also involves an active effort to consider possibilities and form central commitments. Regardless of how one gets there, moratorium is a state where one has no current identity commitments but is seeking to make such commitments.

Unlike identity diffusion and foreclosure, which may continue indefinitely, moratorium is a relatively unstable state. The individual is likely to resolve his or her identity crisis in one of two ways. The positive outcome would be to make commitments, thus leading to the status known as **identity-achieved**. The negative outcome would be to give up the search for identity, thus becoming identity-diffused. According to Marcia's original formulation, however, the individual cannot go back to foreclosure. Once one has genuinely considered identity alternatives, foreclosure is no longer a possible status. One either makes commitments and becomes identity-achieved or fails to commit and becomes identity-diffused.

Identity-achieved is a relatively stable state. An individual who makes new commitments on a weekly or monthly basis is not making genuine identity commitments and should not be considered identity-achieved. Nevertheless, it is possible for an identity-achieved individual to begin questioning his or her commitments, and seriously considering alternatives, thus moving again into moratorium status. This may be a key component of a midlife crisis, for example. It is also possible for identity commitments to lose their vitality, thus leading to a state of identity diffusion. The four identity statuses are not simply stages of development; their potential interrelationships are quite complex. Research indicates that the most active period for identity formation is the period from adolescence through early adulthood (Kroger, 1993, 2003; Kroger & Marcia, in press; Marcia et al., 1993; Meeus, Iedema, Helsen, & Vollebergh, 1999; Whitbourne & VanManen, 1996).

Figure 9.1 shows the possible developmental paths connecting Marcia's four identity statuses. You may wish to consider the meaning of each arrow and to think of an example of an identity transition to illustrate it. Note the absence of certain arrows. Note, in particular, that one cannot get to identity-achieved without going through moratorium and that once one has been in moratorium one cannot return to foreclosure. The difference between foreclosure and identity achievement is not in the content of one's commitments—the specific ideas, goals, and values to which one is committed—but rather in whether those commitments are the outcome of an identity crisis, in the course of which various possibilities have been seriously considered.

Figure 9.2 shows how one determines an individual's identity status. It should be emphasized that the arrows here, unlike those in Figure 9.1, represent not developmental pathways but, rather, aspects of a decision procedure. Two of the identity statuses

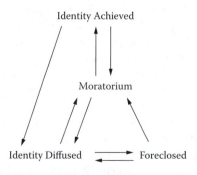

FIGURE 9.1 Developmental pathways in identity formation.

FIGURE 9.2 Determination of identity status.

involve commitment; the other two do not. In each case, distinguishing the two statuses involves inquiry into the active search for commitment (Marcia et al., 1993).

Research on Identity Status

There is extensive research supporting Marcia's claims that adolescents and adults can be categorized into the four identity statuses and that such categorization is useful in understanding their psychological characteristics and development (Årseth, Kroger, Martinussen, & Marcia, 2009; Côté, 2009; Kroger & Marcia, in press; Marcia et al., 1993; Schwartz, Zamboanga, Weisskirch, & Rodriguez, 2009). A major focus of identity research has been identifying personality characteristics associated with each of the four statuses. In a review of this literature, Jane Kroger (1993) summarized the findings:

> Identity achievement individuals showed the highest levels of ego development, moral reasoning, internal locus of control, self-certainty and self-esteem, performance under stress on a concept attainment task, and intimacy in interpersonal relationships. ... Moratorium adolescents consistently appeared as the most anxious and fearful of success among the identity statuses, although maintaining high levels of ego development, moral reasoning, and self-esteem. ... Moratoriums are also most likely to be pre-intimate in their interpersonal relationships. ... Adolescents in the foreclosure identity status evidenced the highest levels of authoritarianism and socially stereotypical thinking, obedience to authority, external locus-of-control, and dependent relationships

with significant others; they also showed the lowest levels of anxiety. ... Diffusion adolescents presented more mixed results, but generally demonstrated low levels of ego development, moral reasoning, cognitive complexity, [and] self-certainty, and poor cooperative abilities. (p. 9)

Marcia's scheme is widely seen as a useful basis for understanding adolescent identity formation (Årseth et al., 2009; Berzonsky & Adams, 1999; Kroger, 2003; Kroger & Marcia, in press; Waterman, 1999). There is also consensus, however, on the need to modify or transcend Marcia's approach (Bosma & Kunnen, 2001; Côté, 2009; Crocetti, Rubini, Luyckx, & Meeus, 2008; Grotevant, 1998; Kunnen & Bosma, 2003; Luyckx, Goossens, Soenens, Beyers, & Vansteenkiste, 2005; Meeus et al., 1999; Schwartz, 2001; van Hoof, 1999a, 1999b).

One set of concerns involves evidence for diverse domains of identity commitment (Grotevant, 1987; Schwartz, 2001). These may include vocation, religion, sexuality, ethnicity, morality, political ideology, family roles, and more. How do we address asynchronous development? How do we classify someone who is identity-achieved with respect to vocational choice, identity-diffused with respect to political ideology, and foreclosed with respect to religion? The Marcia framework can handle inconsistencies across multiple domains by defining identity status on the basis of those domains that a particular person deems central (Blasi & Glodis, 1995). Nevertheless, domain differences complicate the question of classifying individuals.

Another set of concerns involves the conceptualization of the four statuses. Even if adolescents can be divided into four categories of the sort described by Marcia (1966), how exactly should those categories be defined and distinguished? On the basis of a review of the literature and longitudinal analysis of individuals over time, Meeus et al. (1999) proposed reconceptualizations of all four statuses. Probably most theorists of identity formation would agree on the need for reconceptualization, but there is no consensus about just what needs to be reconceptualized and how.

A related complication is that individuals within a given status may differ in ways that the Marcia scheme cannot fully comprehend. Assorted researchers have suggested the need for more differentiated categorizations with regard to foreclosure (Kroger, 1995; Valde, 1996), diffusion (Luyckx et al., 2005), or moratorium

(Crocetti et al., 2008), each of which could be divided into at least two distinguishable statuses. This has led to specific proposals that one of the four standard statuses be divided into two, thus generating five identity statuses. But which one? There is no consensus, and without a consensus there is the danger that going beyond the classic four statuses could lead to a proliferation of identity statuses. The more statuses we have, the more homogeneous each can be but the less parsimonious the overall system. And parsimony, no less than precision, is a major criterion of a good theory.

Two major cluster analyses by overlapping sets of authors (Crocetti et al., 2008; Luyckx et al., 2005) have each attempted to provide a definitive set of identity statuses on empirical grounds. Cluster analysis is a sophisticated statistical technique for analyzing complex multivariate data sets. By grouping participants into relatively homogenous clusters that are maximally distinguishable from each other, cluster analysis provides a basis for a classification system derived directly from patterns in the data. This is not to say that cluster analysis provides an entirely objective answer to theoretical questions about the number and nature of the identity statuses. For one thing, the data themselves reflect researchers' decisions about what to measure and how, which partially reflect their theories of identity formation. Second, cluster analysis generally provides multiple solutions offering a trade-off of precision (many homogenous categories) and parsimony (a smaller number of less homogenous categories); experts may reasonably differ as to the best solution. Finally, whatever number of clusters one settles on, the clusters must still be labeled and theoretically interpreted, which is also a matter of judgment on which experts may reasonably differ. Nevertheless, in contrast to the theoretical derivation of Marcia's four identity statuses from Erikson's writings, cluster analysis is a systematically data-driven approach to the identification of identity statuses.

Koen Luyckx and associates (2005) conducted a cluster analysis based on a conception of identity formation that extends Marcia's emphasis on exploration and commitment. Drawing on earlier work by a variety of theorists and researchers, Luyckx et al. suggested (a) a distinction between originally making a commitment and later identifying with that commitment and (b) a distinction between exploration in breadth of alternative options and exploration in depth of a particular option. On the basis of their theoretical conception, they prepared an assortment of instruments that assessed commitment making, identification with commitment, exploration in breadth, exploration in depth, and various measures of personality and adjustment. The instruments were administered in Dutch to 565 university students, mostly women in psychology and education, in Flanders, the Dutch-speaking part of Belgium. The cluster analysis generated multiple possible sets of clusters, but what was deemed the best solution was a five-cluster outcome with clusters corresponding to Marcia's four statuses except that diffusion was divided between two relatively distinct sets of students: those who were troubled by their lack of identity and those who were carefree about it.

Elisabetta Crocetti and associates (2008) conducted another cluster analysis, on a different population, based on somewhat different theoretical presumptions, and generated somewhat different results. Crocetti et al. devised a battery of instruments based on their process model of identity formation in which the pivotal processes are commitment, in-depth exploration, and reconsideration of commitment. A set of instruments based on this neo-Eriksonian conceptualization was administered in Dutch to 1,952 adolescents in the Netherlands, about equally divided between boys and girls, ranging in age from 10 to 19 years. The sample included 333 adolescents from non-Western countries such as Morocco, Turkey, and Surinam. Once again the solution deemed best was a five-cluster outcome roughly corresponding to Marcia's statuses. In this case, however, it was the moratorium status that required further differentiation, a result consistent with previous observations concerning its dual aspect as a positive search for identity and a period of identity crisis. Thus cluster analyses provide some empirical support for Marcia's statuses and some intriguing suggestions for revision of those statuses but no definitive conclusion concerning the number and nature of the statuses.

Concerns about identity formation are not limited to questions about Marcia's statuses. At a still more fundamental level, theorists have also continued to question what identity means (Blasi & Glodis, 1995). Gregory Valde (1996) observed,

> A careful reading of Erikson leaves one with a somewhat paradoxical understanding of identity. Identity is something one ought to achieve yet can never finish. Identity is preferable to identity confusion, but a total lack of confusion or a total sense of identity is not considered ideal. Identity depends on expanding and opening

one's perspective at the same time that one is limiting and narrowing one's perspective. Identity, as a state of active tension constantly in a process of reevaluation, almost defies operationalization. Yet operationalize identity we must, if we are to apply contemporary scientific methods of examination to it. (p. 252)

And the problems go even deeper. Many theorists have noted that despite the strong emphasis on exploration and commitment in the work of Erikson and Marcia, research in this tradition has not enlightened us very much about how an individual moves from one identity status to another (Bosma & Kunnen, 2001; Côté, 2009; Grotevant, 1987; LaVoie, 1994). Yet this may be the most fundamental question of all. What are the developmental processes involved in constructing an identity?

Conclusion

Research continues in the Erikson–Marcia tradition, with an expanding base of data, evolving instruments and methodologies, and ongoing theoretical refinements. But the assimilation of all identity phenomena to some finite number of identity categories also limits what we see, measure, and theorize about. Some say we need to go back to the original Erikson, whose conception of identity was much richer than what Marcia measured (Côté, 2009). Some remind us there are other conceptions of identity entirely (see Chapter 11).

As we saw in the first four chapters, Piaget's conception of formal operations remains important not as a general theory of adolescent cognition but more specifically as a theory of metalogical development in early adolescence, an important piece of a larger picture. Similarly, as we saw in the chapters on moral development, Kohlberg's theory remains important not as a general theory of moral functioning but rather as a theory of the development of conceptions of justice, central to most conceptions of morality. In like fashion, research and theory in the Erikson–Marcia tradition form the core of a developmental literature on identity that increasingly expands beyond its origin. That developmental literature, in turn, is part of an enormous and rapidly increasing literature on identity that spans the social sciences and humanities. Developmental theorists and researchers since the 1980s have increasingly attempted to provide a fuller picture of the nature and development of identity. We turn now to this work.

CHAPTER **10**

Identity as a Theory of Oneself

Who in the world am I? Ah, *that's* the great puzzle!

—**Alice**
(Carroll, 1865/1949, p. 19)

What appears to be missing in the standard identity measures is the basic identity question "Who am I?"

—**Augusto Blasi**
(1988, p. 228)

Marcia's extension of Erikson's work on identity formation (see Chapter 9) transformed a rather diffuse psychoanalytic concept into a fruitful basis for empirical research. The Marcia framework and associated research continue to be held in high regard (Berzonsky & Adams, 1999; Kroger, 2003; Kroger & Marcia, in press; Waterman, 1999). Since the 1980s, however, there has been increasing concern among adolescent identity theorists that Marcia's identity statuses do not fully encompass Erikson's concept of identity, much less the diverse uses of that concept in theoretical and popular discourse (Bosma & Kunnen, 2001; Grotevant, 1998; Kunnen & Bosma, 2003; Meeus, Iedema, Helsen, & Vollebergh, 1999; Schwartz, 2001; van Hoof, 1999a, 1999b). Efforts to interpret and expand identity research have generated a variety of proposals about what is, or should be, meant by **identity**.

Obviously, no one can dictate how the term **identity** must be used. Nevertheless, if identity meant something utterly different to everyone who used or encountered thc term, there would be a serious failure of communication among theorists, researchers, practitioners, and the general public. Fortunately, although not everyone means precisely the same thing by identity, there does appear to be considerable overlap among various uses of the term. In this chapter I suggest a conception of identity that captures a core of common meaning. I then consider briefly the multiplicity of domains within which, and across which, identity is constructed and note aspects of identity beyond the realm of cognition.

Development of Self-Conceptions

What is identity? Answering this question is complicated by differences among theorists in how they define identity and differences within and among individuals in their various self-conceptions. No definition of identity has ever achieved universal acceptance, and it seems unlikely that any ever will.

Nevertheless, having considered a variety of definitions and conceptions in the current literature, I have devised a brief definition of identity that captures most of the elements highlighted by most contemporary theorists and provides a useful framework for addressing the construction of identity in adolescence: *An identity is, at least in part, an explicit theory of oneself as a person.* Let me explain what I mean by this.

Identity as a Conception of Oneself

Theorists of identity universally agree that identity has some relation to the self (Ashmore & Jussim, 1997; Blasi, 1988). Augusto Blasi and Kimberly Glodis (1995), for example, argued that any defensible definition of identity must acknowledge the subjective awareness of self:

> Central to the description of identity is a special experience of self characterized by the following: a direct focus on one's own person aimed at capturing what is basic about it; the realization of what is true, real, genuine about oneself, namely, the experience that certain aspects are indispensable to the sense of self, while others are marginal and superficial; finally, the subjective experience of unity produced by such a realization. (pp. 406–407)

Conceptions of the self become increasingly sophisticated over the course of development; the emergence and transformation of identity may be explained, in part, in terms of such changes

(Garcia, Hart, & Johnson-Ray, 1997; Harter, 2006). Larry Nucci (1996), for example, proposed five levels in conceptions of personal issues that reflect increasingly advanced conceptions of the self that emerge over the course of childhood, adolescence, and early adulthood, with substantial individual differences in the rate and extent of development:

1. *Establishing concrete self–other distinctions.* The individual conceptualizes the personal domain as an observable body and an equally concrete realm of things and activities ...
2. *Establishing a behavior style ...* The individual extends the conception of the person to include the notion of personality, defined as a set of characteristic behaviors ...
3. *Establishing the self as an individual defined in terms of a unique set of ideas or values.* The individual begins to define the self in terms of internal cognitive processes ...
4. *Coordinating the self esteem.* The individual views control over events within the personal domain as essential to coordinating all aspects of the self into an internally consistent whole. Consciousness is understood as having depth. At the center of consciousness the individual [perceives] an immutable essence around which the self system is constructed ...
5. *Transforming the labile self.* Instead of viewing the self as an essence the individual comes to view the self as labile, as a constantly evolving product of one's personal decisions ... (p. 55)

An identity, however, is not simply a conception of oneself. Even young children have conceptions of themselves (Garcia et al., 1997; Harter, 2006; Nucci, 1996). At least in the Eriksonian sense of **ego identity** or **personal identity**, an identity is an advanced sort of self-conception that would not normally be seen in childhood.

Identity as a Theory of Oneself

An identity, then, is a sophisticated conception of oneself. Taking this a step further, a number of theorists have proposed that an identity is a **theory** of oneself (Berzonsky, 1993; Garcia et al., 1997; Grotevant, 1987). Michael Berzonsky took this to mean that an identity is "a conceptual structure composed of postulates, assumptions, and constructs relevant to the self interacting in the world" (1993, p. 169).

Two characteristics of theories are particularly relevant here. First, theories are organized and (at least ideally) coherent. To say one's identity is a theory of oneself is to say it is not just a collection of beliefs about oneself but rather organized to generate an integrated conception. Second, theories are explanatory. To say one's identity is a theory of oneself is to say it is not just a description of oneself but rather an attempt to explain oneself. That is, an identity is a conception of the self that is structured in such a way as to enhance self-understanding. An identity is not just an attempt to *describe* one's typical behavior; an identity is an account of the core beliefs and purposes that one construes as *explaining* that behavior.

Identity as an Explicit Theory of Oneself

Psychologists have long recognized that even young children have highly structured knowledge, including structured knowledge about themselves. It has become increasingly common to highlight the structured nature of knowledge by referring to structures of knowledge as theories. For example, there is a huge domain of research related to what is commonly referred to as **4-year-olds' theories of mind** (Doherty, 2009; Wellman & Gelman, 1998). Review of this literature, however, suggests that although 4-year-olds use what psychologists call a theory of mind, the children themselves are not aware of their theories *as theories*. To say an individual's identity is, at least in part, explicit is to say it is not simply an implicit theory of self that is inferred by a psychologist to explain behavior. Rather, it is a theory known to the individual.

This is not to deny that a person's identity is deeply interconnected with a variety of implicit assumptions, unconscious dispositions, emotional reactions, and socially imposed roles (Kristjánsson, 2009). These assumptions, dispositions, feelings, and roles may even be considered part of the person's identity, in a broad, Eriksonian sense of that term. Unless there is an explicit theory of self at the core, however, such assumptions, dispositions, feelings, and roles do not constitute an identity.

Construing the Self as a Person

To have an identity is not just to have an explicit theory of oneself. The theory must be of a sort that enables one to see oneself as a person. At a minimum, this means as a rational agent.

Construing the Self as a Rational Agent

To say one's identity is an explicit theory of oneself *as a person* is to say it is a theory that construes the self as a **rational agent** (Rovane, 2004). To see oneself as a rational agent, moreover, is to see oneself as **singular** and **continuous**. Elaborating on this, I consider the nature of agency, rationality, singularity, and continuity and what it means to construe oneself as having such characteristics.

An **agent** is one who acts, who engages in action, and thus who has (or at least attempts to have) an impact on the world (Blasi, 1988, 2004; Blasi & Glodis, 1995; Côté & Levine, 2002). A **rational agent** has **reasons** for his or her actions (see Chapter 3, especially Figure 3.1). Rational agency thus entails autonomy and responsibility (Audi, 1997, 2001). In the words of the distinguished philosopher Isaiah Berlin (1969), to be a rational agent is

> to be a subject, not an object; to be moved by reasons, by conscious purposes, which are my own, not by causes which affect me, as it were, from outside. I wish to be somebody, not nobody; a doer— deciding, not being decided for, self-directed and not acted upon by external nature or by other men as if I were a thing, or an animal, or a slave incapable of playing a human role, that is, of conceiving goals and policies of my own and realizing them. This is at least part of what I mean when I say that I am rational, and that it is my reason that distinguishes me as a human being from the rest of the world. I wish, above all, to be conscious of myself as a thinking, willing, active being, bearing responsibility for my choices and able to explain them by references to my own ideas and purposes. (p. 131)

Ideas and purposes, and thus the content of identity, will of course vary from person to person and culture to culture. To say that an identity is an explicit theory of oneself as a rational agent, however, is to say that identity is necessarily built around a conception of oneself much like what Berlin described. To lack such a self-conception, in other words, is to lack an identity in the present sense of that term. Consciousness of one's rational agency, moreover, entails an orientation toward two additional characteristics that are much discussed in the literature of identity formation: singularity and continuity.

Singularity

Rational agents determine and are responsible for their actions. To have an identity is to conceptualize oneself as a rational agent—that is, as a self that determines and is responsible for its actions (Craig, 1997). If you attribute your actions to multiple autonomous agents, you do not have an identity. To have an identity is to see yourself as singular.

Are singular self-conceptions justified? Researchers and theorists interested in the self have long debated issues of unity and multiplicity (Ashmore & Jussim, 1997; Harré, 1998; Harter, 2006). Does the typical person show a sufficient degree of behavioral consistency across contexts to be construed as a unitary self? Alternatively, is behavior so variable across contexts that each of us is best construed as having or being multiple selves? Given evidence for both consistency and variability, there is no simple resolution to this issue, either for developing individuals trying to make sense of themselves or for theorists trying to understand the developmental process.

But there is, it appears, what some might deem a "standard-issue Euro-American, Judeo-Christian, Post-Enlightenment cultural narrative" (Proulx & Chandler, 2009, p. 261), which goes like this:

> Nobody likes a two-face. Three faces and up are straight out. Rather, we are meant to be of *one* face, inside and out. That is, on pain of things otherwise unravelling, we are each meant to be a coherent self, not only continuous in time, but also unified across whatever contexts in which we find ourselves embedded. If we lend you a fiver while out on the town, we do not want to hear, at home, about how you are no longer the same person who borrowed the money, and so do not owe us a dime. (pp. 261–262)

In a novel study of adolescent conceptions of self-unity, Travis Proulx and Michael Chandler (2009) had 120 Canadian high school and college students ranging in age from 13 to 25 years read a stripped-down version of a Classic Comic Book edition of Robert Louis Stevenson's (1886/2003) *The Strange Case of Dr. Jekyll and Mr. Hyde*. They then asked them (using interviews for the high school students and questionnaires for the college students) whether Jekyll and Hyde could be considered "one and the same person" given the good and bad behaviors observed—and, if so, how this conclusion could be justified. The interview or questionnaire then proceeded to parallel questions of self-unity related to themselves and others they knew. Contrary to what Eriksonian theories of identity seem to suggest, there was no age trend toward seeing the self as unitary. Adolescents commonly saw themselves as multiplicitous, and this tendency, if anything, increased with age. Perhaps we really are multiplicitous, and we rightly recognize that.

So am I still the same person I was while out on the town? No self is fully coherent. Identity formation cannot be the discovery of a preexisting unity, nor is it possible to establish a fully coherent self. This does not mean, however, that coherence, consistency, and unity are irrelevant to identity formation. Identity, by definition, is something we can have only one of. Identity formation is an effort to identify or create a sufficient degree of consistency to justify construing the self as singular (Schachter, 2002). The construction of identity does not begin or end with a fully unitary self, but it does take unity as a guiding ideal.

Continuity

Commitment to a singular or unitary self, moreover, includes a sense of continuity across time. As Blasi and Glodis (1995) observed, "Unity in one's self experience is reflected in the attempt to bring together different elements of one's personality and to find a principle, simple or complex as it might be, by which past and present events as well as future expectations are integrated into a coherent biography" (p. 417). To see myself as a rational agent includes taking responsibility for what I have done and for what I will do. This entails commitment to a conception of myself that extends from the past through the present to the future (Chandler, Lalonde, Sokol, & Hallett, 2003; Côté, 2009; Craig, 1997; Erikson, 1950/1963, 1968; Lalonde & Chandler, 2004).

Since the turn of the century, researchers and theorists concerned with conceptions of the self as continuous across time have increasingly focused their attention on what is commonly called **narrative identity**, a personal life history that is deemed to define the self. One's theory of oneself as a person assumes and encompasses a narrative of a continuous self that extends across time (Grotevant, 1993, 1998; Habermas & Bluck, 2000; Hammack, 2008; McAdams, in press; McLean, Breen, & Fournier, 2010; Pasupathi, Mansour, & Brubaker, 2007; Sarbin, 1997). The narrative aspect of identity has been conceptualized as a **life story**, an autobiographical account connecting one's past to one's theory of self (Pasupathi et al., 2007).

Identity, however, is not simply any old story we choose to tell about our lives. To qualify as an identity, a story of self must have some degree of theoretical coherence and must provide a sense of oneself as a person. At the very least, it must be a story that one believes in and to which one is committed. Many such stories may be possible. But not just any story will do (Neisser, 1994/2008; Schachter, 2002).

Personhood and Identity

Four characteristics of personhood have been suggested—agency, rationality, singularity, and continuity. At the very least, persons are rational agents extending across time, acting in diverse contexts on the basis of their own reasons, and responsible for their actions. There may be other features necessary to any conception of personhood and additional features deemed necessary to personhood in certain social or cultural contexts. Whatever constitutes personhood, however, to have an identity is not just to have an explicit theory of oneself but to have an explicit theory whereby one construes oneself as a person.

Domains of Identity

Four standard domains of identity formation have been stressed in the Erikson and Marcia tradition and related research: career (Marshall, Young, Domene, & Zaidman-Zait, 2008), sexuality (see Chapter 12), religion (Hutnik & Street, 2010; Leak, 2009), and political ideology (Yates & Youniss, 1998). Although research shows that these are all important domains, they are not the only domains in which adolescents explore possibilities, make commitments, and construct theories of themselves. Additional domains that have been proposed and investigated include gender role, ethnicity (see Chapter 11), values, morality (see Chapter 13), marriage, parenting, and friendship (Kroger, 1993; Marcia, Waterman, Matteson, Archer, & Orlofsky, 1993; Schwartz, 2001). There is, not surprisingly, no definitive list.

It is important to keep in mind, moreover, that individuals vary in the domains they explore and in the relative importance of these various domains to their conceptions of who they are. In fact, in addition to constructing specific commitments, adolescents construct the identity domains within which they make those commitments. One has an identity to the extent that one has an explicit theory of oneself that addresses those aspects of the self that one sees as central to personhood. To have an identity, then, is not necessarily to have commitments in every domain that psychologists have identified as potentially relevant to identity. Rather, to have an identity is to have commitments in those domains you yourself see as central to personhood and to have an overriding theory of self that coordinates these commitments (Blasi & Glodis, 1995).

Beyond Cognition

Theories are organized forms of knowledge and thus are cognitive entities. To define identity as a theory of oneself suggests a cognitive theory of identity. But it is not clear that theories must be entirely cognitive, nor is it clear that identities must consist entirely of theories. As defined in this chapter, an identity is "at least in part" a theory, thus including a cognitive component, but may be something richer and more inclusive than that. What more could an identity be?

One response is that emotions, as well as cognitions, are central to identity. Kristján Kristjánsson (2009), for example, argued that there are a variety of self-relevant emotions and that these include "*self-constituting* emotions: emotions that define who we are" (p. 262). Different emotions are self-constituting for different individuals. What makes an emotion self-constituting for a given individual is that "it exemplifies some of his or her core commitments in life, is truly identity-conferring" (p. 262). My emotional reaction to a popular new song may change after I've heard it a hundred times, but I will still be, and will still see myself as, the same person. My compassion for victims of poverty, on the other hand, may be so central to my self and identity that I would see some hypothetical future version of myself who lacked such compassion as being a fundamentally different person than my present self, and I might be right.

Another response to the question of what, beyond cognition, could compose an identity is agency. Augusto Blasi (2004), in particular, argued that the self is rooted developmentally not in cognition or personality but in the immediate experience of agency, which is thus the basis for identity. Strong connections can be made from agency to autonomy to an appreciation of freedom to a conception of a personal domain of choice, all of which can be seen in young children and continue to develop, often long beyond childhood (Helwig, 2006b). At advanced levels, such development may be central to the construction of one's own identity.

Finally, there is **social identity**, a term so common in the social sciences and humanities that it is sometimes simply called **identity**. Identity in the sense of social identity is not the same thing as identity in the sense of personal identity, which is what we have discussed thus far. But they are not altogether different. What does it mean to "belong" to some ethnic group? There is a cognitive sense in which our identities are personally constructed, but there is also a social sense in which they reflect the social reality of our various actual and perceived affiliations. This is the subject of the next chapter.

Conclusion

Developmental research on identity formation continues, as we have seen, extending in multiple directions from the original work of Erikson and Marcia. One direction, highlighted in this chapter, has involved cognitive conceptualizations of identity as an explicit theory of oneself as a person. To see oneself as a person is to see oneself, at least ideally, as a singular and continuous rational agent. A related direction has been research on ethnic identity, much of which, as we will see in the next chapter, is firmly in the developmental tradition. But as developmental research on identity moves in this direction, it encounters the independent (and enormous) literatures of social identity, as we will now see.

CHAPTER **11**

Personal and Social Identity

Vladimir [after the first departure of Pozzo and Lucky]: "How
      they've changed!"
Estragon: "Who?"
Vladimir: "Those two. [...]"
Estragon: "Very likely. They all change. Only we can't."
Vladimir: "Likely! It's certain. Didn't you see them?"
Estragon: "I suppose I did. But I don't know them."
Vladimir: "Yes you do know them."
Estragon: "No I don't know them."
Vladimir: "We know them, I tell you. You forget everything.
      [*Pause. To himself.*] Unless they're not the same ...
      [...] Unless they're not the same ..."

—Samuel Beckett
(1954, p. 32; unbracketed ellipses in original)

In Chapters 9 and 10 the term **identity** was used in a manner typical of its use in the study of adolescent and early adult development.
The developmental literature on identity formation, however, is part
of a much larger identity literature that spans the social sciences
and humanities, including social psychology, sociology, philosophy,
and literary theory (for a "treetops" overview of identity studies, see
Côté, 2006; for a broad-ranging integration, see Hammack, 2008).
A distinction is commonly made between (a) **personal identity**,
which is what developmental psychologists generally have in mind
when they talk about adolescent identity formation, and (b) **social
identity**, which is what most other researchers and theorists have

in mind. Identity is not just about *me*; it is equally about *us* and also about *them*. The discussion of social identity in relation to the formation of personal identity clarifies issues related to both and leads, in the remainder of the chapter, to consideration of ethnic identity formation, diversity, and universality.

Social Identity

Outside the field of developmental psychology, the term **identity** typically refers to one's identification with a salient social group (Appiah, 2005; Côté, 2006; Hammack, 2008; Maalouf, 2001; Postmes & Jetten, 2006; Sen, 2006). This is sometimes called *social* identity to distinguish it from the concept of *personal* identity in the developmental literature. The concept of social identity reminds us that our identities are intrinsically and fundamentally social. It also raises problems, however, that cannot be solved without retaining from the developmental literature a concept of personal identity. As we will now see, personal identity and social identity are best construed as aspects of identity rather than distinct types or forms of identity.

One central issue in the conceptualization of social identity is that people generally identify with multiple groups (Appiah, 2005; Maalouf, 2001; Sen, 2006). Thus we might say that social identity is constituted by the **groups** with which one identifies. Identification with multiple groups requires considerable coordination, however. The reflective coordination of social identities requires rational agency, which brings us back to singularity and personal identity. Thus even as the concept of social identity helps us appreciate the extent to which we define ourselves as members of groups, the concept of personal identity reminds us that it is autonomous individuals who define themselves in this way. We cannot ignore our social affiliations, but they do not determine our identities. The construction of identity takes place within, and is profoundly influenced by, social contexts, but the constructor is a rational agent whose actions also contribute to the outcomes. Thus identity entails individuality and autonomy as well as social connection. Social identity and personal identity may be distinguished for analytical purposes, but we must keep in mind that our identities are simultaneously social and personal.

Correspondingly, we must keep in mind that groups are internally complex and dynamic (Turiel, 2002). Cultures are constituted by multiple agents and voices. We are well aware that cultures change through contact with other cultures but often overlook the fact that they also change as a result of ongoing internal transactions. In the cultural evolution of social identities, we see the role of individuality and autonomy in group processes (Postmes & Jetten, 2006).

Some groups are just collections of people. Among the most important groups in our lives, however, are abstract social entities such as nations, cultures, or religions that, unlike collections of people, have the potential to outlast the individuals who compose them at any given time. Identification with such groups thus provides a deepened sense of continuity, permanence, and meaning. As a result, we are highly motivated to act on behalf of abstract groups central to our social identities.

Although social identity provides the benefits of solidarity within groups, it also generates divides across whatever categories come to be seen as fundamental. Dividing the multifaceted social universe into discrete categories of "us" and "them" often generates stereotypes, suspicion, fear, discrimination, harassment, exclusion, antagonism, and violence. Children and adolescents increasingly recognize and grapple with the myriad moral dilemmas of social identity (Killen, Margie, & Sinno, 2006).

In its most extreme manifestations, social identity is central to group violence such as genocide, ethnic cleansing, and terrorism (Maalouf, 2001; Moshman, 2004a, 2004c, 2007, in press-b; Sen, 2006). Group violence is an act of group against group, but the perpetrators are individuals acting against other individuals. The link connecting the psychological and sociological levels of explanation is social identity. In particular, genocide and other acts of group violence generally proceed in a sequence of four overlapping phases (Moshman, 2007, in press-b). First, there is a dichotomization of identities; everyone is either one of "us" or one of "them." Then "they" are dehumanized to remove them from the universe of moral concern, thus enabling us to deny the moral significance of what we do to them. This may be followed by violence and destruction. Finally, beginning before the violence and destruction and lasting long after, processes of denial preserve the subjective moral identity of the perpetrators against all evidence (see the discussion of false moral identity in Chapter 13). Thus the concept of identity, fully incorporating personal and social aspects, helps us understand how individuals act on behalf of their groups against others in cases ranging from daily experiences to genocide.

The concept of social identity helps us steer between the twin perils of psychological and sociological reductionism (Postmes & Jetten, 2006). An overly psychological conception construes social identity as just another aspect of personal identity. People are seen individually as preexisting autonomous agents who create social groups. An overly sociological conception construes social identity as simply a matter of being part of a group. Groups are seen as preexisting entities that mold the identities of their members. The challenge is to maintain a more dialectical conception of social identity that connects the sociological reality of human groups to the psychological reality of personal identities.

From the standpoint of personal identity, the concept of social identity reminds us that to be a person is to be social and that this usually involves conceptualizing oneself in relation to groups one sees as self-defining. Our identities are deeply rooted in our social roles and connections with others. Thus our conceptions of ourselves as persons cannot help but be, at least in part, conceptions of our social affiliations. Social identities thus unite people (within groups) and divide them (across groups). This is a mixed blessing, to say the least, and perhaps should lead us to reconsider whether and in what sense identity formation is a developmental process (see Chapter 13).

Ethnic Identity

Within the United States a distinction is commonly made between members of the "White" majority and members of various "racial" and "ethnic" minority groups, who since the 1970s have typically been classified into four broad categories: African American, Asian American, Hispanic American, and Native American (Indian). Categories of this sort are social and political rather than biological. That is, although there is substantial genetic diversity among members of the human species, and although such diversity is related to ancestry, there is no empirical justification for the widespread notion that human beings fit naturally into some finite number of races or other such biological categories (Birman, 1994; Fisher, Jackson, & Villarruel, 1998; Garcia, Hart, & Johnson-Ray, 1997; Graves, 2001; Helms, 1994). Even at the social level, ethnic categories and labels are highly imprecise. Regardless of grouping, moreover, there is far more variability within groups than among them on most psychological measures (Fisher et al., 1998; Phinney, 1996). Nevertheless, Americans perceive themselves and each other as members of various racial and ethnic groups, and these perceptions, justified or not, have real psychological consequences. To the extent that one sees one's affiliation with an ethnic or racial group as self-defining one may be said to have an ethnic or racial identity.

The major theorist and researcher in the area of ethnic identity formation is Jean Phinney (Ong, Fuller-Rowell, & Phinney, 2010; Phinney & Rosenthal, 1992), who, along with a variety of associates, has been investigating the construction of ethnic identity since the 1980s (see Burrow, Tubman, & Montgomery, 2006, for a review and integration of research on racial identity). Although Phinney acknowledged that White majority adolescents may see themselves as White or as members of various specific ethnic groups (e.g., Italian American), she argued that such identifications usually play little role in identity formation (Phinney, 1996; Phinney & Rosenthal, 1992; see also Grossman & Charmaraman, 2009; Schwartz, Zamboanga, Weisskirch, & Rodriguez, 2009). For ethnic minority adolescents, in contrast, the situation is quite different:

> For adolescents from ethnic minority groups, the process of identity formation has an added dimension due to their exposure to alternative sources of identification, their own ethnic group and the mainstream or dominant culture. Growing up in a society where the mainstream culture may differ significantly in values and beliefs from their culture of origin, these youth face the task of achieving a satisfactory and satisfying integration of ethnic identity into a self-identity. The ease, or difficulty, with which this task is accomplished depends on a number of factors. ... In particular, minority adolescents may have to confront issues of prejudice and discrimination, structural barriers which limit their aspirations and hinder their achievements, and other features of the mainstream society that differentiate them from the majority. If minority youth are to construct a strong, positive, and stable self-identity, then they must be able to incorporate into that sense of self a positively valued ethnic identity. (Phinney & Rosenthal, 1992, p. 145)

Phinney defines ethnic identity as "an enduring, fundamental aspect of the self that includes a sense of membership in an ethnic group and the attitudes and feelings associated with that membership" (1996, p. 922). This is much more than the sort of label a child might learn (e.g., "I am Black" or "I am a Vietnamese American"). Rather, ethnic identity is constructed in adolescence or beyond as part, and often a core part, of the more general process of identity formation:

> Individuals progress from an early stage in which one's ethnicity is taken for granted, on the basis of attitudes and opinions of others or of society; through a period of exploration into the meaning and implications of one's group membership; to an achieved ethnic identity that reflects a secure, confident sense of oneself as a member of a group. Furthermore, an achieved ethnic identity is not necessarily a static end point of development; individuals are likely to reexamine their ethnicity throughout their lives. (Phinney, 1996, p. 923)

Research with adolescents and young adults has indicated that ethnic identity tends to increase with age (French, Seidman, Allen, & Aber, 2006; Lysne & Levy, 1997; Phinney, Ferguson, & Tate, 1997; Umaña-Taylor, Gonzales-Backen, & Guimond, 2009; see also Burrow et al., 2006, on racial identity). Higher levels of ethnic identity are associated with more positive attitudes toward one's own and other ethnic groups (Phinney, Ferguson, et al., 1997; Phinney, Jacoby, & Silva, 2007; Whitehead, Ainsworth, Wittig, & Gadino, 2009). It also appears that ethnic identity achievement is associated with higher levels of self-esteem and psychological well-being (Abu-Rayya, 2006; Burrow et al., 2006; French et al., 2006; Phinney & Alipuria, 1996; Phinney, Cantu, & Kurtz, 1997; Seaton, Scottham, & Sellers, 2006; Umaña-Taylor et al., 2009).

Central to the challenge of forming a minority ethnic identity, as noted, is coordinating one's relation to a specific ethnic group with one's relation to the mainstream culture (Birman, 1994; Hutnik & Street, 2010; Phinney & Rosenthal, 1992). A variety of resolutions are possible. In a study of African American and Mexican American adolescents, for example, Phinney and Devich-Navarro (1997) concluded that most of the adolescents had bicultural identities but that these identities took a variety of different forms.

For multiethnic or multiracial adolescents, whose parents represent different ethnic or racial groups, the coordination process is potentially even more complex. Although this may create difficulties for some adolescents at some points in their development, multiethnic background does not seem to be associated with marginalization, lower self-esteem, or other indications of maladjustment (Phinney & Alipuria, 1996; Shih & Sanchez, 2005). In fact, the flexibility and cognitive challenge of having more alternatives for identity commitment may, in the long run, enhance one's development.

Ethnic identity formation is also very much influenced, in many cases, by discrimination against one's group and the associated sense of oppression (Fisher et al., 1998). Erikson (1968) lamented "the sad truth that in any system based on suppression, exclusion, and exploitation, the suppressed, excluded, and exploited unconsciously accept the evil image they are made to represent by those who are dominant" (p. 59).

Even if such internalization of a negative self-image is less inevitable than Erikson thought, the experience of oppression may take its toll in other ways. Members of oppressed minority groups may, for example, form an "oppositional identity" that substantially hinders academic performance in schools perceived as White (Ogbu, 1993). Responses to social oppression, moreover, must consider the identity issues of the oppressors. As Erikson noted, "Where dominant identities depend on being dominant it is hard to grant real equality to the dominated" (1968, p. 264).

Sharri Clark (1997) addressed in a personal account many of the complex issues of ethnic identity formation. Clark wrote that her "heritage includes, in order of purported degree: Irish, Cherokee, Choctaw, Scottish, French, and German ancestry" (p. 36). Although her primary ancestry is Irish and she is, by her calculation, more White than Native American, this does not determine her identity. Having heard since early childhood the story of the "Trail of Tears," the deadly expulsion and relocation of the Cherokee from their homeland in 1838, she has constructed an identity that provides her with a sense of continuity, not only with her own past but also with the history of those she takes to be her people. In her own words,

> Who is Native American? Am I? Who has the authority to define the category "Native American?" Do I identify with the majority or the minority, with both or with neither? One fact is indisputable—I am a Native American descendant. I am a descendant of survivors

of a bitter forced migration that has become so integral to the identity of Oklahoma Cherokees and others that I cannot remember a time when I did not know about the Trail of Tears. (p. 37)

Longitudinal studies of ethnic self-identification show that such identification commonly changes across time, presumably as adolescents address issues of identity. One such study analyzed data from students in British Columbia schools who responded annually over 10 years to a series of identifying questions including whether they were "of Aboriginal ancestry" (Hallett et al., 2008). Of 4,307 students who self-identified as Aboriginal at least once, only about half (51%) were consistent in doing so. Some of these (13% of the total) identified as Aboriginal only once, which may have been a mistake in responding, but it appears that many students genuinely changed their self-identifications over this period. The proportion who shifted from never declaring ancestry to consistently declaring it (15% of the total) was substantially greater than the proportion who shifted in the opposite direction (4%), with the rest (17%) showing more complex patterns of change. Other longitudinal research similarly shows that changes in ethnic and racial self-identification over the course of adolescence are common (Hitlin, Brown, & Elder, 2006).

One general conclusion is that, regardless of ancestry or ethnicity, identity formation is neither the discovery of the one defining group you really and truly forever belong to nor the free creation of a personal theory of yourself that just happens to please you. Research on ethnic identity reminds us that identity, personal and social, is always constructed in, but never entirely determined by, social and cultural contexts.

Gender, Culture, and Identity

Many factors are known to influence identity. Gender and culture are two such factors that have been the basis for fundamental critiques. As Patterson, Sochting, and Marcia (1992) noted, "Researchers have questioned the appropriateness of applying the identity construct to women, and whether the construct of identity itself is biased toward the Western, masculine ideal of individualism over relatedness" (p. 14).

Most researchers and theorists are skeptical of the view that identities are constructed only by some categories of individual (e.g., men) or only within certain cultures (e.g., Western culture). It is clear that identities are constructed by women and men in varied cultures. One might nevertheless wonder whether the nature of identity or the processes of identity formation differ for women and men or for members of different cultures. I consider gender first and then culture, keeping in mind that the effects of gender vary across culture, and the influences of culture are often mediated by gender (Cross & Madson, 1997; Rotheram-Borus & Wyche, 1994).

Gender Differences

A number of identity theorists have proposed that women's identities are qualitatively different from those of men. Erikson (1968) suggested that intimacy, which for men is the developmental stage following identity, is a central aspect of identity for women and thus critical to female identity formation. Carol Gilligan (1982) criticized Erikson for identifying the male developmental sequence as the basic stages of human development but agreed with his conception that interconnections with others are typically fundamental to women's identities but not to men's. For women, Gilligan argued, "identity is defined in a context of relationship and judged by a standard of responsibility and care" (p. 160).

In a review of research on "models of the self," Susan Cross and Laura Madson (1997) placed more emphasis than Erikson on cultural (as opposed to biological) bases for gender differences and were more cautious than Gilligan to note that gender differences may be specific to particular cultural contexts rather than reflect differences in the essential natures of women and men. Nevertheless, Cross and Madson concluded that, at least among North Americans toward the end of the 20th century, "social factors … channel the creation and maintenance of divergent self-construals by men and women" (p. 8). Women, they suggested, typically construct **interdependent self-construals**, reflecting self-representations that highlight relatedness to others, whereas men typically construct **independent self-construals**, based on more autonomous self-representations. Closer examination of the data, however, shows that individual differences among women and among men are much greater than the corresponding mean differences between the two genders. Although Cross and Madson reviewed substantial evidence showing statistically significant gender differences, these differences are not nearly substantial enough, compared to the variability within each gender, to justify the categorical conclusions reached or the equally strong claims made by gender-difference theorists such as Erikson and Gilligan.

More generally, the literature on identity formation indicates that mean gender differences, where they exist at all, are usually minimal in relation to the enormous variability within each gender. In other words, gender accounts for surprisingly little of the variability among adolescents in matters of identity formation. Sally Archer (1994) summarized the research as follows:

> Males and females use the processes of exploration and commitment comparably. The timing of their identity activity is comparable. They address the identity task similarly in numerous domains of life [including] career, religion, gender role, marriage, and parenting. ... Females have been found to have engaged in more sophisticated identity activity [in] the areas of sexuality, friendship, and [marriage/career] prioritizing, whereas males have been more likely to become committed to political ideology than have females. (p. 4)

In summary, research shows gender differences with respect to particular identity commitments in particular domains and with respect to the interrelations among these commitments (Archer, 1994; Marcia, Waterman, Matteson, Archer, & Orlofsky, 1993) but disconfirms categorical claims that women and men form fundamentally different types of identities or that identity formation follows qualitatively different routes for males and females (Côté, 1996, 2009; Côté & Levine, 2002; Harter, 2006; Kalakoski & Nurmi, 1998). Rather than hailing from Venus and Mars, respectively, women and men are all from Earth.

Culture

Evidence for cultural differences in matters of self and identity has led to strong claims that people in different cultures have qualitatively different sorts of self-conceptions. The standard distinction, which parallels the gender difference claims just discussed, is between (a) Western conceptions of the self as individual and independent and (b) alternative conceptions of the self as relational and interdependent (Shweder et al., 2006).

Hazel Markus and Shinobu Kitayama (1991), for example, put the matter thus:

> People in different cultures have strikingly different construals of the self, of others, and of the interdependence of the [two]. These construals can influence, and in many cases determine, the very nature of individual experience, including cognition, emotion, and motivation. Many Asian cultures have distinct conceptions of individuality that insist on the fundamental relatedness of individuals to each other. The emphasis is on attending to others, fitting in, and harmonious interdependence with them. American culture neither assumes nor values such an overt connectedness among individuals. In contrast, individuals seek to maintain their independence from others by attending to the self and by discovering and expressing their unique inner attributes. As proposed herein, these construals are even more powerful than previously imagined. (p. 224)

Evidence from diverse cultures, however, suggests that categorical views of this sort are overly simplistic (Brewer & Chen, 2007; Li, 2006; Oyserman, Coon, & Kemmelmeier, 2002; Turiel, 2002, 2006a). "Cultural variability in the structuring of independent and interdependent behavior," concluded Catherine Raeff (2006, p. 106), "may be viewed as variations on universal themes of human separateness and connectedness." Without denying the reality and importance of cultural diversity, many psychologists and anthropologists have concluded that (a) human cultures do not fall neatly into two categories, (b) the influences of culture are subtle and complex, and (c) people within any given culture show much more variability than cultural determinist views lead one to expect. Anthropologist Melford Spiro (1993), for example, argued that

> a typology of self and/or its cultural conception which consists of only two types, a Western and non-Western, even if conceived as ideal types, is much too restrictive. Surely, some non-Western selves, at least, are as different from one another as each, in turn, is different from any Western self. In short, ... there is much more differentiation, individuation, and autonomy in the putative non-Western self, and much more dependence and interdependence in the putative Western self, than these binary opposite types allow. (p. 117)

Similarly stressing intracultural heterogeneity and individual differences, Elliot Turiel (1996) proposed that cultures are not adequately characterized as cohesive or homogeneous, but rather as dynamic and multifaceted, in many instances entailing struggles and disputes among people furthering different values. Varying interests and goals among members of a culture, especially when they hold different roles and status in the social hierarchy, can produce conflict and tensions to go along with sources of cooperation and harmony. Whereas cultures are often portrayed through analyses of social institutions and public ideology as reflecting a cohesive social orientation, ... analyses of individuals' moral, social, and personal concepts ... show that within cultures there is heterogeneity in social orientations and diversity in people's judgments and actions. (pp. 75–76)

Diversity within cultures, it should be emphasized, exists not just *across* individuals but *within* individuals. Explicit conceptions of oneself as individual and interdependent routinely coexist within individual minds. Identity formation is neither the cultural imposition of individualism or interdependence nor a choice between these. Rather it is a coordination of both self-conceptions (Killen & Wainryb, 2000; Schachter, 2002; Shimizu, 2000).

Cultures differ in the opportunities for choice and commitment they provide with respect to various potential domains of identity and in their general level of support for the construction of identities (Côté, 1996; Rotheram-Borus & Wyche, 1994). An adequate theory of the construction of identity must consider "the multitude of ways in which women and men struggle to come to terms with their membership in societies and with their own sense of who they are in the midst of a vast but structured field of signs, symbols, and voices from the culture(s) in which they live" (Penuel & Wertsch, 1995, p. 90). There is little or no evidence, however, to support stronger claims of cultural differences in the basic processes of identity formation or in the fundamental nature of the resulting identities.

In summary, research does not support suggestions of categorical differences in identity formation between women and men or among some finite number of cultures. Rather, it appears that the reflective construction of identity proceeds in multifaceted cultural contexts, with complex patterns of individual and cultural differences in the domains explored, possibilities considered, beliefs constructed, and commitments made.

Conclusion

Our consideration of social identity has led to detailed treatment of ethnic identity and issues of diversity, which lead us right back to the crucial importance of personal identity and its inseparability from social identity. With this enriched conception of identity, we now move to the developmental question of how identities are constructed.

CHAPTER **12**

The Construction of Identity

You raise the blade, you make the change
You rearrange me till I'm sane
You lock the door and throw away the key
There's someone in my head but it's not me

—**Pink Floyd**
(Brain Damage, 1973)

Between what a man calls *me*
and what he simply calls *mine*
the line is difficult to draw.

—**William James**
(1890/1950, Vol. 1, p. 291)

How does identity develop? What developmental processes account for the emergence of an explicit theory of oneself as a person? In this chapter I consider the process of identity formation first at a general level and then, more specifically, with regard to the domain of sexual identity.

Developmental Process

At a time when Marcia's approach still dominated the study of identity formation, Harold Grotevant (1987) complained that "most of the identity status research ... has focused on the

153

correlates of the identity statuses rather than on the processes [of development]" (p. 204). That is, in their zeal to demonstrate how individuals in each of the four identity statuses differ from each other, researchers had largely overlooked the fundamental question of how one achieves an identity. Grotevant noted, as the basis for a stronger focus on developmental processes, that "the identity status work has pointed to the importance of two key processes involved in identity formation: *exploration* of alternatives and *commitment* to choices" (p. 204).

Taking this as a starting point, Grotevant (1987) devised what he called a **process model of identity formation**. Exploration, he proposed, is a process of gathering information and testing hypotheses about oneself, one's roles, and one's relationships. Consideration of multiple possibilities and consequences ideally leads to choices that represent self-conscious long-term commitments.

Grotevant discussed in detail a variety of individual and contextual factors that affect identity formation. The extent and success of identity formation depends, he argued, on (a) personality factors such as flexibility, self-esteem, tendency to monitor one's behavior, and openness to experience; (b) cognitive competence to consider possibilities, draw appropriate inferences, and coordinate multiple perspectives; (c) characteristics of one's social context such as cultural support for making personal choices, family communication patterns, peer reactions, educational and career opportunities, and exposure to multiple options and viewpoints; and (d) the individual's general orientation, at a given point in his or her life, to engage in or avoid identity exploration and commitment.

Oddly, although Grotevant's model succeeds in focusing attention on the process of identity formation, it has much more to say about factors affecting that process than about the dynamics of the process itself. Michael Berzonsky (1993, 2004, in press) provided a model that extends Grotevant's process orientation to highlight the internal dynamics of constructing an identity. Elaborating the conception of identity as a theory of self, Berzonsky suggested that we view the individual as a **self-theorist**, engaged in a process of theorizing about the self. Taking a constructivist view of theorizing, he argued that theorizing is not simply a matter of gathering and summarizing data and testing predictions. Rather, theorizing involves an active process of interpreting one's experiences and generating new ones.

Berzonsky (1993) distinguished three types of self-theorists marked by different styles of theorizing: **scientific self-theorists**, **dogmatic self-theorists**, and **ad hoc self-theorists**. Scientific self-theorists

> tend to be self-reflective, skeptical about self-constructions, and open to self-relevant information. ... Such information-oriented individuals deal with personal decisions and identity concerns by deliberately seeking out, processing, and evaluating self-relevant information. (p. 173)

Dogmatic self-theorists, in contrast, conform to "the values and expectations of significant others (including parents)." This includes

> self-serving efforts ... to defend against potential threats to their self-constructions. Individuals who utilize this protectionist approach to self-theorizing have been found to endorse authoritarian views, to possess rigid self-construct systems, and to be closed to novel information relevant to hard core values and beliefs. (p. 174)

Finally, ad hoc self-theorists

> react continually to situational demands. A poorly organized, fragmented self-theory leads them to procrastinate and avoid dealing with personal conflicts and decisions. If one waits long enough, situational demands and consequences will eventually determine behavioral reactions. ... Situation-specific accommodations are likely to be short-term, ephemeral acts of behavioral or verbal compliance, rather than long-term, stable revisions in the identity structure. (p. 174)

On the basis of Marcia's characterization of his four identity statuses, one might expect that scientific self-theorists would be most likely to be in moratorium or to have an achieved identity, that dogmatic self-theorists would tend to have foreclosed identities, and that ad hoc self-theorists would tend to have diffused identities. Berzonsky (1993) summarized research demonstrating precisely these relationships; subsequent research has supported and extended his analysis (Berzonsky, 2004, 2008, in press;

Berzonsky & Ferrari, 2009; Berzonsky & Luyckx, 2008; Good, Grand, Newby-Clark, & Adams, 2008; Seaton & Beaumont, 2008). It appears, then, that Berzonsky's theory is largely continuous with the earlier work of Marcia but with a shift of focus, as urged by Grotevant, from the characteristics of various identity statuses to the nature of the processes involved in the construction of identity.

Theory and research since the 1990s extend the constructivist approach to identity formation seen in the work of Grotevant and Berzonsky (Berman, Schwartz, Kurtines, & Berman, 2001; Habermas & Bluck, 2000; LaVoie, 1994; Schwartz, 2002). As we have seen, however, constructivism is a metatheoretical orientation that can give rise to a variety of specific theories (see Chapter 14 for further discussion). With respect to identity, some theorists have highlighted the creative nature of constructive processes, whereas others have tried to devise rigorous psychological models of such processes. Sarbin (1997), for example, emphasized the creative construction of narratives about our lives. The various stories we encounter in novels, plays, movies, and other art forms, he suggested, provide the plot structures for our own self-narratives. Kerpelman, Pittman, and Lamke (1997), in contrast, presented a cybernetic "control theory," involving ongoing comparison of immediate self-perceptions with the self-definitions that compose identity. Incongruities are typically resolved via behavioral changes, but if such changes are repeatedly inadequate, the individual may restore equilibrium by engaging in fundamental transformations of the identity itself. Constructivist theories of identity formation continue to flourish and diversify (Kunnen, 2006; Kunnen, Bosma, & van Geert, 2001; Luyckx, Goossens, & Soenens, 2006; Luyckx, Schwartz, & Goossens, in press).

Discovery or Creation

Perhaps the major critique of the constructivist view of identity formation comes from those who see identity formation as a process of discovery. Alan Waterman (1992; see also 2004, in press), for example, proposed that

> a person's search for identity is an effort to identify those potentials that correspond to the "true self." The metaphor for identity

development used here is one of discovery ... rather than one of construction. ... According to the discovery metaphor, for each person there are potentials, already present though unrecognized, that need to become manifest and acted upon if the person is to live a fulfilled life. For many people, the task of recognizing and acting upon these potentials is not an easy one, as evidenced by the stresses associated with an identity crisis. Feelings of eudaimonia or personal expressiveness can serve as a basis for assessing whether identity elements are well-chosen. The presence of such feelings can be used as a sign that identity choices are consistent with an individual's potentials and thus can provide a basis for self-fulfillment. (p. 59)

In a similar vein, Blasi and Glodis proposed that identity formation consists of "the 'discovery' that one is, inevitably and necessarily, a certain kind of person" (1995, p. 412; see also Waterman, 2004). It is noteworthy, however, that Waterman, in the first sentence of the quoted passage, put scare quotes around the term **true self** and that Blasi and Glodis did the same with respect to the term **discovery**. It seems clear that we do not "discover" our "true selves" in the same straightforward way that a child might find a ball that has been hidden under a couch.

Theodore Sarbin (1997), in fact, doubted that we discover true selves in any sense at all. Explaining how he came to his title "The Poetics of Identity," he wrote,

My first pass at a title was "The Narrative Construction of Identity." While this title conveys my general meaning, the use of "construction" carries a nuance reminding us of the precise manipulation of materials by architects and carpenters. A more apt metaphor is "poetics," a word that calls up images of a person creating, shaping and molding multidimensioned *stories*. (p. 67, italics in original)

Thus, for Sarbin, identity is created, not discovered.

James Marcia sees identity formation as involving both discovery *and* creation, although acknowledging the difficulties this poses for both the individual and the theorist. In a discussion published as part of Berzonsky (1993), Marcia said,

It seems to me that there are some elements that have the characteristic of feeling as if they emerge. There are some grooves in which you find yourself moving that feel as if this is the right place to be, and when you begin to deviate from those situations, it feels as if you are out of sync with something. Now that something, whether or not it is totally constructed or whether there is some part that is given, has a quality for me of just being given. Then there is the additional task of somehow constructing an identity, accounting for that rut- or pathlike quality of one's life. So for me, I have got a kind of a mixed model that relies heavily on construction but with allowance for things that seem also to thrust themselves on my experience that I cannot account for by construction. (p. 189)

Without denying genuine and interesting differences among identity theorists, I think that part of the problem in this debate is ambiguity concerning what it means to take a constructivist view. As discussed in the introduction, constructivism is best understood with respect to how it differs from the more traditional **nativist** and **empiricist** perspectives. A nativist view of identity formation would suggest that our identities are innate. Even if they are not present at conception, they emerge, regardless of later experience, in a manner determined by our genetic programming. An empiricist, in contrast, would suggest that our identities are imposed on us by our environments, shaped by our specific experiences in various cultural contexts.

Contemporary identity theorists agree that neither of these alternatives is adequate. At the very least, identity emerges out of a complex interaction of hereditary and environmental factors. A constructivist would go beyond this, however, to insist that individuals play an active role in generating their own identities through their actions, interpretations, reflections, and coordinations (Lerner, Freund, De Stefanis, & Habermas, 2001). A radical constructivist, taking this position to its extreme, might deny the possibility of any sort of real self and thus see the creation of an identity as an unconstrained act of free will.

Within the field of developmental psychology, however, most constructivists take a position I term **rational constructivism** (see Chapter 8). Rational constructivists assume that there exist realities outside our constructed cognitions. Thus, although such realities do not determine our cognitions, some constructions are indeed more justifiable than others. As Berzonsky (1993) put it,

We ... live and act within an objective reality that exists independent from our construction of it, even though we have no way of directly understanding it. ... Objective reality does constrain the utility and viability of the constructs or theories we generate: We cannot simply make up and continue to use any "story." (p. 170)

With respect to selves and identities, then, I suggest that there is a reality within us that bears a complex relation to the reality outside us. Our efforts to construct an identity are constrained not only by external social factors but also by a need to be true to ourselves (Kristjánsson, 2009; Schwartz, 2002; Waterman, 2004, in press). But we can never know ourselves in a direct, simple, and final sense, any more than we can know the reality outside us. We have no choice but to **construct** our understanding of who we are. To the extent that we focus on the identification of alternatives, and on autonomous interpretations and commitments, such construction looks and feels like a process of creation. To the extent that we focus on the necessary relation of identity to a preexisting though dimly perceived self, such construction looks and feels like a process of discovery. The actual construction of identity may sometimes partake more of creation, and sometimes more of discovery, but in general it involves elements of both. Identity, then, is a construction, but it is a construction constrained by realities without and realities within (Schachter, 2002).

Having proposed the existence of a real self that constrains, without determining, the construction of identity, I hasten to add that the real self should not be viewed as an intrinsic, unalterable part of the person; the self itself is subject to change. The construction of identity may involve processes of reflection and coordination that increase the level of agency, rationality, unity, and continuity manifested in one's behavior. Somewhere at the border of metacognition and metaphysics lies the possibility that the reflections and coordinations involved in constructing and reconstructing my identity may change not only who I think I am but who I *really* am.

Sexual Identity

Sexuality is a domain in which scientific understanding has been especially hindered by unjustified and misleading assumptions that reflect a discovery versus creation dichotomy. Part of the reason for this is political. Both supporters and opponents of gay rights often assume that the case for gay rights depends on sexual orientation being an innate and unchangeable characteristic.

Specifically, it is assumed that if sexual orientation is genetically determined, there is a strong case for laws forbidding discrimination on the basis of this characteristic, whereas if sexual orientation is a free choice to engage in certain behaviors, the case for gay rights is undermined. Given this widely shared assumption, some supporters of gay rights accept flimsy evidence as a basis for strong claims that sexual orientation is genetically determined, whereas opponents of gay rights often maintain, without evidence, that people simply choose to engage in homosexual behavior and could choose to be heterosexual instead. In effect, many supporters of gay rights view **sexual identity formation** as the discovery of one's innate sexual orientation; many opponents of gay rights view sexual identity formation as a creation, a series of choices that society should channel in socially, morally, and religiously acceptable directions.

The association of gay rights with genetic determinism, however, is dubious. Although it is indeed true that we often forbid discrimination on the basis of innate characteristics such as skin color, it is not true that genetic determination of a characteristic is central to the case against discrimination. For example, hardly anyone believes that political or religious commitments are genetically determined, but almost everyone agrees that it is wrong to discriminate against people on the basis of their personal beliefs, religious practices, or political activities. Similarly, racial discrimination remains fully objectionable even if race is a set of sociopolitical categories rather than a biological reality. Thus, scientific conclusions about the development of sexual orientation and identity do not mandate particular positions on issues of gay rights.

Turning, then, to the scientific issues, what can be said about the development of sexual identity? Sexual identity, it appears, is constrained, but not determined, by sexual orientation. It will be useful to begin with the development of sexual orientation and then turn to the construction of sexual identity.

Research in many domains of development has convinced most psychologists that complex psychological characteristics are virtually always the result of complex interactions of (a) hereditary influences, (b) environmental (including cultural) influences, and (c) the individual's actions, interpretations, and constructions. Nativists stress the role of genes, empiricists stress the role of environment, and constructivists stress the role of the individual, but most developmentalists agree that all three considerations are important.

There is no reason to think that the development of sexual orientation is an exception to this general rule. There is evidence that hereditary variations influence sexual orientation but no evidence that any gene or set of genes causes a person to be heterosexual or homosexual (Bailey, 1995; Hershberger, 2001). Similarly, it is likely that environmental factors influence sexual orientation, but there is no evidence that particular events or experiences cause people to become homosexual or heterosexual. Finally, it appears that behaviors and interpretations over the course of childhood play a role in the emergence of later sexuality, but it is clear that people do not simply choose their sexual orientations.

Daryl Bem (1996, 2001) provided a developmental theory of sexual orientation consistent with this general perspective. He proposed that

> biological variables, such as genes, prenatal hormones, and brain neuroanatomy, do not code for sexual orientation per se but for childhood temperaments that influence a child's preferences for sex-typical or sex-atypical activities and peers. These preferences lead children to feel different from opposite- or same-sex peers—to perceive them as dissimilar, unfamiliar, and exotic. This, in turn, produces heightened nonspecific autonomic arousal that subsequently gets eroticized to that same class of dissimilar peers: Exotic becomes erotic. (1996, p. 320)

Bem added that the extent to which sexual orientation is organized around gender may depend on the extent to which the culture in which the child develops is organized around gender. Critics of Bem's theory have noted a variety of other theoretical possibilities and empirical uncertainties (Peplau, Garnets, Spalding, Conley, & Veniegas, 1998; for a reply, see Bem, 1998). Whatever the fate of Bem's specific theory, however, it seems likely at a general level that children in various cultures move into adolescence with varied and complex patterns of sexual dispositions and desires that result from the interactions of genetic, environmental, and cognitive influences over the course of childhood (Carver, Egan, & Perry, 2004).

Sexual orientation does not determine sexual identity, however. Rather, the construction of sexual identity in adolescence and beyond is influenced not only by sexual orientation, the inner reality of one's sexual dispositions and desires, but also by the categories of sexuality fostered by one's culture and cultural attitudes toward these various categories (Floyd & Stein, 2002; Hammack, 2005). Cultural categories and attitudes, moreover, change over time and vary widely across cultures (Bem, 1996; Hammack, 2005; Herdt, 2001; Jagose, 1996).

In the mid-20th-century United States, for example, there was a widely accepted cultural distinction between **heterosexuals**, who were construed as normal, and **homosexuals**, who were construed as pathological. Homosexuality was deemed at best a mental illness and at worst a sin; homosexual behavior was illegal in every state. Although this state of affairs did not by itself determine sexual identities, it restricted the potential self-conceptions of anyone whose sexual orientation did not fit the category of "normal heterosexuality."

In the 1960s and 1970s, however, the term **gay** became increasingly accepted for those who would earlier have been classified as homosexual. This was not merely a change of label. Although the term **homosexual** continued to be used in a neutral sense, the term **gay** reflected a more positive evaluation of homosexuality and thus made it easier for many people to define themselves positively. To be sure, simply calling oneself gay does not generate a positive sexual identity. The existence of a "gay" category, however, enhances the prospects for many individuals to construct positive theories of themselves as sexual persons and thus to construct positive identities that encompass their sexual orientations.

A simple distinction between heterosexuals and gays, however, is inadequate to encompass human sexual diversity. Gay women, for example, often label themselves **lesbians** to highlight that they are a distinct group (Diamond, 2000; Jagose, 1996; McConnell, 1994; Schneider, 2001). This yields three potential categories of sexual identity: heterosexual, lesbian, and gay male. But some individuals are attracted to both opposite-sex and same-sex individuals, leading to a fourfold set of categories common in the 1980s: heterosexual, lesbian, gay male, and **bisexual** (Fox, 1995; Herdt, 2001). There are, moreover, transsexuals, transvestites, and others who cannot be assimilated to these categories; they have often been grouped since the 1990s into a fifth category termed **transgender**. Such categories do not determine sexual identity but create a richer set of options for individuals trying to construct a conception of themselves that is true to their own pattern of sexual dispositions and desires.

The use of five categories rather than some smaller number, however, does not resolve the problems of categorization. Heterosexuals, for example, are highly diverse in their sexual inclinations and desires. At the very least, we could distinguish male from female heterosexuals; further distinctions within the heterosexual category could surely be justified. Bisexuals, to take another example, are attracted to both women and men, but this does not mean that bisexuals are attracted to everyone—Woody Allen was joking when he said being bisexual doubles one's chances of getting a date. Bisexual orientations may be organized on the basis of characteristics other than gender. There may, in fact, be a variety of little-understood dimensions of sexual orientation that cut across, and thus undermine, the standard gender-based categories (Jagose, 1996). The transgender category gets at some of this complexity, but transgenderism itself is an umbrella for a variety of potential sexual categories.

And that's not all. To complicate matters further, many people, especially women, change their sexual self-categorizations over the course of adolescence and early adulthood (Diamond, 2008). And many people, especially younger people in recent years, reject the traditional categories altogether, defining themselves instead as "queer" or "mostly straight" or as just not fitting any category at all (Savin-Williams, 2005; Thompson & Morgan, 2008).

Human beings, then, do not come in some finite number of sexual categories, nor do they choose from some universal set of such categories. The construction of a sexual identity is neither the discovery of one's true sexual self nor the free creation of an ideal sexual self. Rather it is a creative act constrained, but not determined, by the complex interrelations of (a) one's sexual dispositions and desires and (b) the categories and dimensions of sexuality highlighted by one's culture. Although the standard categories of gay, lesbian, and bisexual remain influential in identity development (Russell, Clarke, & Clary, 2009), we should not attribute them directly to biology or expect them to remain fixed over time.

For sexual minorities, as for ethnic minorities, the construction of identity is further complicated by social disapproval, discrimination, and oppression (Rivers & D'Augelli, 2001;

Savin-Williams, 1995, 1998). Although many sexual minority youth, especially in recent years, construct their sexual identities in supportive environments without serious difficulty (Cohler & Hammack, 2007; Savin-Williams, 2005), the construction of sexual identity remains a major challenge for many others (Bos, Sandfort, de Bruyn, & Hakvoort, 2008; Busseri, Willoughby, Chalmers, & Bogaert, 2006). To extend Erikson's (1968) observation about the internalization of a negative image, sexual minorities may "accept the evil image they are made to represent by those who are dominant" (p. 59). This problem is likely exacerbated by the fact that children often internalize negative images of homosexuals before they have any inkling of their own sexuality. As Anthony D'Augelli (1994) put it, "In contrast to other groups, lesbians, gay men, and bisexual people have grown up absorbing a destructive mythology before they appreciate that it is meant for them" (p. 315).

Most individuals succeed in constructing positive adult identities. But to do this they must survive adolescence, a period when suicide is common, especially among sexual minorities (Hershberger, Pilkington, & D'Augelli, 1997). Depending on cultural reactions to their sexual dispositions and desires, some adolescents find the construction of sexual identity more difficult than others, and some find themselves in circumstances where it appears to be impossible.

Conclusion

We have come a long way since Erik Erikson's theoretical proposal that identity formation is central to adolescent development (Chapter 9), not to mention since Piaget's conclusion that adolescents reason at a qualitatively higher level than children (Chapter 1). The work of James Marcia has been central in generating empirical research on the nature and development of identity. In many ways, however, the field is now moving beyond Marcia's four identity statuses. As we have seen, there is increasing emphasis on developmental processes. Contrary to traditional and current stereotypes, there are strong indications that the basic processes and outcomes of identity formation are common to women and men in diverse cultural contexts. There is also increasing research on the specifics of identity formation in an increasing number of domains.

Identity formation cannot be fully understood, however, without considering its interrelations with rationality and morality, nor can the development of rationality and morality in adolescence and beyond be fully understood without reference to each other and to identity formation. We now turn to the intersection of rationality, morality, and identity, leading to a more general treatment of the developmental transformations of adolescence and beyond.

DEVELOPMENT BEYOND CHILDHOOD

In the study of psychological development, it is useful to distinguish advanced development from basic development. **Basic development** is child development—the universal and predictable progress of the first 10 to 12 years of life. **Advanced development** refers to the developmental changes of adolescence and beyond—changes that are neither universal nor tied to age. Despite the subtle nature of advanced development, we have seen evidence in the first three parts of this book for developmental changes beyond childhood in rationality, morality, and identity. We now consider, in a more general sense, the nature and process of advanced psychological development (Chapters 13–14), its promotion in secondary education (Chapter 15), and the nature of adolescence (Chapter 16).

CHAPTER 13

Rational Moral Identity

If you knew who I was and who you were, you would not have killed me.

—Sign outside a Catholic church in Nyamata, Rwanda, where as many as 10,000 people are estimated to have been killed on a single day during the 1994 genocide
(Packer, 2002, p. 140)

Everywhere there is a need for calm and thorough reflection on the best way to tame the wild beast of identity.

—Amin Maalouf
(2001, p. 157)

To speak of development, we must specify what constitutes progress (Sen, 1999). With regard to development beyond childhood, a conception of rational moral identity is useful for this purpose. Rational moral identity, however, is not a state of maturity achieved by some or all persons. Rather it is a developmental ideal that enables us to identify psychological progress, and thus development, at advanced levels.

Rational moral identity is not just the sum of rationality, morality, and identity. In the first three sections of this chapter, I discuss moral rationality, rational identity, and moral identity. Having partially integrated rationality, morality, and identity, two at a time, I then turn to rational moral identity.

Moral Rationality

Rationality is central to Kohlberg's theory of moral development (Arnold, 2000) and arguably central to any developmental conception of morality (Moshman, 1995b; Turiel, 2006b; see also Rawls, 1971, 2001; Sen, 2009). If morality is nothing more than conformity to the norms of your social group, then moral change is simply the learning of those norms, whatever they happen to be. It is the rational aspect of morality, if there is one, that has the potential to develop (see Chapter 5).

Perspective taking, which is widely seen as crucial to the development of both rationality (see Chapter 4) and morality (see Chapter 7), has often been highlighted as a particularly important link between them. To be rational is to transcend your own perspective, and to be moral is, in large part, the same thing. Thus, the development of perspective taking connects cognitive and moral development (Gibbs, 2010).

Moral rationality includes not just rational judgments about what actions are right or wrong but **meta-ethical cognition** concerning the basis for and justification of moral judgments. A judgment about what Heinz should do in response to his dilemma may be considered rational to the extent that it is supported by reasons, but the reasons are moral reasons directly related to the judgment. In contrast, meta-ethical cognition addresses epistemological questions in the domain of morality. In thus connecting the moral domain to the domain of epistemology, research on the development of meta-ethical cognition addresses the development of **moral epistemologies**.

Tobias Krettenauer (2004) provided the most systematic research on the development of meta-ethical cognition in adolescence. First, on the basis of the existing literature and a series of pilot studies, he identified three moral epistemologies: (a) intuitionism, (b) subjectivism, and (c) transsubjectivism. These correspond to the more general epistemologies identified in research and theory on the development of epistemic cognition (see Chapter 3). **Intuitionism**, corresponding to the more general stance of objectivism, holds that moral rightness or wrongness can be determined by moral intuitions, which serve a role parallel to direct perception in the determination of truth. **Subjectivism** holds that moral judgments are neither right nor wrong but simply a matter of opinion, a position that may be part of a more general subjectivist epistemology that questions the meaning and possibility of truth. Finally, **transsubjectivism** holds moral judgments to be justifiable but fallible, a position that may be associated with a more general rationalist stance regarding judgments of truth and falsity.

Krettenauer (2004) used a semistructured interview procedure to assess meta-ethical cognition in 200 German high school students in Grades 7, 9, 11, and 13 (with mean ages of 13, 15, 17, and 19, respectively). The students were presented with moral dilemmas as a basis for initial judgments and were then asked about the sources, certainty, and justification of their judgments and the possibility of equally justifiable alternatives. Krettenauer found that responses could be reliably classified with regard to the three moral epistemologies and that individual adolescents were somewhat (though not perfectly) consistent across dilemmas in their moral epistemology. Age differences were consistent with developmental expectations of a general trend from intuitionism to subjectivism. Transsubjectivism was seen in some of the older students and was the predominant meta-ethical stance in a comparison group of graduate students with a background in moral philosophy. Moral epistemologies were substantially, but not perfectly, correlated with general epistemologies.

In sum, rationality is central to morality, and adolescents increasingly understand the ways in which this is so. But whatever the relation of rationality to morality, why be rational or moral in the first place? Many theorists believe identity plays a major role in providing the motivation to formulate, and act on the basis of, your own reasons, moral or otherwise.

Rational Identity

Constructivist views of identity formation all assume an individual operating at an advanced level of cognitive competence. Erikson (1968) himself proposed that formal operations may be a necessary, but not sufficient, condition for the construction of identity:

> The cognitive gifts developing during the first half of the second decade add a powerful tool to the tasks of youth. Piaget calls the gains in cognition made toward the middle teens the achievement of "formal operations." This means that the youth can now operate on hypothetical propositions and can think of possible

variables and potential relations—and think of them in thought alone, independent of certain concrete checks previously necessary. As Jerome S. Bruner puts it, the child now can "conjure up systematically the full range of alternative possibilities that could exist at any given time." Such cognitive orientation forms not a contrast but a complement to the need of the young person to develop a sense of identity, for, from among all possible and imaginable relations, he must make a series of ever-narrowing selections of personal, occupational, sexual, and ideological commitments. (p. 245)

Formal operations, as discussed in Chapter 1, includes the ability to systematically generate a framework of possibilities that are not merely direct extensions of a given reality and to use hypothetico-deductive reasoning to infer the consequences of such hypothetical possibilities. Identity formation, correspondingly, involves consideration of multiple potential selves and the consequences of commitment to a particular conception of oneself. It does seem plausible, then, that formal operations would be a prerequisite for identity formation. Many researchers see the construction of possible selves in adolescence and beyond as central to identity formation (Marshall, Young, Domene, & Zaidman-Zait, 2008).

As we saw in Chapters 2 and 3, however, current theory and research provide a complex picture encompassing advanced forms of rationality far more diverse than anticipated in Piaget's conception of formal operations. Recent research on the relation of cognitive development to identity formation has accordingly focused on identifying the specific cognitive abilities associated with the construction of identity. Given that the construction of identity raises questions of being true to oneself, one might expect conceptions of knowledge and truth would play a key role in such construction. With this in mind, several researchers have investigated the relation of epistemic cognition (see Chapter 3) to identity (Boyes & Chandler, 1992; Chandler, Boyes, & Ball, 1990; Krettenauer, 2005; Peterson, Marcia, & Carpendale, 2004).

Michael Boyes and Michael Chandler (1992), for example, identified 61 high school students who could be clearly classified with respect to Piagetian stage, level of epistemic cognition, and Marcia identity status. With respect to Piagetian stage, 12 students were classified as concrete operational and 49 as formal operational. With respect to epistemic level, 22 students showed the sort of epistemic orientation that was described in Chapter 3 as objectivist, and 39 showed more sophisticated epistemic orientations of the sort described in Chapter 3 as subjectivist or rationalist, involving explicit insight into the constructed nature of knowledge. Finally, with respect to identity status, 28 were classified as diffused or foreclosed (the less advanced identity statuses), and 33 were classified as in moratorium or as identity-achieved (the more advanced identity statuses).

Of central interest were the interrelations of (a) Piagetian stage with identity status, (b) Piagetian stage with epistemic level, and (c) epistemic level with identity status. Comparison of Piagetian stage and identity status suggested that formal operational thinkers may be more likely to be in one of the more mature statuses, but the relationship was not statistically significant. The other two interrelationships, however, were clear and significant. Formal operational thinking was strongly associated with higher epistemic levels, and higher epistemic level, in turn, was strongly associated with more advanced identity status. A more fine-grained analysis indicated that rationalist epistemologies were most strongly associated with identity achievement.

These results indicate that cognitive development is indeed important to the construction of identity but that the traditional distinction between concrete and formal operations, though perhaps relevant, provides an insufficient account of this relationship. Epistemic cognition appeared to be a critical connecting link in the cognition–identity relationship. That is, students who saw knowledge as simple and absolute were likely either to have foreclosed identities or to be unconcerned with identity formation. Students who understood that knowledge is a subjective construction, in contrast, typically were constructing or had constructed identities. Among this latter group, moreover, students who understood the potential for rational judgment despite subjectivity were most likely to have constructed an identity.

Research on young adults' narratives of their own identity formation has shown a constructive process in which individuals constrain their choices and commitments on the basis of what they deem to be rational criteria for a "good" identity. They may insist, for example, that identity must "allow for a sense of consistency, sameness and continuity," and/or "include all significant identifications," and/or "allow for mutual recognition between individual and society," and/or "allow for feelings of authenticity and vitality" (Schachter, 2002, p. 422).

Also highlighting the rational construction of identity, Michael Berzonsky (2004, 2008, in press) and colleagues (Berzonsky & Adams, 1999; Berzonsky, Macek, & Nurmi, 2003; see also Berman, Schwartz, Kurtines, & Berman, 2001; Klaczynski, 2004; Schwartz, Mullis, Waterman, & Dunham, 2000) found that rational identity processing orientations are associated with the sort of active exploration that typifies moratorium individuals and enables identity achievement:

> Information-oriented individuals negotiate identity issues by actively processing, evaluating, and utilizing self-relevant information. They are skeptical about their self-constructions and willing to test and revise aspects of their identity structure when confronted with self-discrepant information. ... They have been found to engage in high levels of effortful self-exploration, introspection, and private self-awareness and to have high levels of need for cognition, problem-focused coping, cognitive complexity, and openness to experience. ... Self-exploring individuals, classified as being identity achieved or moratoriums according to the identity status paradigm, have been found to rely on this social-cognitive orientation. (Berzonsky & Adams, 1999, p. 579)

But if some types, forms, or levels of rationality are prerequisite for some types, forms, or levels of self-conception—such as Eriksonian identity—it is equally true that the construction of identity contributes, in turn, to rationality by providing increasingly organized and justified reasons for belief and action. Consider, for example, the role of the **life story**—the narrative aspect of identity—in enabling **autobiographical reasoning**:

> The life story is usually used in a piecemeal fashion ... through what we term autobiographical reasoning. Autobiographical reasoning is a process of self-reflective thinking or talking about the personal past that involves forming links between elements of one's life and the self in an attempt to relate one's personal past and present. ... Autobiographical reasoning indicates the evolution of a biographical perspective that frames one's individuality in terms of a specific developmental history. It relies on autobiographical remembering but goes beyond it by enhancing understanding

through actively creating coherence between events and the self. (Habermas & Bluck, 2000, p. 749)

Although identity may enhance rationality in ways such as these, identity is also a serious and ongoing threat to rationality. Paul Klaczynski and others have shown that self-serving biases incline us uncritically to accept and accumulate evidence and arguments consistent with our beliefs, especially those beliefs central to our identities, while critically scrutinizing and dismissing evidence and arguments threatening to our beliefs and identities (Klaczynski, 1997, 2000, 2004; Klaczynski & Fauth, 1997; Klaczynski & Gordon, 1996a, 1996b; Klaczynski & Narasimham, 1998; Kuhn, Amsel, & O'Loughlin, 1988; Moshman, 2004a; Paul, 1990; Schauble, 1996; Stanovich & West, 1997). Identity commitments may thus undermine rationality, and the strongest identities may pose the most serious problem.

If identity poses a problem, however, it may also present a solution. We all see ourselves, to varying degrees, as rational agents, which is why we try to explain and justify our actions to ourselves and others (Stanovich, 2008). To the extent that you come to see your rational agency as central to who you are, you have a **rational identity**. Rational identity does not guarantee good reasoning, but it does motivate efforts to be rational, including deliberate efforts to identify and overcome biases in seeking and processing information.

Individuals whose identities are strong but for whom rationality is not a self-conscious commitment may fail to engage in good reasoning because they identify too strongly with their present beliefs. As philosopher Jerry Cederblom (1989) put it, "The chief drawback of identifying myself with my set of beliefs is that this view leads me to see a mistaken belief as a defect in myself. This inclines me to reject a belief that conflicts with my own, even when I have good reason to accept it" (p. 149). A better alternative, he suggested, is to identify oneself as a "belief-forming process." Individuals who see themselves this way are more likely to change their beliefs appropriately, in light of evidence and argument, because they see such change not as acknowledgment of a fundamental shortcoming but as an affirmation of themselves as rational agents.

Critical scrutiny of one's identity, then, is more likely if one has the sort of identity that values such scrutiny. This may be a key difference between foreclosed and achieved identities (Marcia, Waterman, Matteson, Archer, & Orlofsky, 1993; see Chapter 9). Thus identities may undermine rationality or may support it, or both.

We now turn from rational identity to moral identity. Identities may differ not only in the extent to which we see ourselves as rational but also in the extent to which we see ourselves as moral.

Moral Identity

Chapter 8, concluding four chapters on morality, ended with a suggestion that we need to study identity because, among other things, identity may be important in motivating moral perception, reflection, and behavior. Identity, to be sure, can motivate many things, not all of them morally justifiable (Maalouf, 2001; Moshman, 2004a, 2004c; Sen, 2006). Many people, however, have explicit theories whereby they construe themselves as moral agents, and for some, to varying extents, commitment to moral agency is central to the organization of their self-conceptions. Augusto Blasi (1984, 2004) and others have proposed that such persons be understood as having **moral identities** (Arnold, 2000; Bergman, 2002, 2004; Colby & Damon, 1992; Frimer & Walker, 2009; Hardy, Bhattacharjee, Reed, & Aquino, 2010; Hardy & Carlo, 2005, in press; Hart, 2005; Hart & Fegley, 1995; Lapsley, 1996; Moshman, 2004a, 2005; Mustakova-Possardt, 1998; Walker & Hennig, 1997; Walker & Pitts, 1998).

To have a moral identity is to have an explicit theory of yourself as a moral agent—as one who acts on the basis of respect and/or concern for the rights and/or welfare of others. Several aspects of this definition warrant explanation and elaboration.

As discussed in Chapter 8, to have an identity is to see yourself as a rational agent—as one who acts on the basis of beliefs and values of your own. Even if your beliefs and values are demonstrably wrong or evil, if you are consciously committed to acting on the basis of those beliefs and values because you see them as fundamental to who you are, then you have an identity.

To have a moral identity is to see yourself as a moral agent—as one who acts on the basis of moral beliefs and values. Regardless of whether your moral beliefs or values are correct or justifiable, your fundamental commitment to them as central to your personhood constitutes a moral identity. If you see yourself as the sort of person who notices, reflects on, and acts on moral issues, then you have a moral identity, regardless of the accuracy of your perceptions, the quality of your reasoning, or the justifiability of your judgments and actions.

But what counts as a moral issue? What beliefs and values fall within the moral domain? How can we accommodate individual and cultural diversity in moral perception, reasoning, and judgment? Is morality what anyone says it is?

As we have seen, there is substantial evidence that, beginning in early childhood, people in normal human environments, regardless of specific cultural contexts, construct some conception of a moral domain encompassing respect and/or concern for the rights and/or welfare of others (Gibbs, 2010; Moshman, 1995b; Nucci, 2001; Piaget, 1932/1965; Rest, Narvaez, Bebeau, & Thoma, 1999; Turiel, 2002). Some conceptions of the moral domain may highlight respect for rights and justice as most fundamental, some may put more emphasis on care and compassion for others, and some may see these as deeply interconnected with each other and/or with related values; but there is sufficient agreement on the meaning of morality among diverse children, adolescents, adults, and theorists to justify an objective specification of the moral domain.

Thus to have a moral identity is to have an explicit theory of yourself as systematically acting on the basis of respect and/or concern for the rights and/or welfare of others. This definition does not require a commitment to any particular set of moral beliefs, values, rules, or principles and is thus consistent with moral diversity among those who have strong moral identities. It does, however, require that one's theoretical commitment be objectively moral, not in the sense of being morally correct but in the sense of falling with an objectively defined moral domain.

People cannot be neatly divided into those who have moral identities and those who do not. On the contrary, people have moral identities to varying degrees. Probably almost all people, beginning in childhood, have moral self-conceptions entailing commitments to others (Nucci, 2004). In cases of moderate moral identity, the commitment to others is an important aspect of a person's explicit theory of self but may be colored or compromised by other identity commitments. In cases of strong moral identity, the commitment to others is so central as to direct and coordinate other commitments, in which case moral identity may be seen as a type, not just an aspect, of identity (Colby & Damon, 1992).

Research on moral identity is consistent with this depiction of its nature and development (Frimer & Walker, 2009) but too sparse to provide a more detailed picture (for reviews, see Hardy & Carlo, 2005, in press; Hart, 2005). Moral self-conceptions and moral behavior are undoubtedly related in interesting and changing ways over the course of development, but relevant evidence is difficult to obtain for a variety of methodological, practical, and ethical reasons.

Larry Nucci was initially sympathetic to the concept of moral identity (2001) but later grew skeptical (2004), insisting that genuine morality involves acting out of respect and concern for others, not to maintain one's own self-consistency. If I choose to be moral because I perceive it to be all about me, is that really morality at all? Isn't the motivation for morality intrinsic to our understanding of its objective demands regarding the rights and welfare of others? Blasi (2004) and other advocates for the concept of moral identity acknowledged that genuine morality requires moral understanding and that such understanding can be a basis for action. After all, even children act morally. Nevertheless, they continue to see the development of moral identity in adolescence and beyond as an important supplementary source of motivation.

Even people with strong moral identities, however, may fail to act morally. Powerful commitments to what we see as the rights or welfare of others may motivate actions that cannot be justified on the basis of such commitments. Theories can be false, and this includes theories of ourselves as moral agents. That is, we can have **false moral identities** (Moshman, 2004a; see also Uhlmann, Pizarro, Tannenbaum, & Ditto, 2009).

False theories are still theories, and false moral identities are moral identities. If you have an explicit theory of yourself as a moral agent, then you have a moral identity. If your theory is false—if you do not really act on the basis of respect and/or concern for the rights and/or welfare of others, although you think you do—then you have a false moral identity. This raises the question of how moral identities can be true, reminding us once again that issues of morality and identity immediately raise questions of epistemology and rationality (Moshman, 2004a).

Rational Moral Identity

The phenomenon of false moral identity reminds us that the construction of identity does not necessarily entail progress toward more advanced forms of rationality or morality. Identity formation may entrench and reinforce irrational and biased commitments and ideologies. If by progress in identity we simply mean progress toward stronger identity structures, then identity formation is by definition a developmental process. From the broader perspective of advanced psychological development, however, it is clear that the construction of identity may undermine rationality and/or morality and thus does not always constitute progress. Identities can motivate oppression and violence, for example, up to and including genocide (Maalouf, 2001; Moshman, 2004a, 2004c, 2007, in press-b; Sen, 2006).

The development of identity, then, is not simply the formation of whatever identity you happen to form. The developmental aspect of identity formation is the rational construction of theories that enable us to explain ourselves to ourselves and others. Much of what must be explained, moreover, pertains to our relations to others and our roles within social institutions. Rationality and morality are thus intrinsic to identity formation, at least to the extent that it is a developmental process. The developmental ideal is to construct identities that not only are rooted in rationality and morality but also enable us to see ourselves as rational and moral agents. The developmental ideal for identity formation is the self-regulated construction of a **rational moral identity**.

Rational moral identity, it should be clear, is not a state of maturity. There is no stage of rational moral identity reached by some or all people. Self-conceptions qualify as identities in multiple aspects and to varying degrees. Identities, in turn, vary in the strength and self-consciousness of their commitments to rationality and to morality and in the extent to which these commitments are intertwined such that the moral commitments have a rational basis. Identity formation is progressive to the extent that our theories of ourselves increasingly highlight and motivate our rationality and morality. This is the sense in which rational moral identity is a developmental ideal.

The concept of rational moral identity overlaps with related conceptions of advanced psychological development that construe rationality as much more than a set of advanced cognitive skills.

Harvey Siegel (1988, 1997) and other philosophers of education have addressed the broader aspects of rational functioning in terms of the **critical spirit**:

> The "critical spirit" … refers to a complex of dispositions, attitudes, habits of mind, and character traits. It includes … the dispositions to seek reasons and evidence in making judgments and to evaluate such reasons carefully; … a respect for the importance of reasoned judgment and for truth, and rejection of partiality, arbitrariness, special pleading, [and] wishful thinking; … habits of reason seeking and evaluating, of engaging in due consideration of principles of reason assessment, of subjecting proffered reasons to critical scrutiny, and of engaging in the fairminded and non-self-interested consideration of such reasons; and character traits consonant with all of this. People who possess the critical spirit *value* good reasoning, and are disposed to believe, judge and act on its basis. (1997, pp. 35–36)

Others have highlighted the development of autonomy (Goossens, 2006; Helwig, 2006b; Silverberg & Gondoli, 1996). An autonomous individual is not one whose behavior is never influenced by others, or whose thoughts are never influenced by emotions, or who has transcended the need for relationships and intimacy. Rather, to be autonomous is to be **self-directed** or **self-governed**—that is, to make one's own choices and to be responsible for the consequences of those choices. This is central to what it means to be a rational and moral agent (Appiah, 2005; Audi, 1997, 2001; Berlin, 1969; Rovane, 2004), and your autonomy is enhanced to the extent that you are consciously committed to this vision of yourself.

Conclusion

Advanced psychological development is not simply the sum of cognitive development, moral development, and identity formation, nor does it end with the attainment of maturity in one or more of these domains. Development beyond childhood encompasses the development of rationality, including rational aspects of morality, and the development of identities committed to rationality and morality. Rationality and morality each come in diverse forms, however, and diverse identities can be committed to these ideals in multiple ways. Thus we return to pluralist rational constructivism, a metatheory of advanced psychological development.

CHAPTER 14

Pluralist Rational Constructivism

pluralism, yes;
radical relativism, no.

—Harvey Siegel
(1987, p. 159)

Theories of development invariably rest on metatheoretical assumptions about the nature of developmental processes. In the Introduction, I presented constructivism as a metatheory distinct from the more traditional nativist and empiricist perspectives. In the subsequent chapters, I showed the utility of a constructivist approach for explaining various aspects of adolescent psychological development. As we have seen, however, a variety of constructivist theories and perspectives are possible. They vary with respect to whether the constructive process is construed as rational and whether its outcomes are assumed to be universal (Chiari & Nuzzo, 1996, 2010; Marshall, 1996; Overton, 2006; Phillips, 1997; Prawat, 1996). We now revisit these issues. Drawing on theory and research regarding the development of rationality, morality, and identity, I identify and discuss a metatheoretical perspective I term **pluralist rational constructivism**.

Constructivism

Constructivism has been presented in the context of the historic nature–nurture debate. On the nature side, nativism proposes that development is a causal process directed by our genes. That is, the mature forms of our knowledge, reasoning, and behavior are determined by hereditary factors that direct the development of our species. On the nurture side, empiricism proposes that development is a long-term process of learning from, or being shaped by, our environments. Thus, knowledge, reasoning, and behavior are determined by cultural and other environmental forces.

Developmentalists generally agree that both hereditary and environmental factors are important in development and that the effects of each depend on the other. Thus, although some developmentalists put more emphasis on genetic considerations, and others on environmental considerations, most take an interactionist position somewhere along the continuum from nativism to empiricism.

As we have seen, however, constructivists believe an interactionist position does not go far enough. Constructivist metatheory assumes that individuals play an active role in constructing their own knowledge and reasoning and in generating their own behavior. As we have seen, there is substantial evidence for the active role of adolescents in the construction of rationality, morality, and identity. Thus, it appears that neither nature nor nurture, nor an interaction of the two, is sufficient to explain adolescent psychological development. Rather, we must move off the nature–nurture continuum into a dimension that recognizes the active role of the individual.

If we think of the three corners of the triangle in Figure 14.1 as representing theories that recognize only a single type of developmental factor—**genes, environment,** or **individual construction**—it is safe to say that few contemporary theories fall into one of these corners. Most posit the importance of at least two of these potential influences. Annette Karmiloff-Smith (1992), for example, suggested a theory that might fit midway along the nativism–constructivism side of the triangle.

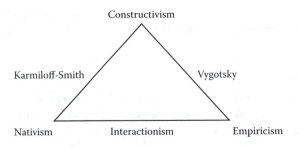

FIGURE 14.1 Nativism, empiricism, and constructivism.

She argued that heredity provides a more substantial starting point for cognition than Piaget was willing to acknowledge but that further development is, as he insisted, an active, constructive process. Alternatively, Lev Vygotsky's theory of development (Penuel & Wertsch, 1995), which emphasizes the active roles of both individual and culture, might be placed along the empiricism–constructivism side of the triangle. Theories that encompass the roles of all three potential considerations would fall somewhere inside the triangle, although genuinely integrating all three sets of considerations is easier said than done.

Constructivism, then, need not deny the role of heredity or environment, but it insists that the individual is an active agent in his or her own development and that this third factor cannot be reduced to heredity, environment, or an interaction of both. Developmental changes, a constructivist would argue, must be understood, at least in part, from the point of view of the developing person.

Rational Constructivism

If individuals construct their own knowledge and cognitive processes, it might seem that each individual would construct his or her own idiosyncratic beliefs and modes of processing, with no legitimate basis for evaluating the adequacy of such constructions. A **radical constructivist** would argue that our conceptions, moralities, and identities are indeed free creations, and there can never be neutral criteria for evaluating the adequacy of whatever we choose to believe or however we choose to think.

Radical constructivism, however, undermines the fundamental conception of development as progress (Chandler, 1997; see Introduction). Developmental constructivists generally maintain a view that I have termed **rational constructivism** (Chapters 8 and 12). Rational constructivism construes the construction of knowledge and reasoning as a rational process that generates justifiable outcomes. Given an individual at a certain stage of moral development, for example, potential reconstructions of the moral reasoning associated with that stage can be evaluated with respect to whether they provide a more defensible moral framework—for example, a perspective that can resolve a wider range of moral issues. Developing individuals make such judgments about their own constructions. Thus, they increasingly commit to conceptions that, both from their own perspective and from the external perspective of a moral theorist, represent moral progress. Moral change is thus constrained by rational considerations that render such change developmental in nature.

Rational constructivists highlight reflection, coordination, and peer interaction as key developmental processes. Reflection on one's inferential processes, for example, may enable the abstraction of logical necessities (Smith, 1993). Reflection on one's beliefs and/or behaviors may enable the abstraction of common patterns that one comes to see as aspects of one's identity (Erikson, 1968). Coordination of two social perspectives may enable an individual to construct a structure of moral understanding that accommodates both (Piaget, 1932/1965, 1995). Peer interaction may enable two or more individuals to construct a line of reasoning that they could not have constructed individually (Moshman & Geil, 1998). Although there is much more to be learned about such processes, it does seem plausible that they might constrain our constructions in such a way as to enable developmental progress (Piaget, 1985, 2001).

Like any metatheory, rational constructivism has a variety of advantages and limitations. The relative balance of advantages and limitations depends on the phenomena to be explained. In particular, rational constructivism directs attention to the active role of rational agents in constructing higher levels of understanding and reasoning. As suggested throughout this volume, this may be critically important in explaining the development of advanced forms of rationality, morality, and identity in adolescence and early adulthood. Attention to rational agency may also be helpful (along with other considerations) in explaining other aspects of psychological development, including development in earlier and later portions of the life span, in a variety of social and cultural contexts. A rational constructivist approach may be unhelpful or even misleading, however, in explaining (a) processes of anatomical or physiological maturation that are strongly guided by the genes or (b) processes of social influence or cultural indoctrination that circumvent or undermine rational choice.

Another limitation of rational constructivism, it may be argued, is that its commitment to universal developmental sequences cannot accommodate the reality of individual and cultural diversity. Elaborating on the analysis in Chapter 8, however, I now return to my proposal that such a limitation is not inherent to rational constructivism.

Pluralist Rational Constructivism

Rational constructivist theories have traditionally posited universal sequences of development. As we saw in Chapter 1, for example, Piaget believed that a particular logical structure—formal operations—is the basis for adolescent and adult cognition; construction of this structure, in his view, is the only pathway beyond concrete operations. Similarly, Kohlberg believed there are six possible structures of moral reasoning, and these develop in a fixed sequence (see Chapter 5). An individual can transcend the form of moral reasoning Kohlberg labeled Stage 4, for example, only by constructing the form of moral reasoning he labeled Stage 5.

The rational constructivist perspective, however, does not require a commitment to universal pathways of development or universal forms of psychological maturity. There could, for example, be two or more justifiable logical structures that transcend concrete operations; a rational agent might construct either or both. Similarly, we cannot rule out the possibility that some individuals at Kohlberg's Stage 4 may construct a form of moral understanding that is demonstrably superior to Stage 4 but different from Kohlberg's conception of Stage 5. Pluralist rational constructivism shares with universalist rational constructivism a developmental vision of justifiable reconstructions that constitute progress in rationality. It differs, however, in highlighting the possibility of diversity in the pathways and/or outcomes of development (see Figure 14.2).

Thomas Bidell and his collaborators (Bidell, Lee, Bouchie, Ward, & Brass, 1994), for example, proposed a five-step sequence in the development of conceptions of racism among young White

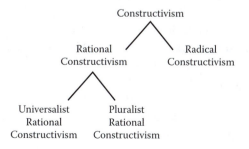

FIGURE 14.2 Constructivist metatheories.

adults participating in cultural diversity course work. Their sequence involves progress toward increasingly differentiated and coordinated conceptions, each of which is more justifiable than the previous one. Thus, they posited a developmental process of rational construction. Nevertheless, they did not claim that their proposed sequence is universal across persons or contexts. On the contrary, they argued that

> researchers seeking to decide the sequence of constructions through which individuals make sense of a problem such as racism must also carefully define the context in which the individuals under study are attempting to construe the problem. It cannot be assumed that the same sequence of understandings observed in one context would emerge in a different context. For example, the present model is tightly restricted to the description of conceptual development in the specific context of cultural diversity course-work on a predominately white, affluent college campus. Other developmental pathways, leading to different conceptions of the problem than we have described, are both possible and likely. It would be a mistake, for instance, to assume that the sequence of ideas about racism constructed by middle to upper-middle class white students in the context of cultural diversity coursework would replicate the construction of ideas about racism among young white adults from a working class neighborhood where racial tensions have been exacerbated by competition for scarce social resources. (pp. 189–190)

Diversity and universality were both salient in a study of identity formation in Canadian adolescents that included both culturally mainstream youth and Aboriginal youth affiliated with Canadian First Nations. Michael Chandler and his associates (Chandler, Lalonde, Sokol, & Hallett, 2003; Lalonde & Chandler, 2004) found no reason to doubt that identity is important in diverse cultural contexts and universally involves issues of continuity over time (see Chapter 10). Two distinct approaches to establishing personal continuity were identified, however, with a hierarchy of developmental levels within each. **Essentialist accounts of continuity** construe the self as an essence unaffected by time. **Narrative accounts of continuity** are people's stories of their lives. Some accounts of continuity over time—whether postulated fundamental essences or life stories—are more abstract and/or self-conscious than others. Thus the two approaches to continuity may be considered two parallel developmental tracks.

Must each of us take one track? Not necessarily. In fact, Chandler et al. (2003) found that some adolescents were taking both tracks. There were also individual and cultural differences, however. First Nations youth were substantially more likely to offer narrative accounts of their own continuity, whereas mainstream Canadian youth tended to favor essentialist accounts, but there were exceptions within each cultural category. Thus, as is often the case, there was evidence for diversity within individuals, across individuals, and across cultures.

Consistent with such research and theory, Charles Helwig (1995b) endorsed perspectives that

> chart a middle ground between global stage theory and recently emerging contextualist perspectives. ... The role of social context in social cognition can be adequately addressed neither through abstract, decontextualized global structures of reasoning, nor by a narrow contextualism that essentially equates individuals with their environments. In between these two extremes may be a local-structural analysis of development that maintains important distinctions between individuals and environments, between structural and functional processes. (p. 194)

As we have seen throughout this volume, there is a great deal of diversity in the beliefs, values, self-conceptions, and forms of reasoning individuals construct and thus in the developmental pathways they traverse. A rational constructivist in the universalist tradition would not deny the clear evidence for such diversity but would question its importance. The universalist might, for example, dismiss such diversity as representing superficial variations that fall outside the realm of rational justification and are, thus, secondary to the universal stages and outcomes of development. Pluralist rational constructivism, in contrast, suggests that rational construction may lead in more than one direction, that differences are no less important than universals, and that many aspects of diversity can and should be explained within a rational constructivist framework.

Outside the realm of rational constructivism are radical or "postmodern" versions of constructivism, contextualism, and relativism that not only accept the reality and importance of diversity but deny the existence of universals and the possibility of rational evaluation (Gergen, 2001; for critiques of such views, see Bickhard, 1995; Chandler, 1997; Kahn & Lourenço, 1999; Lynch, 1998; Perry, 1997;

Phillips, 1997; Shestack, 1998; Siegel, 1987, 1997, 2004). Pluralist rational constructivism does not go this far. There may indeed be forms of reasoning, morality, or identity that represent advanced levels of development in any cultural context, and there may be important commonalities across individuals and cultures in the pathways to advanced forms of rationality. On the general question of diversity and universality, pluralist rational constructivism takes a middle ground, open to both universals and differences (Chandler et al., 2003; Moshman, 2003; Norenzayan & Heine, 2005; Perry, 1997; Saltzstein, 1997).

Three Aspects of Diversity

Taking diversity seriously requires recognition of three potential aspects of diversity and careful scrutiny, with respect to these aspects, of all claims of variation. Diversity may exist within individuals, across individuals, and across groups.

Research in many domains of performance shows that individuals of all ages typically have at their disposal a variety of ideas, strategies, and perspectives. These observations have led a number of researchers and theorists to highlight the importance of diversity *within* individuals (Fischer & Bidell, 2006; Killen & Wainryb, 2000; Kuhn, Garcia-Mila, Zohar, & Andersen, 1995; Siegler, 1996; Turiel, 2006a; Wark & Krebs, 1997). As seen in Chapter 2, for example, multiple types of reasoning coexist in any given adolescent. Any account of thinking must explain how the individual selects from, or coordinates, diverse types of reasoning in responding to a given task or dilemma (Kuhn, 1999, 2000).

Diversity can also be seen *across* individuals. That is, people differ from each other. Specific claims of differences across or among individuals must be critically scrutinized, however. In particular, such claims must be evaluated with regard to the relation of these differences to differences *within* individuals.

Extending distinctions made in Chapter 6, for example, suppose it were proposed that, with respect to morality, some adolescents are justice reasoners, some are care reasoners, and some are virtue reasoners. A universalist in the Kohlberg tradition might try to show either (a) that care and virtue reasoning are special cases of justice reasoning rather than distinct forms of morality or (b) that considerations of care and virtue represent nonrational values outside the domain of morality. A pluralist version of rational constructivism acknowledges the possibility that there are indeed three justifiable forms of morality but would require both philosophical and empirical justification of the proposed distinctions.

Suppose we were convinced that the proposed three types of morality are indeed philosophically distinct and meaningful. Suppose, in addition, we had data showing statistically significant differences among adolescents in the use of such reasoning on a range of moral dilemmas. Does it follow that we can meaningfully distinguish teenage Kohlbergs, Gilligans, and Aristotles? Before accepting the idea that individuals can be usefully classified into the three proposed moral categories, we should consider the relationship of differences *across* individuals to differences *within* individuals.

Imagine, for example, that careful scrutiny of our data showed that 30% of all adolescents use justice reasoning at least 80% of the time, 30% use care reasoning at least 80% of the time, and 30% use virtue reasoning (whatever that means) at least 80% of the time (with nondominant forms of reasoning rare in each case). Such results would support the utility of distinguishing justice, care, and virtue reasoners, with the understanding that a few adolescents may be hard to classify and that even those who clearly fit one of the categories will not be 100% consistent in using the reasoning associated with their category.

Actual research on moral reasoning, however, does not generate such results (Wark & Krebs, 1996, 1997). A more likely finding across a range of moral dilemmas might be that most adolescents use each of the three kinds of reasoning at least 25% of the time, and few favor one particular kind of reasoning most of the time. In this case, classification of the adolescents as justice, care, or virtue reasoners would be highly misleading. A better conclusion would be that most people use a combination of justice, care, and virtue reasoning. Individuals may differ somewhat from each other in the relative frequency of the three types of reasoning, but it would be important to emphasize that these differences across individuals are minor compared to the substantial variability *within* individuals. In this case, we should emphasize distinct types of moral *reasoning* but not distinct types of moral *reasoners*.

Claims of diversity across various biological and social groupings require similar scrutiny with respect to how the group differences compare to (a) differences across individuals and (b) differences within individuals. As we have seen in the first three sections of this book, strong claims have been made about gender and cultural differences with regard to rationality, morality, and identity, but such claims are not supported by empirical research.

Consider, for example, Carol Gilligan's much cited association of justice reasoning with men and care reasoning with women. Many studies have failed to show such a difference (for reviews, see Brabeck & Shore, 2003; Dawson, 2002; Hyde, 2005; Jaffee & Hyde, 2000; Walker, 1984, 1991, 2006). Even if research consistently showed statistically significant gender differences in this regard, however, that would not suffice to support Gilligan's claim. Rather, we would need to consider the magnitude of the gender difference relative to the extent of variability among and within individuals. If, for example, we found that 80% of all women use care reasoning rather than justice reasoning at least 80% of the time and 80% of all men use justice reasoning rather than care reasoning at least 80% of the time, it would be reasonable to assert (with due allowance for exceptions) that women construe morality as a matter of care whereas men construe it as a matter of justice. As noted in Chapter 6, however, the association of gender and morality is not nearly this strong. At most, one might conclude that in the United States in the late 20th and early 21st centuries, women have been slightly more likely than men to be among those individuals who use care reasoning slightly more often than justice reasoning, whereas men have been slightly more likely than women to be among those who use justice reasoning slightly more often than care reasoning. Even this modest conclusion, moreover, overlooks the fact that most moral reasoning involves coordinating diverse moral and nonmoral considerations, not simply choosing among them (Turiel, 2002, 2006a).

Pluralist rational constructivism, then, can accommodate diversity within individuals, across individuals, and across various social and biological groupings of individuals, but it need not, and should not, accept all claims uncritically. In addition to the obvious question of whether an asserted difference really exists, we must consider what the evidence shows about the locus and extent of variability. In particular, substantial variability within individuals often undermines categorical claims about differences among individuals and groups.

Conclusion

Part of the reason for rational constructivism's traditional commitment to universalist conceptions of development may be an assumption that to give up universality is to abandon rationality. Given that appreciation of human diversity has so often been associated with radical forms of constructivism, contextualism, and relativism, this is an understandable and appropriate concern.

There is no need, however, to choose between (a) a conception of change as progress through universal pathways toward universal outcomes and (b) a conception of change as an arbitrary process with no particular direction and without justifiable outcomes. Pluralist rational constructivism accommodates diversity in pathways and outcomes without relinquishing a rationalist conception of progress. To say more than one pathway is justifiable is not to say all pathways are equally progressive. To identify multiple forms of advanced reasoning, morality, and identity is not to say all inferences, frameworks, and self-conceptions are equally sophisticated. Evidence for diversity need not undermine a rational constructivist conception of psychological development (Chandler et al., 2003; Clinchy, 2002; Demetriou, Christou, Spanoudis, & Platsidou, 2002; Floyd & Stein, 2002; Lalonde & Chandler, 2004; Schachter, 2002).

Rational constructivism, moreover, in contrast to nativism, empiricism, and radical constructivism, provides a conception of socially facilitated rational change that enables education to be distinguished from training and indoctrination. In Chapter 15, applying a rational constructivist perspective to secondary education, I propose that the promotion of rationality should be the primary purpose of education and that the construction of rationality is best facilitated in a context of intellectual freedom.

CHAPTER 15

Rationality, Liberty, and Education

> Freedom to differ is not limited to things that do not matter much. That would be a mere shadow of freedom. The test of its substance is the right to differ as to things that touch the heart of the existing order.
>
> —*West Virginia State Board of Education v. Barnette*
> *(1943, p. 642)*

Adolescents spend much of their lives in secondary schools, an environment that may promote or inhibit development, and often does both. In this chapter we consider issues of rationality, liberty, and development in the context of secondary education.

Secondary schools present information, ideas, and perspectives in abundance and expect students to express themselves orally and in writing. At the same time, secondary schools routinely exclude politically unacceptable ideas and perspectives from the curriculum, limit student access to alternative sources of information, and censor or punish students and teachers who address controversial topics or express views that school authorities deem offensive or dangerous (Brown, 1994; Gaddy, Hall, & Marzano, 1996; Lent & Pipkin, 2003; Moshman, 1989, 1993, 2009b; Pipkin & Lent, 2002).

Within the United States, historic Supreme Court decisions set important restrictions on censorship and indoctrination in public schools. In *West Virginia v. Barnette* (1943), the Supreme Court recognized freedom from indoctrination as a First Amendment right and thus provided the constitutional foundation for intellectual freedom in public education. The case involved the objection of Jehovah's Witnesses—parents and children—to a requirement that all students salute the flag and pledge their allegiance. In ruling for the Jehovah's Witnesses, the plurality opinion appealed not just to religious freedom (as did two concurring justices) but to a First Amendment principle it deemed even more fundamental: "If there is any fixed star in our constitutional constellation," maintained the Court, "it is that no official, high or petty, can prescribe what shall be orthodox in politics, nationalism, religion, or other matters of opinion or force citizens to confess by word or act their faith therein" (p. 642).

In *Tinker v. Des Moines Independent Community School District* (1969), the Supreme Court rejected the proposition "that either students or teachers shed their constitutional rights to freedom of speech or expression at the school house gate" (p. 506). In a case involving secondary school students suspended for wearing black armbands in school to protest the U.S. military intervention in Vietnam, the Court ruled that students "may not be confined to the expression of those sentiments that are officially approved" (p. 511). Unless a school can demonstrate a constitutionally valid basis for regulation, "students are entitled to freedom of expression of their views" (p. 511). For nearly two decades, *Tinker* provided broad protection for intellectual freedom in public education (Moshman, 1989).

In *Hazelwood School District v. Kuhlmeier* (1988), however, the Court reversed course. Schools have broad authority, it ruled, not only to formulate curriculum but also to censor and punish ideas they deem inconsistent with their message. Although *Hazelwood* involved censorship of a high school newspaper, it has served as the basis for numerous decisions restricting student and faculty expression and discussion in all academic contexts at all levels of education. *Tinker* now applies only on the margins, to speech outside the curriculum. Education is deemed by the Court to be a special activity that requires special restrictions on intellectual freedom. Or at least school officials are free to act that way. Fortunately, although the decision permits censorship and indoctrination, it does not require either. School officials remain free to respect the intellectual freedom of students at all levels of education, and there are strong educational and developmental reasons for doing so (Moshman, 2009b).

Any systematic approach to education must consider what we are trying to achieve through education and how we can best achieve it. I have suggested throughout this volume that adolescent psychological development is best understood from the perspective of **rational constructivism**. Extending the rational constructivist perspective to education, I propose here that the primary purpose of education should be the promotion of rationality. I then argue that the single most important thing secondary schools can do to promote rationality is to provide an environment of intellectual freedom. In contrast to the Supreme Court, I conclude that censorship and indoctrination are never necessary to education. In fact, they are counterproductive, at least if education is conceived as the promotion of rationality.

Education for Rationality

Education, it is often suggested, should aim at the promotion of development (Baker, 1999). With respect to adolescent development, this appears to mean it should aim at the promotion of rationality, morality, and identity. With regard to morality, however, what develops is largely moral rationality. With regard to identity, it is the development of a rational basis for identity that constitutes progress rather than foreclosure. Identity formation is truly developmental when it makes progress toward rational moral identities (Chapter 13). Thus the promotion of advanced psychological development is fundamentally the promotion of rationality, broadly conceived to encompass the realms of morality and identity.

Although education potentially serves many purposes, a number of theorists have argued that its core purpose should be the promotion of rationality (Lipman, 1991; Moshman, 1990b; Paul, 1990; Scheffler, 1997; Siegel, 1988, 1997; Stanovich, 2001; see also Kuhn, 2005, on education for thinking, and Sternberg, 2001, on teaching for wisdom). For philosopher Harvey Siegel, this is most fundamentally a matter of moral obligation to students. There is simply no distinction between the sort of education that promotes rationality and the sort that respects students as persons:

> Conceiving and conducting education in ways which do not take as central the fostering of students' abilities and dispositions to think critically fails to treat students with respect as persons, and so fails to treat them in a morally acceptable way. (1997, p. 4)

What does it mean for a teacher to recognize the equal moral worth of students and to treat them with respect? Among other things, it means recognizing and honoring the student's right to question, to challenge, and to demand reasons and justifications for what is being taught. (1988, p. 56)

Education for rationality can also be justified on the basis of the needs and progress of society, especially in a democratic society. Philosopher Israel Scheffler (1997) argued,

To choose the democratic ideal for society is wholly to reject the conception of education as an *instrument* of rule; it is to surrender the idea of shaping or molding the mind of the pupil. The function of education in a democracy is rather to liberate the mind, strengthen its critical powers, inform it with knowledge and the capacity for independent inquiry, engage its human sympathies, and illuminate its moral and practical choices. This function is, further, not to be limited to any given subclass of members, but to be extended, in so far as possible, to all citizens, since all are called upon to take part in processes of debate, criticism, choice, and co-operative effort upon which the common social structure depends. (p. 29)

A strong case can be made, in fact, that any form of education not aimed at the promotion of rationality tends to undermine genuine democracy. In the World War II flag salute case, the U.S. Supreme Court ruled that the use of public schools to indoctrinate students is forbidden by the Constitution:

There is no mysticism in the American concept of the State or of the nature or origin of its authority. We set up government by consent of the governed, and the Bill of Rights denies those in power any legal opportunity to coerce that consent. Authority here is to be controlled by public opinion, not public opinion by authority. (*West Virginia v. Barnette*, 1943, p. 641)

Both concern for individual students and concern for the welfare of society thus lead to the conclusion that we want our educational institutions to contribute to the development of rationality. To paraphrase Isaiah Berlin (1969), whose conception of the rational agent was quoted in Chapter 10, we want the graduates of our educational institutions to be subjects, not objects; to be moved by reasons, by conscious purposes, of their own, not by external causes. We want them to be doers—deciding and not being decided for, self-directed and not acted on by external nature or by other people as if they were things, or animals, or slaves, incapable of playing a human role, that is, of conceiving goals and policies of their own and realizing them. We want them, above all, to be conscious of themselves as thinking, willing, active beings, bearing responsibility for their choices and being able to explain those choices by references to their own ideas and purposes.

Education for rationality, then, rests on a vision of educated persons as rational and moral agents with rational moral identities. If something like this is indeed our guiding ideal, how can we promote the construction of rationality?

The Role of Liberty in the Construction of Rationality

As seen throughout this volume, rationality is neither the inevitable result of genetically directed maturation nor a set of thinking skills internalized from the environment. Rather, the rational agent applies forms of epistemic cognition that are constructed by the individual in the course of social interaction, especially with peers, and self-reflection. Thus, one would expect the construction of rationality to be facilitated by social environments in which individuals have free access to information and ideas and are encouraged to formulate, express, discuss, and justify ideas of their own (for related research and theory, see Dimant & Bearison, 1991; Kuhn, Garcia-Mila, Zohar, & Andersen, 1995; Levesque, 2007; Moshman, 1995a, 1995b, 1998, 2009b; Silverberg & Gondoli, 1996; Youniss & Damon, 1992).

Recall, for example, the five students in Chapter 4 who were discussing which cards to turn over on the selection task. Consider four important features of this discussion. First, each student had multiple opportunities to present and defend his or her views. Second, each student was exposed to a variety of alternative views and justifications. Third, students were encouraged to reach agreement on a conclusion they all deemed most justifiable. And fourth, students were not required to change their views if they remained unconvinced by the critiques and alternatives. Thus freedoms of belief and expression were fully respected, but there was no presumption that all views are equally good. As we saw, groups operating under such conditions were surprisingly successful in solving a notoriously difficult logical task (Moshman & Geil, 1998).

In contrast to this idealized experimental context, actual school discussions, especially with regard to controversial matters, often take place in contexts where (a) the presentation of disfavored viewpoints is subtly discouraged or explicitly forbidden, (b) access to disfavored alternatives is similarly restricted or prevented, and (c) teacher authority and peer pressure channel thinking in socially acceptable directions (Brown, 1994; Chomsky, 1989; Gaddy et al., 1996; Moshman, 1989, 1993, 2009b; Pipkin & Lent, 2002). A rational constructivist perspective suggests that such contexts may maximize behavioral and ideological conformity but will not promote the rational construction of justifiable beliefs, moralities, identities, and forms of reasoning. Rationality is encouraged and enhanced by an environment of intellectual freedom.

Intellectual Freedom in Secondary Education

Even if one accepts the argument that intellectual freedom is essential to the development of rationality, and thus to any educational program that aims to promote rationality, one might wonder how this applies to students of various ages. If children and adolescents do not understand the nature and purpose of intellectual freedom, they may be unable to operate effectively in an environment that presents multiple viewpoints and encourages them to think and speak for themselves.

Research indicates, however, that children as young as age 6 show meaningful conceptions of intellectual freedom (Helwig, 1997, 1998; Helwig & Yang, in press) and that adolescents do not differ substantially from college students in this regard (Dunkle, 1993; Helwig, 1995a; Wainryb, Shaw, Laupa, & Smith, 2001; Wainryb, Shaw, & Maianu, 1998). Charles Helwig (1995a), for example, assessed conceptions of freedoms of speech and religion in eight males and eight females at each of Grades 7 and 11 and at the college level. Students were asked to evaluate potential laws restricting these freedoms and to evaluate various applications of these freedoms, including cases where the freedom was exercised in a manner potentially offensive or harmful to others (such as speech involving racial slurs). In each case, students were asked to justify their responses.

Virtually all students at all three age levels showed substantial support for freedoms of speech and religion. Although there were differences in opinion with regard to the more complex dilemmas in which freedom conflicted with other values, these individual differences were found at each of the three ages. Even the seventh graders justified their responses in ways that showed clear appreciation of the issues involved. The results, concluded Helwig,

> show that sophisticated conceptions of civil liberties emerge by early adolescence and are used to evaluate social events. … Abstract conceptions of rights were judged in accordance with moral criteria … and justified by diverse and sophisticated rationales differentiated according to type of freedom. These abstract rights were also applied to judgments of social events in context. … These aspects of individuals' judgments and reasoning were found to be continuous across the age-span studied. (1995a, p. 162)

Other research has generated similar results (Dunkle, 1993; Ruck, Abramovitch, & Keating, 1998; Verkuyten & Slooter, 2008; Wainryb et al., 1998, 2001). Cecilia Wainryb and her associates (1998), for example, interviewed 20 males and 20 females at each of Grades 1, 4, 7, and college level about hypothetical cases in which a parent or teacher (a) holds a dissenting belief, (b) expresses such a belief, or (c) acts on such a belief. The dissenting beliefs were views that every participant disagreed with (e.g., that children learn best by being ridiculed for their mistakes or that girls are not as smart as boys and thus more likely to get into trouble). Overall there was greater tolerance for the holding of dissenting beliefs than for the expression of those beliefs and, in turn, more tolerance for the expression of dissenting beliefs than for actions based on those beliefs. These results suggest that rather than being generally tolerant, or generally intolerant, individuals across a wide age range make differentiated judgments about when tolerance is appropriate and when it is not.

More specifically, participants at all ages showed little or no tolerance for cases in which (a) a teacher, on the basis of her beliefs about children, ridicules students who make mistakes or (b) a father, on the basis of his beliefs about girls, denies his daughters freedoms available to his sons. Most saw these actions as harmful or unfair to others and therefore not to be tolerated. There were substantial age differences, however, in tolerance for the underlying beliefs. Most notably, first graders were less likely than the three older groups to be tolerant of the holding and expression of the beliefs in question and more likely to be concerned that the holding or expression of these beliefs would lead to harmful action. Differences between seventh graders and college students, in contrast, were minimal: Most seventh graders and college students were tolerant not only of the holding of these beliefs but also of the expression of these beliefs, explaining that the mere expression of a belief does not harm others and/or that the exchange of opinions may generate progress toward better ideas. Wainryb et al. (2001) found similar patterns of results for dissenting views about a wide variety of topics and showed that adolescents, like college students, made reasonable judgments about when intellectual diversity should be celebrated (e.g., with regard to metaphysical beliefs) and when it should be merely tolerated (e.g., with regard to beliefs that are clearly false and potentially harmful).

Research also shows that over the course of elementary school, children increasingly recognize and object to indoctrination. In a study of students' developing philosophies of education, Helwig, Ryerson, and Prencipe (2008) assessed judgments and reasoning about four distinct methods of teaching two distinct values to hypothetical students of two different ages. The values were racial equality and patriotism, the hypothetical students were in third or eighth grade, and the methods varied in the extent to which they provided for rational autonomy, active involvement, and choice. Participants in the study were 12 males and 12 females in each of the age ranges 7–8 years, 10–11 years, 13–14 years, and college (ranging from 18 to 53 years). In the course of individual interviews, they made and justified judgments about various hypothetical teaching scenarios varying systematically in methods, values, and ages of the hypothetical students. The major age break among the participants, it turned out, was between the three older groups (ages 10 and over) and the youngest group (ages 7–8). Older participants were more likely to distinguish methods that stimulate rational thought processes and active involvement and to take reasonable account of age and context in evaluating various methods. Of course even philosophers debate the fine points of just what constitutes indoctrination and just what is wrong with it (Callan & Arena, 2009). It appears that even by age 10, however, children understand the role of intellectual freedom in education and the dangers of indoctrination.

Developmental research, then, suggests that intellectual freedom is meaningful and important even in elementary schools and that there is little or no basis for distinguishing secondary from higher education in this regard. To promote advanced psychological development, secondary schools should facilitate access to all sources of information and should actively encourage reflection and discussion (Helwig & Yang, in press; Moshman, 1989, 1993, 2009b).

Educational theorists have elaborated on this general theme. Keating and Sasse (1996) argued that secondary schools should actively encourage critical thinking and critical habits of mind. Dreyer (1994) proposed that secondary schools should systematically foster identity formation and that "an identity-enhancing curriculum [is one that] promotes exploration, responsible choice, and self-determination by students" (p. 129). Lipman (1991) argued that the ideal classroom would be a "community of inquiry" in which students challenge each other to supply reasons, assist each other in drawing inferences and identifying assumptions, and coordinate their various ideas. Silverberg and Gondoli (1996), noting the hierarchical structure of authority in secondary schools, suggested that extracurricular activities are often more likely than the curriculum itself to permit the sort of peer interactions that foster autonomy. In some cases, however, depending on students' cultural backgrounds and home situations, a high school classroom that encourages free discussion of meaningful topics may be an oasis of intellectual freedom (Sarroub, 2005).

Although rational constructivism is a metatheory of psychological development, its application to education is fully consistent with the acquisition of traditional academic content. In a review of the literature on the use of peer groups in classrooms, for example, Cohen (1994) concluded that freedom of expression and discussion are critical to higher levels of conceptual learning. It is important to note, moreover, that rational constructivism does not preclude the direct presentation of specific facts or systematic training in particular skills (Harris & Alexander, 1998). In fact, rational constructivism can encompass a variety of instructional strategies. What marks a rational constructivist approach is an overarching context of liberty, where students are free to disagree with what is presented and ultimately to decide for themselves what to believe (Moshman, 2009b).

Education for rationality is not just the absence of censorship and indoctrination. It also includes a meaningful and challenging curriculum and active encouragement of learning, thinking, discussion, reflection, and creative expression (Kuhn, 2005). To fully promote rationality, moreover, educators must confront the universal human tendency to shield favored views from serious critique (Chomsky, 1989; Klaczynski, 1997, 2000, 2004; Klaczynski & Fauth, 1997; Klaczynski & Gordon, 1996a, 1996b; Klaczynski & Narasimham, 1998; Kuhn, Amsel, & O'Loughlin, 1988; Moshman, 2004a; Schauble, 1996; Stanovich & West, 1997; see Chapter 13). In its stronger forms, education for rationality involves active efforts to foster a critical spirit (Siegel, 1988, 1997) or rational identity (Chapter 13) by encouraging students to identify their fundamental assumptions and commitments and subject them to critical evaluation (Paul, 1990). Intellectual freedom is, of course, crucial to all of this.

In summary, there is good reason to believe that restrictions on intellectual freedom are antithetical to development and education; there is no reason to believe that adolescents or secondary schools are exceptions to this general rule. Contrary to the Supreme Court's decision in *Hazelwood* (1988), secondary education is a setting that requires strict protection of, rather than special restrictions on, the right of adolescents to formulate, express, and discuss their own ideas. Ideally, secondary education would not just respect students' rights but actively encourage reflection, coordination, and peer interaction to foster advanced psychological development.

Conclusion

Rational constructivism suggests that education should be aimed at the promotion of rationality and that rationality is promoted by intellectual freedom. It follows, then, that schools should present multiple perspectives and justifications, facilitate student access to all viewpoints and sources of information, and encourage students to formulate, express, discuss, and justify their own ideas. "Such a direction in schooling," noted Israel Scheffler (1997),

> is fraught with risk, for it means entrusting our current conceptions to the judgment of our pupils. In exposing these conceptions to their rational evaluation we are inviting them to see for themselves whether our conceptions are adequate, proper, fair. Such a risk is central to scientific education, where we deliberately subject our current theories to the test of continuous evaluation by future generations of our student scientists. It is central also to our moral

code, *in so far as* we ourselves take the moral point of view toward this code. And, finally, it is central to the democratic commitment which holds social policies to be continually open to free and public review. In sum, rationality liberates, but there is no liberty without risk. (p. 32)

How great are those risks? If we convey to adolescents that they are free to believe and do what they choose because we have no basis for our own beliefs and actions, we may undermine rationality, including the rational construction of morality and identity. If, on the other hand, we communicate the reasons for our commitments and encourage adolescents to form justifiable commitments of their own, much of what we value will endure. To think otherwise, as the Supreme Court noted in *West Virginia v. Barnette* (1943, p. 641), "is to make an unflattering estimate of the appeal of our institutions to free minds."

CHAPTER 16

Adolescents as Young Adults

Our beliefs about teenagers are deeply contradictory: They should be free to become themselves. They need many years of training and study. They know more about the future than adults do. They know hardly anything at all. They ought to know the value of a dollar. They should be protected from the world of work. They are frail, vulnerable creatures. They are children. They are sex fiends. They are the death of culture. They are the hope of us all.

—**Thomas Hine**
(1999, p. 11)

I t appears from Chapter 15 that secondary school students do not differ substantially from college students in their ability to understand, operate in, and profit from an environment of intellectual freedom. More generally, research discussed throughout this volume indicates that with respect to a wide range of basic psychological competencies, adolescents are far more easily distinguished from children than from adults.

As discussed in Chapter 14, categorical distinctions between groups of people—men are this way, women are that way—require more than evidence of statistically significant differences. To support a categorical distinction, evidence should show that the difference between the groups is qualitative or at least very substantial compared to the diversity among and within individual members of the groups.

With regard to a distinction between adolescents and children, even the more stringent criterion of qualitative difference is easily met. Adolescents routinely show forms and levels of knowledge and reasoning rarely seen in children before age 10 or 11. These include hypothetico-deductive reasoning, explicit conceptions of inferential validity, dialectical reasoning, reflective coordinations of theories and evidence, reflective epistemologies, third-party perspective taking, principled forms of moral reasoning, and reflective self-conceptions (Basseches, 1984; Boyes & Chandler, 1992; Campbell & Bickhard, 1986; Chandler, Boyes, & Ball, 1990; Efklides, Demetriou, & Metallidou, 1994; Erikson, 1968; Franks, 1996, 1997; Habermas & Bluck, 2000; Inhelder & Piaget, 1958; King & Kitchener, 1994; Klaczynski, Schuneman, & Daniel, 2004; Kohlberg, 1984; Kuhn, 1989; Marcia, Waterman, Matteson, Archer, & Orlofsky, 1993; Markovits & Vachon, 1989; Moshman, 1990a, 1993, 1998, 2004b, 2005, 2008, 2009a, 2009c, in press-a; Moshman & Franks, 1986; Overton, 1990; Selman, 1980).

Development does continue over the course of adolescence and early adulthood; many individuals construct concepts and forms of reasoning that go far beyond the competencies they had in early adolescence. I am not aware, however, of any form or level of knowledge, reasoning, or psychological functioning that is routine among adults but rarely seen in adolescents. On the contrary, there is enormous cognitive variability among individuals beyond age 12, and it appears that age accounts for surprisingly little of the variance. Adolescents often fail to reason logically, but the same is true of adults. Adolescents often fail to adequately test and revise their theoretical understandings, but adults fail in the same ways. Adolescents often show simplistic conceptions of knowledge and primitive forms of social and moral reasoning, but so do adults. Adolescent thinking is subject to peer pressure, emotional biases, cognitive distortions, and self-serving denial, but so is that of adults. Adults as well as adolescents can be found in all four of the Marcia identity statuses. Adolescents are still developing (Cauffman & Woolard, 2005; Steinberg, Cauffman, Woolard, Graham, & Banich, 2009; Steinberg & Scott, 2003), but development extends well into adulthood (Fischer, Stein, & Heikkinen, 2009; Moshman, 2003).

Research simply does not support categorical distinctions between adolescents and adults in rationality, morality, or identity (Millstein & Halpern-Felsher, 2002; Moshman, 1993). The distinction between adolescence and adulthood is more a matter of cultural expectations and restrictions than of intrinsic biological or psychological characteristics (Epstein, 2007; Hine, 1999; see also Levesque, 2000, 2007). With the understanding that development is not limited to childhood, adolescence may best be construed as the first phase of adulthood.

This is not a popular view, however, among those whose adulthood is not in question. Genuine adults, we assume, differ qualitatively and categorically from adolescents. Research considered in Chapter 15, however, suggests that adolescents are no less capable than college students of functioning in and profiting from an environment of intellectual freedom. In this final chapter we look more generally at adolescent rationality, which is central to any consideration of their rights and responsibilities. To clarify the issue of age comparisons, I present a thought experiment in which panels of developmental psychologists attempt to distinguish individuals of various ages. We then proceed to further discussion of adolescent rationality, including current research and popular claims about adolescent brains. I conclude that development beyond childhood should be considered adult development, as distinct from child development, and that adolescence should be seen as the first phase of adulthood.

A Thought Experiment: The Developmental Panel

Experiments are done to see how they turn out. Sometimes, however, even if an experiment cannot be carried out for practical or ethical reasons, simply thinking about possible and likely outcomes can be useful. Such experiments are known as thought experiments.

Here's a thought experiment, which I will refer to as "the developmental panel." Suppose we round up a group of 100 children, half of them 3-year-olds and the other half 6-year-olds, and convene a panel of developmental psychologists who specialize in developmental change during this age range. The developmentalists are not permitted to see the children. Their charge is to develop a psychological measure of rationality or maturity that will distinguish the older from the younger children as accurately as possible. How well would the panel do?

I would expect them to do very well indeed. Research on young children shows that virtually all 6-year-olds have attained forms and levels of rationality rarely achieved before the age of 4 years. The developmental literature describes many means of assessing such developmental changes. For example, research on preschool children's theories of mind includes tasks assessing the ability to understand that people can hold false beliefs. Children under age 4 almost always fail stringent false belief tasks, whereas 5-year-olds almost always pass them (Doherty, 2009; Wellman, Cross, & Watson, 2001). If one gave four such tasks to each of the 100 children, it is likely that nearly 50 of them would pass all four tasks and that virtually all of these would be 6-year-olds. Correspondingly, nearly 50 children would likely fail all four tasks, and virtually all of these would be 3-year-olds. Even if a few of the older 3-year-olds passed one or more of the tasks, and even if a distracted 6-year-old occasionally failed a task, discrimination of the older from the younger children would be excellent. In a case like this, where an age difference meets the developmental panel test, we have a basis for describing the difference between two age groups as categorical, at least with respect to some ability or domain of understanding. Categorical differences between groups may justify differential treatment, responsibilities, and rights.

What about other age ranges? If the 100 children consisted of 50 children age 3 and 50 infants still short of their first birthday, we wouldn't need to worry about the expertise of the panel; anyone familiar with children could devise a measure (e.g., of language) that would be passed by all the older children and none of the younger.

What about 6-year-olds and 9-year-olds? Here we would certainly want a panel of experts familiar with the developmental literature. And we ought to expect something less than perfection; the distribution of any ability among the 6-year-olds will surely overlap with its distribution among the 9-year-olds. To be realistic, let's say the developmental panel is successful if at least 40 of the 50 top-scoring children are in the older group. This is well short of a perfect score of 50 but substantially higher than the chance score of 25 that would result, on average, from picking 50 students randomly. By this criterion, I would expect the panel to succeed. The Piagetian concrete operations literature, for example, provides multiple tasks assessing the comprehension of logical necessities intrinsic to classification and seriation that are rarely passed before age 7 but relatively easy for 9-year-olds. I expect the developmental panel could devise a measure of what develops most rapidly in this age range and set a criterion that would be met by a substantial majority of 9-year-olds but very few 6-year-olds. Administering this measure to the present 100 children would probably distinguish the older from the younger children with sufficient accuracy that the panel would meet the 80% criterion for success.

And now, moving into the domain of this book, what about 9-year-olds and 12-year-olds? As age increases, 3 years becomes a smaller portion of one's life so far. Thus the task of the developmental panel may become increasingly difficult with increasing age. But I would expect the panel regarding the 9-year-olds versus 12-year-olds to succeed, especially if I were on it or if they had at least read this book. For example, nearly all 12-year-olds are capable of distinguishing valid from invalid inferences, given some explanation or feedback to clarify the distinction of logic from empirical truth, whereas few 9-year-olds grasp this distinction even after comparable explanation and feedback. Research on the development of this metalogical insight (Moshman & Franks, 1986, Experiment 3; see Chapter 1) showed that 75% of a group of seventh graders (ages 12 and 13) met a 90% criterion of success in distinguishing valid from invalid inferences, whereas only 10% of a comparable group of fourth graders (ages 9 and 10) were able to do so. Surely an expert panel charged with distinguishing 12-year-olds from 9-year-olds could come up with a successful measure.

A panel charged with distinguishing 12-year-olds from 15-year-olds, however, would have a much greater challenge. In fact, with the confidence of knowing that this experiment is not about to be done, I predict they would fail. I am not aware of any basis in the literature for a measure with a criterion of success that would be met by a substantial majority of 15-year-olds but very few 12-year-olds. This is not to say there is no development in this age range. As we have seen throughout this book, young adolescents are generally developing in a variety of ways. There are many measures on which the mean performance of 15-year-olds will be significantly higher than that of 12-year-olds. Given the statistical association of age with performance, I would expect the developmental panel could design a measure such that well over half of the top 50 scores would come from the 15-year-olds. But I see no evidence to suggest it could come anywhere close to the level achievable in distinguishing 9-year-olds from 12-year-olds or any set of younger children 3 years apart.

As for 15-year-olds versus 18-year-olds, the developmentalists, with careful work, could probably manage to distinguish the older individuals from the younger at better than chance level (at least

26 of the top 50 in performance would indeed be older), but I doubt they would do much better than that, regardless of whether I was on the panel. Even if one compares 15-year-olds to 30-year-olds, there is far too much diversity within each age group to permit successful sorting by age. However competent the developmental panel, it cannot get around the fact that development beyond childhood is highly individualized in direction and rate. Performance, moreover, is always a function of context. Beyond the age of about 12, the statistical relation of age to performance is not nearly sufficient to predict one from the other accurately in the case of specific individuals in specific contexts. Whatever measure we use, any criterion met by most of the older group will also be met by many of the younger.

Of course this has been only a thought experiment. Perhaps someone will in fact carry out some portion of it with individuals beyond the age of 12, and perhaps the developmental panel will succeed. On the basis of current evidence, however, the thought experiment suggests that there are sufficient grounds for categorically distinguishing children from each other on the basis of age (e.g., allowing 6-year-olds to do things forbidden to 3-year-olds), but categorical distinctions beyond the age of about 12 cannot be justified on the basis of existing developmental data. There is developmental change beyond age 12, but it is not tied to age.

Adolescent Rationality

When does a boy become a man? In Judaism, as noted in the Introduction, the bar mitzvah has for centuries marked 13 years as the age when full rights and responsibilities are attained and officially recognized by the community. In contemporary societies, the bar mitzvah boy (or bat mitzvah girl) is typically a middle school student with 4 years of high school and many years of higher education ahead. For most of human history, however, most teens in most societies have been deemed adults, so the age of maturity set in traditional Judaism is by no means anomalous. On the contrary, adolescence as we know it is largely a cultural construction famously defined and delineated in G. Stanley Hall's (1904) classic work by that title. Prior to the late 19th century, individuals of both sexes beyond the age of 12 or 14 were deemed adults and were expected, depending on gender, to work, marry, have children, run a household, and perform other adult roles.

Developing this theme, Robert Epstein (2010) argued that the trend since Hall (1904) has been to construe teenagers increasingly as children, subject to an astonishing variety of parental and governmental determinations and restrictions that were unknown before the 20th century and would clearly violate the rights of any adult. The central problem of teens, he argued, is that we infantilize them by treating them as if they were children. Contemporary restrictions on their liberty, privacy, and autonomy make it impossible for them to take control of their lives. The solution is to recognize them as adults. This is not to say they should be free to do as they please; no one has such freedom. Adults of all ages live within social networks encompassing a variety of expectations, responsibilities, entitlements, and liberties, including basic rights of personhood recognized by the state. Rather than isolate and marginalize teens within oppressive secondary schools and an artificial adolescent culture, Epstein proposed, we should integrate them into multigenerational social networks.

This is unlikely to happen any time soon, however. Although Epstein is far from alone in his view of adolescence (for related analyses, see Hine, 1999; Levesque, 2000, 2007; Males, 2009, 2010; Nichols & Good, 2004; Quadrel, Fischhoff, & Davis, 1993; Umeh, 2009), stereotypical conceptions of teens became so well entrenched over the course of the 20th century that adolescence has come to be seen as a natural and universal stage with its own intrinsic characteristics. Claims supposedly based on developmental research have often been accepted uncritically because they conform to what parents, adult authorities, and government officials already believe. Traditional challenges to adolescent rationality have included unjustified developmental claims concerning adolescent egocentrism, susceptibility to peer pressure, inclination to risk taking, impulsivity, and limited future orientation.

Notions of adolescent egocentrism can be traced to a theoretical claim by David Elkind (1967) that young adolescents, relatively new to formal operational thinking, are uniquely susceptible to special forms of egocentrism associated with what he called the "imaginary audience" and the "personal fable." The imaginary audience involves an acute and unjustified sense of being the center of attention—for better or worse. The personal fable involves a sense of being special, even more special than anyone else, including a special sense of invulnerability. Research has not supported such claims of adolescent egocentrism, however.

Adolescents do indeed show various forms of egocentrism, but so do adults. There is no evidence that adolescents are uniquely egocentric or even much different from adults in this regard; on the contrary, research has shown age differences to be minimal or nonexistent (Millstein & Halpern-Felsher, 2002; Quadrel et al., 1993; Smetana & Villalobos, 2009). As for the specific assertion that adolescents see themselves as invulnerable, it appears instead that adolescents routinely, and often drastically, *overestimate* their actual vulnerability (Millstein & Halpern-Felsher, 2002). Allegations of adolescent egocentrism, then, have been disconfirmed by empirical research. We're all egocentric in various ways and to differing degrees, but there is no type or degree of egocentrism special to adolescence.

A second counter to conceptions of adolescent rationality is that however well adolescents think on their own, they are uniquely subject to peer pressure and thus substantially less rational in their behavior. There are two points worth noting immediately. First, attention to peer reactions and willingness to go along with a group are often beneficial. Second, deleterious peer pressures are common and influential among people of all ages. Claims that adolescents have some special susceptibility to peer pressure resonate with adults because they fit adult stereotypes of adolescents, but there is no empirical basis for categorical claims of this sort. People of all ages are highly susceptible to peer influences of various sorts, and this is not always a bad thing. Even in the case of deleterious peer pressure, there is no evidence that adolescents are uniquely susceptible compared to children or adults of any age.

Adolescent risk taking (Beyth-Marom, Austin, Fischhoff, Palmgren, & Jacobs-Quadrel, 1993; Males, 2009, 2010; Michels, Kropp, Eyre, & Halpern-Felsher, 2005; Moilanen, Crockett, Raffaelli, & Jones, 2010; Reyna, Adam, Poirier, LeCroy, & Brainerd, 2005; Reyna & Farley, 2006; Sercombe, 2010; Steinberg, 2007; Van Leijenhorst & Crone, 2010) is a popular concept that deserves similar analysis. The phrase "adolescent risk taking" calls up an image of an adolescent doing something foolish and dangerous, which readily connects to additional images we all have of adolescents doing foolish and dangerous things. But risk taking is not always bad, and adolescents are not uniquely prone to it. People of all ages take risks of all sorts, including foolish and dangerous risks; there is no empirical basis for the common assumption that risk taking is a special phenomenon of adolescence. On the contrary, direct comparisons of adolescents and adults show minimal age differences (Beyth-Marom et al., 1993). Sociological data indicate that when covariates such as poverty are controlled, adolescents are no more prone to risk taking than adults, who in fact take plenty of dubious risks (Males, 2009, 2010). There is, to my knowledge, no standard of rational risk taking that is met by most adults but few 15-year-olds. A developmental panel charged with distinguishing 15-year-olds from 30-year-olds on the basis of the ability to deploy risk-related competencies would almost surely fail.

Another allegation against adolescents is that they are impulsive, which is to say they lack self-control, which is presumed to explain why they take risks they should not. Whereas **risk taking** seems to me a vague and value-laden term, impulsivity and self-control are important developmental concepts related to what is commonly called **executive control**, one's capacity for intentional or metacognitive self-regulation, which is widely seen as central to cognition and development (Gestsdottir & Lerner, 2008; Kuhn, 2006, 2009). Adolescents function at levels unseen in children in large part because of qualitatively more advanced forms of executive control. But beyond the age of 12 to 14 years, individual differences and intraindividual variation in functioning are far more substantial than mean differences between age groups. With regard to executive functioning, self-control, and impulsivity, adolescents are categorically distinct from children but not from adults.

Research on the development of future orientation provides a picture consistent with the above discussions of adolescent egocentrism, peer pressure, risk taking, impulsivity, self-control, and executive control. Laurence Steinberg and collaborators (Steinberg, Graham, et al., 2009) showed statistically significant increases in several aspects of future orientation in a sample of 935 individuals ranging from 10 to 30 years, but most of these differences were between ages 10 and 15. The study provided no evidence of a state of mature future orientation achieved by most individuals beyond some age but rare before some earlier age. Quite the contrary, it simply documented statistically detectable increases in early adolescence and in some cases beyond that. A developmental panel charged with distinguishing adolescents from adults on the basis of future orientation, it appears, would fall far short of success.

Actual adolescent responses to their social environments are generally rational and not sharply distinguishable from those of adults (Goossens, 2006; Helwig, 2006b; Kakihara & Tilton-Weaver, 2009; Levesque, 2000, 2007; Smetana, 2006; Smetana & Bitz, 1996; Smetana & Villalobos, 2009). Research by Judith Smetana and others (reviewed in Goossens, 2006; Smetana, 2006; Smetana & Villalobos, 2009) shows that adolescents distinguish a personal domain from domains of morality and social convention in their ongoing negotiations with parents, teachers, and other authorities over issues of personal autonomy. Far from mindlessly asserting a general right to do as they please, they make reasonable distinctions—based on genuine respect for moral obligations and legitimate authority—between legitimate and illegitimate restrictions. Of course adolescents fall far short of perfect rationality in family interactions, but so do their parents. More generally, the problems adolescents face in the adult world are not entirely, or even mostly, the fault of adolescents (Nichols & Good, 2004). Indeed, adolescents often show remarkable insight and competence even as victims of extreme group violence in adult political contexts for which they are not responsible (Barber, 2009; Daiute, 2010).

In summary, psychological research on adolescents clearly disconfirms adult stereotypes of adolescent irrationality and immaturity. Such stereotypes persist, however. In the absence of supportive behavioral evidence, many now argue that the basis for distinguishing adolescents from adults can be seen directly in their brains.

Adolescent Brains?

Claims about brains have been popular for centuries, including claims about the relative size and merit of the brains of various sorts of people (Graves, 2001). Such claims have commonly served as a basis or excuse for oppression of women, racial minorities, and others with brains deemed inferior. Thus there are strong historical reasons for approaching claims about brains with caution. The problem, we should keep in mind, is not brain research itself, which provides useful scientific findings, but interpretations and applications that go far beyond what the data justify.

Brain development and functioning in adolescence has been an active area of research since the turn of the millennium (Crone &

Westenberg, 2009; Kuhn, 2006, 2009; Luciana, 2010; Males, 2009, 2010; Paus, 2009; Sercombe, 2010; Spear, 2010; Steinberg, 2007, 2009, 2010). Results of such research are generally consistent with the psychological findings reported throughout this book. Anatomical and physiological changes beyond age 12 are consistent with the view that development remains possible long beyond childhood. Such changes, however, are highly individualized and are to a large extent the result of experience. Popular assumptions notwithstanding, brain research has not shown an age-related maturation of brain structures and modes of functioning that generate new forms or levels of cognition or behavior. Quite the contrary, the findings of brain research fully support theoretical views in which the brain is part of a developing system with complex multidirectional and interactive causal influences.

There appear to be at least four fallacies in interpreting adolescent brain research: (a) unjustified categorical claims, (b) reductionism, (c) determinism, and (d) the myth of maturity. I consider each in turn.

First, statistically significant differences are an inadequate basis for categorical claims. Brain research does not support categorical claims about adolescent brains as fundamentally distinct from those of adults or about brains of any age group beyond age 12 to 14 as distinct from those of any older age group. Developmental changes beyond age 12 to 14 are much too subtle and individualized, it appears to me, for a developmental panel, even if it included brain experts, to succeed in distinguishing age groups on the basis of their brain development.

Second, there is the reductionist fallacy. Brain data seem more scientific than behavioral data, but they are not, nor do they provide us with ultimate explanations. Even if psychology can in principle be reduced to biology, a dubious proposition, we are a very long way from achieving such reduction. If we want to know what is going on in a brain, relying on data about the brain would be more direct than making inferences from behavioral evidence. But if we want to know about adolescent behavior and cognition, data on behavior and reasoning are a more direct basis for knowledge than inferences from brain data, especially given how little we know about the relation of brain to behavior.

Related to this is the determinist fallacy, based on a nativist view of maturation in which the direction of causality proceeds from genes to brain maturation to developmental advances in psychological functioning. Parents in the grip of this fallacy can be seen in a 2006 *New Yorker* cartoon ordering their teenage son to go to his room until his cerebral cortex matures (Steinberg, 2009). Contrary to such parental assumptions, research shows that the brain is part of a dynamic developing system with a complex interactive causality involving the actions of the developing agent and a variety of internal and external forces (Stiles, 2009). The brain must be part of any complete explanation of behavior and development but is not the ultimate explanation. Brain changes are in large part the result of thinking, action, and experience. Whatever the problems of adolescence, waiting for adolescent brains to mature is not the solution.

In a review of adolescent brain development, Tomáš Paus (2009) concluded,

> Overall, there is an increasing body of evidence that challenges a simple, deterministic view of genes influencing the brain directly and, in turn, the individual's behavior. As indicated by a number of studies on the effect of experience on brain structure, ... anatomical measures may very well reflect a cumulative effect of the differential experience (behavior) rather than the other way around. This point speaks directly to the issue of biological determinism. Quite often, we view developmental changes in brain structure as (biological) prerequisites of a particular cognitive ability. For example, the common logic assumes that cognitive/executive control of behavior emerges in full only after the prefrontal cortex reaches the adult-like level of structural maturity. But given the role of experience in shaping the brain, it might also be that high demands on cognitive control faced, for example, by young adolescents assuming adult roles due to family circumstances may facilitate structural maturation of their prefrontal cortex. (p. 110)

Finally, there is the myth of maturity. It seems almost irresistible for adults to see themselves as having achieved a state of maturity that adolescents (and even younger adults) have not yet reached, but brain research provides no evidence to support the postulation of advanced states of maturity attained by most or all adults but few adolescents. Many people continue to develop long beyond childhood, and their brains reflect those changes, but beyond age 12 there is no natural and universal state of maturity waiting to be achieved.

Brain research is presently flourishing and has much potential to contribute to the understanding of adolescent development. But we know far more about behavior from behavioral research than we are likely to learn any time soon from brain research. We should continue to be wary of claims about brains, which often sound much more definitive and scientific than they are.

Development Beyond Childhood

Development continues beyond childhood, but development beyond childhood is different from child development. As we have seen throughout this book, it is less predictable, less universal, less tied to age, and more a function of the individual's specific actions and experiences. The social context does not cause developmental change but does influence its likelihood and direction. This suggests both the possibility and the limits of intervention. We can encourage, promote, and facilitate development, but development by definition is not externally controlled.

In the context of sentencing adolescent criminals, it is often argued that whatever they have done, there remains the possibility of further development. This is no doubt true, but there is no age at which development is no longer possible. Our concern with development should not end with childhood, but this does not mean we should treat adolescents as children. To see adolescents as young adults, with adult rights and responsibilities, is not at all to deny their developmental potential. In the case of an adolescent criminal sentenced to death or life imprisonment, a compelling argument can be made that such a sentence fails to consider the possibility of developmental change (*Graham v. Florida*, 2010). But that remains true far beyond adolescence.

Adolescent development can profit from active adult support, in some ways even more than child development, which proceeds on a stronger course (Kuhn, 2005, 2009). Children in any normal human environment, for example, proceed through a predictable age-related sequence in constructing the basic theory of mind seen universally by age 4 or 5 years (Doherty, 2009; Wellman et al., 2001). Whether and how far adolescents and adults progress in their scientific or moral reasoning, in contrast, or how far they proceed toward rationalist epistemologies and rational moral identities, are far more dependent on their opportunities, actions, and experiences. Recognizing the need for ongoing support beyond childhood, some researchers and theorists have examined the coconstructive aspects of later development, emphasizing that the developing individual is not the only active and reflective agent (Hardy, Bhattacharjee, Reed, & Aquino, 2010; Marshall, Young, Domene, & Zaidman-Zait, 2008; Schachter & Ventura, 2008). For adolescents and adults, development remains a cognitive and social process.

Conclusion

A developmental approach to adolescence has shown that development may continue throughout adolescence and well into adulthood—or not. There is no state of maturity beyond early adolescence waiting to emerge at some later age. Many adolescents in many societies and educational contexts achieve forms and levels of reasoning and understanding beyond those universally achieved by young teens, but there is nothing automatic or inevitable about this process. To recognize adolescents as young adults is to see that development beyond childhood is up to all of us, and it needn't end with adolescence.

Glossary

Accommodation: Adjusting to the environment.

Adolescence: The period following childhood in which one is not yet accepted as an adult.

Advanced development: Development beyond childhood.

Agent: An actor or subject. One who acts or knows.

Argument: In logic, a set of one or more premises plus a conclusion. In reasoning or social interaction, a justification.

Argumentation: A process of reciprocal justification.

Assimilation: Understanding something new on the basis of what one already knows.

Autonomy: Self-direction or self-governance. Capacity for rational choice.

Care: Concern or compassion for others.

Categorical difference: A difference in kind, not just magnitude.

Cognition: Knowledge and inference.

Competence: Potential performance under optimal conditions.

Concrete operations: In Piaget's theory, the necessary logic of classes, relations, and numbers, typically understood by children beginning about age 7.

Conditional reasoning: Deductive reasoning with conditional premises (of the form *If p then q*).

Constructivism: A metatheory emphasizing the active role of the agent in the construction of knowledge.

Continuity: In identity formation, a postulated property of the self as the same rational agent over time, extending from the past through the present to the future.

Coordination: In constructivist theories, a process of developmental change involving structural integration and reorganization.

Critical spirit: A disposition to value and engage in good reasoning.

Culture: A social system.

Deductive reasoning: Logical reasoning in the strict sense of reaching only logically necessary conclusions. Reasoning in accord with strict rules of deduction that respect the constraints of logical necessity.

Development: Change that is extended, self-regulated, qualitative, and progressive.

Dialectical operations: A conception of postformal operations as dialectical reasoning.

Dialectical reasoning: A form of reasoning that makes progress in understanding by transcending current perspectives rather than mechanically applying rules of logic.

Diversity: Differences across groups, across individuals, or within individuals.

Domain: A broad topic or area of concern.

Dual processing theories: Theories of cognition that postulate parallel processes, one more deliberate than the other.

Ego identity: Personal identity, especially as originally theorized by Erikson.

Empathy: Emotional perspective taking. Feelings congruent with another's situation.

Empiricism: A metatheory emphasizing processes of learning from the (physical or social) environment.

Epistemic cognition: Knowledge about the nature and justification of knowledge.

Epistemic development: Development of epistemic cognition.

Epistemic doubt: Radical skepticism about the possibility of knowledge or justification.

Epistemology: A theory of knowledge focused especially on its most fundamental nature and justification.

Equilibration: In Piaget's theory, restoring or enhancing equilibrium.

Ethnic identity: A social identity focused on ethnic affiliation.

Eudaimonism: A philosophy of character, virtue, and human flourishing.

Executive control: Capacity for metacognitive self-regulation.

False moral identity: An identity centered on a false conception of the self as moral.

Falsification strategy: A (logical) strategy of testing hypotheses by seeking evidence that would falsify them.

Foreclosure: In Marcia's identity statuses, the state of having an unreflectively internalized identity.

Formal logic: Logic based on the forms of propositions as distinct from their content.

Formal operations: In Piaget's theory, the stage of formal (hypothetico-deductive) reasoning following concrete operations.

Formal reasoning: Reasoning on the basis of logical form rather than content.

Heteronomous morality: In Piaget's and Kohlberg's theories, a morality of following externally imposed rules, typical of young children.

Hypothetico-deductive reasoning: Deductive reasoning from premises deemed to be hypothetical or false.

Identity: An explicit theory of oneself as a person.

Identity achievement: In Marcia's identity statuses, the state of having a self-constructed identity.

Identity crisis: In Eriksonian identity theory, the period of forming an identity.

Identity diffusion: In Marcia's identity statuses, a state of neither identity nor search for identity.

Identity status: In Marcia's theory, one of four possible states with respect to identity.

Indoctrination: Causing changes in belief through means that bypass rational agency.

Inference: Going beyond the data.

Intellectual freedom: Freedoms of belief, expression, discussion, inquiry, and access to information and ideas.

Interactionism: The metatheoretical view that development cannot be the sum of genetic and environmental influences because the effect of each depends on the other.

Intersubjective: Coordinating two subjectivities.

Justice: Fairness, principled action, and respect for fundamental rights.

Justification: A basis for belief or action.

Life story: A narrative identity.

Logic: Strict norms of good reasoning.

Logical necessity: Truth based on logical proof rather than empirical evidence.

Logical reasoning: Reasoning in accord with logical norms.

Maturity: The endpoint of ontogenesis. A state achieved by all members of a species at the culmination of development.

Metacognition: Cognition about cognition.

Meta-ethical cognition: Knowledge about the epistemological basis for and justification of moral judgments.

Metalogical understanding: Explicit knowledge about logic.

Metasubjective objectivity: Progress in objectivity through (subjective) reflection on and reconstruction of one's subjectivity.

Microgenetic method: A developmental research methodology that speeds developmental progress to study it over a briefer period.

Moral epistemology: A theory concerning the justification and rationality of moral knowledge and action.

Moral identity: An identity centered on a conception of the self as moral.

Moral reasoning: Reasoning about moral matters.

Morality: At the very least, respect or concern for the rights or welfare of others (some would define it more broadly).

Moratorium: In Marcia's identity statuses, the period of identity crisis.

Narrative identity: A self-defining narrative of one's life.

Nativism: A developmental metatheory that highlights the role of genes in directing developmental change.

Norm: A rule, principle, or ideal against which action, inference, or reality can be evaluated.

Objectivism: An epistemology that holds there to be ultimate truths that are directly observable, provable, or known to the authorities.

Objectivity: Truth in relation to reality regardless of perspective.

Peer interaction: Interaction with others of roughly equal status, authority, and power.

Person: At minimum, a rational agent.

Personal identity: Identity as studied in the literature of developmental psychology beginning with Erikson and Marcia.

Perspective: An orientation or point of view.

Perspective taking: Seeing from perspectives other than one's own.

Pluralism: An epistemological perspective that acknowledges meaningful diversity but not radical relativism.

Postconventional morality: A morality rooted in a prior-to-society perspective.

Postformal operations: A postulated stage of development beyond formal operations.

Principle: A metarule. A rule explicitly applied on the basis of knowledge about its applicability.

Principled reasoning: Reasoning on the basis of explicit principles.

Prior-to-society perspective: A moral perspective more fundamental than any particular social system (central to Kohlberg's Stage 5).

Progressive change: Change that can be normatively judged to make progress (e.g., toward rationality or maturity).

Qualitative change: Change in kind, not just amount.

Rational: Minimally, acting on the basis of reasons. More stringently, having good reasons for one's beliefs and actions.

Rational constructivism: A form of constructivism in which the active agents are seen as rational agents making developmental progress.

Rational identity: An identity centered on a conception of the self as rational.

Rational moral identity: A rational and moral identity (a developmental ideal for identity formation).

Rationalism: A postsubjectivist epistemology in which reasons short of proof provide bases for beliefs and actions.

Rationality: Qualitatively, a characteristic of rational agents. Quantitatively, the justifiability of one's reasoning and action.

Reasoning: Epistemologically self-constrained thinking. Thinking aimed at reaching justifiable conclusions.

Reflection: A strong, self-conscious form of metacognition seen by rational constructivist theories as a basis for developmental change.

Relativism: A subjectivist epistemology claiming that truth is fundamentally relative to perspective.

Scientific reasoning: Reasoning as a scientist does, which includes attention to theory and evidence.

Self-regulated change: Change that is directed or regulated from within.

Sexual identity: One's theory of oneself as a sexual person.

Sexual orientation: One's fundamental pattern of sexual dispositions and desires.

Singularity: In identity formation, a postulated property of the self as the same rational agent across multiple contexts.

Social contract morality: In Kohlberg's theory, a postconventional (Stage 5) morality in which social systems can be rationally evaluated from a prior-to-society perspective on the basis of postconventional moral principles.

Social identity: Identification with a salient social group.

Social system morality: In Kohlberg's theory, an advanced conventional (Stage 4) morality in which upholding the social system (whatever one perceives that system to be) is one's fundamental moral obligation.

Subjectivism: An epistemology in which knowledge is seen as constructed from, and thus determined by, one's point of view.

Subjectivity: Perspective. Contribution of mind to knowledge.

Symmetric social interaction: Interaction with others of equal status, authority, and power (an important basis for development in rational constructivist theories).

Thinking: The deliberate application and coordination of one's inferences to serve one's purposes.

Third-party perspective taking: Seeing one's intersubjective relation to another from a third-party perspective.

Universality: Claims of generality across groups, domains, perspectives, and so on.

Valid argument: An argument in which the conclusion follows logically from the premises.

Verification strategy: A (logically flawed) strategy of supporting hypotheses by seeking and accumulating evidence consistent with them.

Virtue: A trait of good character.

References

Abu-Rayya, H. M. (2006). Ethnic identity, ego identity, and psychological well-being among mixed-ethnic Arab-European adolescents in Israel. *British Journal of Developmental Psychology, 24*, 669–679.

Akatsuko, N. (1997). On the co-construction of counterfactual reasoning. *Journal of Pragmatics, 28*, 781–794.

Alves, J. A. L. (2000). The Declaration of Human Rights in postmodernity. *Human Rights Quarterly, 22*, 478–500.

Amsel, E. (in press). Hypothetical thinking in adolescence: Its nature, development, and applications. In E. Amsel & J. Smetana (Eds.), *Adolescent vulnerabilities and opportunities: Constructivist developmental perspectives*. New York: Cambridge University Press.

Amsel, E., & Brock, S. (1996). The development of evidence evaluation skills. *Cognitive Development, 11*, 523–550.

Amsel, E., Goodman, G., Savoie, D., & Clark, M. (1996). The development of reasoning about causal and noncausal influences on levers. *Child Development, 67*, 1624–1646.

Amsel, E., Klaczynski, P. A., Johnston, A., Bench, S., Close, J., Sadler, E., & Walker, R. (2008). A dual-process account of the development of scientific reasoning: The nature and development of metacognitive intercession skills. *Cognitive Development, 23*, 452–471.

Amsel, E., & Renninger, K. A. (Eds.). (1997). *Change and development: Issues of theory, method, and application*. Mahwah, NJ: Lawrence Erlbaum.

Amsel, E., Trionfi, G., & Campbell, R. (2005). Reasoning about make-believe and hypothetical suppositions: Towards a theory of belief-contravening reasoning. *Cognitive Development, 20*, 545–575.

Appiah, K. A. (2005). *The ethics of identity*. Princeton, NJ: Princeton University Press.

Appiah, K. A. (2008). *Experiments in ethics*. Cambridge, MA: Harvard University Press.

Archer, S. L. (1994). An overview. In S. L. Archer (Ed.), *Interventions for adolescent identity development* (pp. 3–11). Thousand Oaks, CA: Sage.

Aristotle. (1985). *Nicomachean ethics*. Indianapolis, IN: Hackett.

Arlin, P. K. (1975). Cognitive development in adulthood: A fifth stage? *Developmental Psychology, 11*, 602–606.

Arnold, M. L. (2000). Stage, sequence, and sequels: Changing conceptions of morality, post-Kohlberg. *Educational Psychology Review, 12*, 365–383.

Arsenio, W. F., & Lemerise, E. A. (2004). Aggression and moral development: Integrating social information processing and moral domain models. *Child Development, 75*, 987–1002.

Årseth, A. K., Kroger, J., Martinussen, M., & Marcia, J. E. (2009). Meta-analytic studies of identity status and the relational issues of attachment and intimacy. *Identity, 9*, 1–32.

Ashmore, R. D., & Jussim, L. (Eds.). (1997). *Self and identity.* Oxford: Oxford University Press.

Audi, R. (1997). *Moral knowledge and ethical character.* New York: Oxford University Press.

Audi, R. (1998). *Epistemology.* New York: Routledge.

Audi, R. (2001). *The architecture of reason: The structure and substance of rationality.* Oxford: Oxford University Press.

Bailey, J. M. (1995). Biological perspectives on sexual orientation. In A. R. D'Augelli & C. J. Patterson (Eds.), *Lesbian, gay, and bisexual identities over the lifespan* (pp. 102–135). Oxford: Oxford University Press.

Baker, B. (1999). The dangerous and the good? Developmentalism, progress, and public schooling. *American Educational Research Journal, 36,* 797–834.

Barber, B. K. (Ed.). (2009). *Adolescents and war: How youth deal with political violence.* Oxford: Oxford University Press.

Baron, J., & Brown, R. V. (Eds.). (1991). *Teaching decision making to adolescents.* Hillsdale, NJ: Lawrence Erlbaum.

Barrouillet, P., Markovits, H., & Quinn, S. (2001). Developmental and content effects in reasoning with causal conditionals. *Journal of Experimental Child Psychology, 81,* 235–248.

Basseches, M. (1980). Dialectical schemata: A framework for the empirical study of the development of dialectical thinking. *Human Development, 23,* 400–421.

Basseches, M. (1984). *Dialectical thinking and adult development.* Norwood, NJ: Ablex.

Baxter Magolda, M. B. (1992). *Knowing and reasoning in college: Gender-related patterns in students' intellectual development.* San Francisco, CA: Jossey-Bass.

Baxter Magolda, M. B. (2002). Epistemological reflection: The evolution of epistemological assumptions from age 18 to 30. In B. K. Hofer & P. R. Pintrich (Eds.), *Personal epistemology: The psychology of beliefs about knowledge and knowing* (pp. 89–102). Mahwah, NJ: Lawrence Erlbaum.

Beckett, S. (1954). *Waiting for Godot.* New York: Grove Press.

Belenky, M., Clinchy, B., Goldberger, N. R., & Tarule, J. (1986). *Women's ways of knowing: The development of self, mind, and voice.* New York: Basic Books.

Bem, D. J. (1996). Exotic becomes erotic: A developmental theory of sexual orientation. *Psychological Review, 103,* 320–335.

Bem, D. J. (1998). Is EBE theory supported by the evidence? Is it androcentric? A reply to Peplau et al. (1998). *Psychological Review, 105,* 395–398.

Bem, D. J. (2001). Exotic becomes erotic: Integrating biological and experiential antecedents of sexual orientation. In A. R. D'Augelli & C. J. Patterson (Eds.), *Lesbian, gay, and bisexual identities and youth: Psychological perspectives* (pp. 52–68). New York: Oxford University Press.

Berg, C. A. (2005). Commentary: Lessons from a life-span perspective to adolescent decision making. In J. E. Jacobs & P. A. Klaczynski (Eds.), *The development of judgment and decision making in children and adolescents* (pp. 241–249). Mahwah, NJ: Lawrence Erlbaum.

Bergman, R. (2002). Why be moral? A conceptual model from developmental psychology. *Human Development, 45*, 104–124.

Bergman, R. (2004). Identity as motivation: Toward a theory of the moral self. In D. K. Lapsley & D. Narvaez (Eds.), *Moral development, self, and identity* (pp. 21–46). Mahwah, NJ: Lawrence Erlbaum.

Berlin, I. (1969). *Four essays on liberty*. Oxford: Oxford University Press.

Berman, A. M., Schwartz, S. J., Kurtines, W. M., & Berman, S. L. (2001). The process of exploration in identity formation: The role of style and competence. *Journal of Adolescence, 24*, 513–528.

Berzonsky, M. D. (1993). A constructivist view of identity development: People as postpositivist self-theorists. In J. Kroger (Ed.), *Discussions on ego identity* (pp. 169–203). Hillsdale, NJ: Lawrence Erlbaum.

Berzonsky, M. D. (2004). Identity processing style, self-construction, and personal epistemic assumptions: A social-cognitive perspective. *European Journal of Developmental Psychology, 1*, 303–315.

Berzonsky, M. D. (2008). Identity formation: The role of identity processing style and cognitive processes. *Personality and Individual Differences, 44*, 643–653.

Berzonsky, M. D. (in press). A social-cognitive perspective on identity construction. In S. J. Schwartz, K. Luyckx, & V. L. Vignoles (Eds.), *Handbook of identity theory and research*. New York: Springer.

Berzonsky, M. D., & Adams, G. R. (1999). Reevaluating the identity status paradigm: Still useful after 35 years. *Developmental Review, 19*, 557–590.

Berzonsky, M. D., & Ferrari, J. R. (2009). A diffuse-avoidant identity processing style: Strategic avoidance or self-confusion? *Identity, 9*, 145–158.

Berzonsky, M. D., & Luyckx, K. (2008). Identity styles, self-reflective cognition, and identity processes: A study of adaptive and maladaptive dimensions of self-analysis. *Identity, 8*, 205–219.

Berzonsky, M. D., Macek, P., & Nurmi, J.-E. (2003). Interrelationships among identity process, content, and structure: A cross-cultural investigation. *Journal of Adolescent Research, 18*, 112–130.

Beyth-Marom, R., Austin, L., Fischhoff, B., Palmgren, C., & Jacobs-Quadrel, M. (1993). Perceived consequences of risky behaviors: Adolescents and adults. *Developmental Psychology, 29*, 549–563.

Bickhard, M. H. (1995). World mirroring versus world making: There's gotta be a better way. In L. P. Steffe & J. Gale (Eds.), *Constructivism in education* (pp. 229–267). Hillsdale, NJ: Lawrence Erlbaum.

Bickhard, M. H., & Campbell, R. L. (1996). Developmental aspects of expertise: Rationality and generalization. *Journal of Experimental and Theoretical Artificial Intelligence, 8*, 399–417.

Bidell, T. R., Lee, E. M., Bouchie, N., Ward, C., & Brass, D. (1994). Developing conceptions of racism among young White adults in the context of cultural diversity coursework. *Journal of Adult Development, 1*, 185–200.

Birman, D. (1994). Acculturation and human diversity in a multicultural society. In E. J. Trickett, R. J. Watts, & D. Birman (Eds.), *Human diversity: Perspectives on people in context* (pp. 261–284). San Francisco: Jossey-Bass.

Blasi, A. (1984). Moral identity: Its role in moral functioning. In W. M. Kurtines & J. L. Gewirtz (Eds.), *Morality, moral behavior, and moral development* (pp. 128–139). New York: Wiley.

Blasi, A. (1988). Identity and the development of the self. In D. K. Lapsley & F. C. Power (Eds.), *Self, ego, and identity: Integrative approaches* (pp. 226–242). New York: Springer-Verlag.

Blasi, A. (2004). Moral functioning: Moral understanding and personality. In D. K. Lapsley & D. Narvaez (Eds.), *Moral development, self, and identity* (pp. 335–347). Mahwah, NJ: Lawrence Erlbaum.

Blasi, A., & Glodis, K. (1995). The development of identity: A critical analysis from the perspective of the self as subject. *Developmental Review, 15*, 404–433.

Blasi, A., & Hoeffel, E. C. (1974). Adolescence and formal operations. *Human Development, 17*, 344–363.

Bond, T. (2001). Building a theory of formal operational thinking: Inhelder's psychology meets Piaget's epistemology. In A. Tryphon & J. Vonèche (Eds.), *Working with Piaget: Essays in honour of Bärbel Inhelder* (pp. 65–84). Hove, UK: Psychology Press.

Boom, J. (2010). Measuring moral development: Stages as markers along a latent developmental dimension. In W. Koops, D. Brugman, T. J. Ferguson, & A. F. Sanders (Eds.), *The development and structure of conscience* (pp. 151–167). New York: Psychology Press.

Boom, J., Brugman, D., & van der Heijden, P. G. M. (2001). Hierarchical structure of moral stages assessed by a sorting task. *Child Development, 72*, 535–548.

Boom, J., Wouters, H., & Keller, M. (2007). A cross-cultural validation of stage development: A Rasch re-analysis of longitudinal socio-moral reasoning data. *Cognitive Development, 22*, 213–229.

Bos, H. M. W., Sandfort, T. G. M., de Bruyn, E. H., & Hakvoort, E. M. (2008). Same-sex attraction, social relationships, psychosocial functioning, and school performance in early adolescence. *Developmental Psychology, 44*, 59–68.

Bosma, H. A., & Kunnen, E. S. (2001). Determinants and mechanisms in ego identity development: A review and synthesis. *Developmental Review, 21,* 39–66.

Boyes, M. C., & Chandler, M. (1992). Cognitive development, epistemic doubt, and identity formation in adolescence. *Journal of Youth and Adolescence, 21,* 737–763.

Boyes, M. C., & Walker, L. J. (1988). Implications of cultural diversity for the universality claims of Kohlberg's theory of moral reasoning. *Human Development, 31,* 44–59.

Brabeck, M. M., & Shore, E. L. (2003). Gender differences in intellectual and moral development? The evidence that refutes the claim. In J. Demick & C. Andreoletti (Eds.), *Handbook of adult development* (pp. 351–368). New York: Kluwer Academic/Plenum.

Braine, M. D. S., & O'Brien, D. P. (Eds.). (1998). *Mental logic.* Mahwah, NJ: Lawrence Erlbaum.

Brems, E. (1997). Enemies or allies? Feminism and cultural relativism as dissident voices in human rights discourse. *Human Rights Quarterly, 19,* 136–164.

Brewer, M. B., & Chen, Y. (2007). Where (who) are collectives in collectivism? Toward conceptual clarification of individualism and collectivism. *Psychological Review, 114,* 133–151.

Brugman, D. (2010). Moral reasoning competence and the moral judgment-action discrepancy in young adolescents. In W. Koops, D. Brugman, T. J. Ferguson, & A. F. Sanders (Eds.), *The development and structure of conscience* (pp. 119–133). New York: Psychology Press.

Brown, J. E. (Ed.). (1994). *Preserving intellectual freedom: Fighting censorship in our schools.* Urbana, IL: National Council of Teachers of English.

Burrow, A. L., Tubman, J. G., & Montgomery, M. J. (2006). Racial identity: Toward an integrated developmental psychological perspective. *Identity, 6,* 317–339.

Busseri, M. A., Willoughby, T., Chalmers, H., & Bogaert, A. R. (2006). Same-sex attraction and successful adolescent development. *Journal of Youth and Adolescence, 35,* 563–575.

Byrnes, J. P. (1988a). Formal operations: A systematic reformulation. *Developmental Review, 8,* 1–22.

Byrnes, J. P. (1988b). What's left is closer to right: A response to Keating. *Developmental Review, 8,* 385–392.

Byrnes, J. P. (1998). *The nature and development of decision making: A self-regulation model.* Mahwah, NJ: Lawrence Erlbaum.

Byrnes, J. P. (2005). The development of self-regulated decision making. In J. E. Jacobs & P. A. Klaczynski (Eds.), *The development of judgment and decision making in children and adolescents* (pp. 5–38). Mahwah, NJ: Lawrence Erlbaum.

Callan, E., & Arena, D. (2009). Indoctrination. In H. Siegel (Ed.), *Oxford handbook of philosophy of education* (pp. 104–121). Oxford: Oxford University Press.

Campbell, R. L., & Bickhard, M. H. (1986). *Knowing levels and developmental stages*. Basel, Switzerland: Karger.

Campbell, R. L., & Christopher, J. C. (1996a). Beyond formalism and altruism: The prospects for moral personality. *Developmental Review, 16*, 108–123.

Campbell, R. L., & Christopher, J. C. (1996b). Moral development theory: A critique of its Kantian presuppositions. *Developmental Review, 16*, 1–47.

Carlo, G. (2006). Care-based and altruistically based morality. In M. Killen & J. Smetana (Eds.), *Handbook of moral development* (pp. 551–579). Mahwah, NJ: Lawrence Erlbaum.

Carlo, G., Koller, S. H., Eisenberg, N., Da Silva, M. S., & Frohlich, C. B. (1996). A cross-national study on the relations among prosocial moral reasoning, gender role orientations, and prosocial behaviors. *Developmental Psychology, 32*, 231–240.

Carpendale, J. I. (2000). Kohlberg and Piaget on stages and moral reasoning. *Developmental Review, 20*, 181–205.

Carroll, L. (1949). *Alice's adventures in wonderland*. New York: Avenel. (Original work published 1865)

Carver, P. R., Egan, S. K., & Perry, D. G. (2004). Children who question their heterosexuality. *Developmental Psychology, 40*, 43–53.

Case, R. (1998). The development of conceptual structures. In W. Damon & R. M. Lerner (Series Eds.) & D. Kuhn & R. Siegler (Vol. Eds.), *Handbook of child psychology: Vol. 2. Cognition, perception, and language* (5th ed., pp. 745–800). New York: Wiley.

Cauffman, E., & Woolard, J. (2005). Crime, competence, and culpability: Adolescent judgment in the justice system. In J. E. Jacobs & P. A. Klaczynski (Eds.), *The development of judgment and decision making in children and adolescents* (pp. 279–301). Mahwah, NJ: Lawrence Erlbaum.

Cederblom, J. (1989). Willingness to reason and the identification of the self. In E. P. Maimon, B. F. Nodine, & F. W. O'Connor (Eds.), *Thinking, reasoning, and writing* (pp. 147–159). White Plains, NY: Longman.

Chandler, M. J. (1987). The Othello effect: Essay on the emergence and eclipse of skeptical doubt. *Human Development, 30*, 137–159.

Chandler, M. (1997). Stumping for progress in a post-modern world. In E. Amsel & K. A. Renninger (Eds.), *Change and development: Issues of theory, method, and application* (pp. 1–26). Mahwah, NJ: Lawrence Erlbaum.

Chandler, M., Boyes, M., & Ball, L. (1990). Relativism and stations of epistemic doubt. *Journal of Experimental Child Psychology, 50*, 370–395.

Chandler, M. J., Hallett, D., & Sokol, B. W. (2002). Competing claims about competing knowledge claims. In B. K. Hofer & P. R. Pintrich (Eds.), *Personal epistemology: The psychology of beliefs about knowledge and knowing* (pp. 145–168). Mahwah, NJ: Lawrence Erlbaum.

Chandler, M. J., Lalonde, C. E., Sokol, B. W., & Hallett, D. (2003). Personal persistence, identity development, and suicide. *Monographs of the Society for Research in Child Development, 68,* Serial No. 273.

Chandler, M. J., & Proulx, T. (2010). Stalking young persons' changing beliefs about belief. In L. D. Bendixen & F. C. Feucht (Eds.), *Personal epistemology in the classroom: Theory, research, and implications for practice* (pp. 197–219). New York: Cambridge University Press.

Chen, Z., Sanchez, R. P., & Campbell, T. (1997). From beyond to within their grasp: The rudiments of analogical problem solving in 10- and 13-month-olds. *Developmental Psychology, 33,* 790–801.

Chiari, G., & Nuzzo, M. L. (1996). Psychological constructivisms: A metatheoretical differentiation. *Journal of Constructivist Psychology, 9,* 163–184.

Chiari, G., & Nuzzo, M. L. (2010). *Constructivist psychotherapy: A narrative hermeneutic approach.* New York: Routledge.

Chinn, C. A., & Anderson, R. C. (1998). The structure of discussions that promote reasoning. *Teachers College Record, 100,* 315–368.

Chomsky, N. (1989). *Necessary illusions: Thought control in democratic societies.* Boston: South End Press.

Clark, S. (1997). Representing native identity: The Trail of Tears and the Cherokee Heritage Center in Oklahoma. *Cultural Survival Quarterly, 21*(1), 36–40.

Clinchy, B. M. (2002). Revisiting *Women's ways of knowing.* In B. K. Hofer & P. R. Pintrich (Eds.), *Personal epistemology: The psychology of beliefs about knowledge and knowing* (pp. 63–87). Mahwah, NJ: Lawrence Erlbaum.

Cohen, D. H. (2001). Evaluating arguments and making meta-arguments. *Informal Logic, 21,* 73–84.

Cohen, E. G. (1994). Restructuring the classroom: Conditions for productive small groups. *Review of Educational Research, 64,* 1–35.

Cohler, B. J., & Hammack, P. L. (2007). The psychological world of the gay teenager: Social change, narrative, and "normality." *Journal of Youth and Adolescence, 36,* 47–59.

Colby, A., & Damon, W. (1992). *Some do care: Contemporary lives of moral commitment.* New York: Free Press.

Commons, M. L., & Richards, F. A. (2003). Four postformal stages. In J. Demick & C. Andreoletti (Eds.), *Handbook of adult development* (pp. 199–219). New York: Kluwer Academic/Plenum.

Commons, M. L., Richards, F. A., & Armon, C. (Eds.). (1984). *Beyond formal operations: Late adolescent and adult cognitive development.* New York: Praeger.

Conry-Murray, C. (2009). Adolescent and adult reasoning about gender roles and fairness in Benin, West Africa. *Cognitive Development, 24,* 207–219.

Côté, J. E. (1996). Identity: A multidimensional analysis. In G. R. Adams, R. Montemayor, & T. P. Gullotta (Eds.), *Psychosocial development during adolescence: Progress in developmental contextualism* (pp. 130–180). Thousand Oaks, CA: Sage.

Côté, J. E. (2006). Identity studies: How close are we to developing a social science of identity? An appraisal of the field. *Identity, 6,* 3–25.

Côté, J. E. (2009). Identity formation and self-development in adolescence. In R. M. Lerner & L. Steinberg (Eds.), *Handbook of adolescent psychology* (3rd ed., Vol. 1, pp. 266–304). Hoboken, NJ: Wiley.

Côté, J. E., & Levine, C. G. (2002). *Identity formation, agency, and culture: A social psychological synthesis.* Mahwah, NJ: Lawrence Erlbaum.

Craig, A. P. (1997). Postmodern pluralism and our selves. *Theory and Psychology, 7,* 505–527.

Crocetti, E., Rubini, M., Luyckx, K., & Meeus, W. (2008). Identity formation in early and middle adolescents from various ethnic groups: From three dimensions to five statuses. *Journal of Youth and Adolescence, 37,* 983–996.

Crone, E. A., & Westenberg, P. M. (2009). A brain-based account of developmental changes in social decision making. In M. de Haan & M. R. Gunnar (Eds.), *Handbook of developmental social neuroscience* (pp. 378–396). New York: Guilford.

Cropper, D. A., Meck, D. S., & Ash, M. J. (1977). The relation between formal operations and a possible fifth stage of cognitive development. *Developmental Psychology, 13,* 517–518.

Cross, S. E., & Madson, L. (1997). Models of the self: Self-construals and gender. *Psychological Bulletin, 122,* 5–37.

Cushman, F., Young, L., & Hauser, M. (2006). The role of conscious reasoning and intuition in moral judgment: Testing three principles of harm. *Psychological Science, 17,* 1082–1089.

Daiute, C. (2010). *Human development and political violence.* New York: Cambridge University Press.

Daniel, D. B., & Klaczynski, P. A. (2006). Developmental and individual differences in conditional reasoning: Effects of logic instructions and alternative antecedents. *Child Development, 77,* 339–354.

D'Augelli, A. R. (1994). Identity development and sexual orientation: Toward a model of lesbian, gay, and bisexual development. In E. J. Trickett, R. J. Watts, & D. Birman (Eds.), *Human diversity: Perspectives on people in context* (pp. 312–333). San Francisco: Jossey-Bass.

Dawson, T. L. (2002). New tools, new insights: Kohlberg's moral judgement stages revisited. *International Journal of Behavioral Development, 26,* 154–166.

Dawson-Tunik, T. L. (2004). "A good education is …": The development of evaluative thought across the life span. *Genetic, Social, and General Psychology Monographs, 130,* 4–112.

Day, J. M., & Tappan, M. B. (1996). The narrative approach to moral development: From the epistemic subject to dialogical selves. *Human Development, 39*, 67–82.

De Fuccio, M., Kuhn, D., Udell, W., & Callender, K. (2009). Developing argument skills in severely disadvantaged adolescent males in a residential correctional setting. *Applied Developmental Science, 13*, 30–41.

De Lisi, R., & Golbeck, S. L. (1999). Implications of Piagetian theory for peer learning. In A. M. O'Donnell & A. King (Eds.), *Cognitive perspectives of peer learning* (pp. 3–37). Mahwah, NJ: Lawrence Erlbaum.

DeLoache, J. S., Miller, K. F., & Pierroutsakos, S. L. (1998). Reasoning and problem solving. In W. Damon & R. M. Lerner (Series Eds.) & D. Kuhn & R. Siegler (Vol. Eds.), *Handbook of child psychology: Vol. 2. Cognition, perception, and language* (5th ed., pp. 801–850). New York: Wiley.

Demetriou, A., Christou, C., Spanoudis, G., & Platsidou, M. (2002). The development of mental processing: Efficiency, working memory, and thinking. *Monographs of the Society for Research in Child Development, 67*, Serial No. 268.

De Neys, W., & Everaerts, D. (2008). Developmental trends in everyday conditional reasoning: The retrieval and inhibition interplay. *Journal of Experimental Child Psychology, 100*, 252–263.

Dewey, J. (1997a). *Democracy and education: An introduction to the philosophy of education.* New York: Free Press. (Original work published 1916)

Dewey, J. (1997b). *How we think.* Mineola, NY: Dover. (Original work published 1910)

De Wolff, M. S., & Brugman, D. (2010). Moral atmosphere and moral behaviour: A study into the role of adolescents' perception of moral atmosphere for antisocial behaviour. In W. Koops, D. Brugman, T. J. Ferguson, & A. F. Sanders (Eds.), *The development and structure of conscience* (pp. 135–150). New York: Psychology Press.

Diamond, L. M. (2000). Sexual identity, attractions, and behavior among young sexual-minority women over a 2-year period. *Developmental Psychology, 36*, 241–250.

Diamond, L. M. (2008). Female bisexuality from adolescence to adulthood: Results from a 10-year longitudinal study. *Developmental Psychology, 44*, 5–14.

Dimant, R. J., & Bearison, D. J. (1991). Development of formal reasoning during successive peer interactions. *Developmental Psychology, 27*, 277–284.

Doherty, M. J. (2009). *Theory of mind: How children understand others' thoughts and feelings.* New York: Psychology Press.

Dominus, S. (2008, December 28). The color of love. *New York Times Magazine*, p. 21.

Doyle, A. C. (2000). The crooked man. In *The memoirs of Sherlock Holmes.* Oxford: Oxford University Press. (Original work published 1893)

Dreyer, P. H. (1994). Designing curricular identity interventions for secondary schools. In S. L. Archer (Ed.), *Interventions for adolescent identity development* (pp. 121–140). Thousand Oaks, CA: Sage.

Dunkle, M. E. (1993). The development of students' understanding of equal access. *Journal of Law and Education, 22,* 283–300.

Efklides, A., Demetriou, A., & Metallidou, Y. (1994). The structure and development of propositional reasoning ability: Cognitive and metacognitive aspects. In A. Demetriou & A. Efklides (Eds.), *Intelligence, mind, and reasoning: Structure and development* (pp. 151–172). Amsterdam: North-Holland.

Eisenberg, N. (1996). Caught in a narrow Kantian perception of prosocial development: Reactions to Campbell and Christopher's critique of moral development theory. *Developmental Review, 16,* 48–68.

Eisenberg, N. (2005). The development of empathy-related responding. In G. Carlo & C. P. Edwards (Eds.), *Moral motivation through the life span: Nebraska symposium on motivation* (Vol. 51, pp. 73–117). Lincoln: University of Nebraska Press.

Eisenberg, N., Carlo, G., Murphy, B., & Van Court, P. (1995). Prosocial development in late adolescence: A longitudinal study. *Child Development, 66,* 1179–1197.

Eisenberg, N., Cumberland, A., Guthrie, I. K., Murphy, B. C., & Shepard, S. A. (2005). Age changes in prosocial responding and moral reasoning in adolescence and early adulthood. *Journal of Research in Adolescence, 15,* 235–260.

Eisenberg, N., Fabes, R. A., & Spinrad, T. L. (2006). Prosocial development. In W. Damon & R. M. Lerner (Series Eds.) & N. Eisenberg (Vol. Ed.), *Handbook of child psychology: Vol. 3. Social, emotional, and personality development* (6th ed., pp. 646–718). Hoboken, NJ: Wiley.

Eisenberg, N., Guthrie, I. K., Cumberland, A., Murphy, B. C., Shepard, S. A., Zhou, Q., & Carlo, G. (2002). Prosocial development in early adulthood: A longitudinal study. *Journal of Personality and Social Psychology, 82,* 993–1006.

Eisenberg, N., Morris, A. S., McDaniel, B., & Spinrad, T. L. (2009). Moral cognitions and prosocial responding in adolescence. In R. M. Lerner & L. Steinberg (Eds.), *Handbook of adolescent psychology* (3rd ed., Vol. 1, pp. 229–265). Hoboken, NJ: Wiley.

Eisenberg, N., Zhou, Q., & Koller, S. (2001). Brazilian adolescents' prosocial moral judgment and behavior: Relations to sympathy, perspective taking, gender-role orientation, and demographic characteristics. *Child Development, 72,* 518–534.

Elkind, D. (1967). Egocentrism in adolescence. *Child Development, 38,* 1025–1034.

Epstein, R. (2010). *Teen 2.0: Saving our children and families from the torment of adolescence.* San José, CA: Quill Driver Books.

Erikson, E. H. (1963). *Childhood and society* (2nd ed.). New York: Norton. (Original work published 1950)

Erikson, E. H. (1968). *Identity: Youth and crisis.* New York: Norton.

Evans, J. St. B. T. (1989). *Bias in human reasoning.* Hillsdale, NJ: Lawrence Erlbaum.

Evans, J. St. B. T. (2002). Logic and human reasoning: An assessment of the deduction paradigm. *Psychological Bulletin, 128,* 978–996.

Evans, J. St. B. T. (2007). *Hypothetical thinking: Dual processes in reasoning and judgement.* New York: Psychology Press.

Felton, M. K. (2004). The development of discourse strategies in adolescent argumentation. *Cognitive Development, 19,* 35–52.

Fischer, K. W., & Bidell, T. R. (2006). Dynamic development of action and thought. In W. Damon & R. M. Lerner (Series Eds.) & R. M. Lerner (Vol. Ed.), *Handbook of child psychology: Vol. 1. Theoretical models of human development* (6th ed., pp. 313–399). Hoboken, NJ: Wiley.

Fischer, K. W., Stein, Z., & Heikkinen, K. (2009). Narrow assessments misrepresent development and misguide policy: Comment on Steinberg, Cauffman, Woolard, Graham, & Banich (2009). *American Psychologist, 64,* 595–600.

Fisher, C. B., Jackson, J. F., & Villarruel, F. A. (1998). The study of African American and Latin American children and youth. In W. Damon & R. M. Lerner (Series Eds.) & R. M. Lerner (Vol. Ed.), *Handbook of child psychology: Vol. 1. Theoretical models of human development* (5th ed., pp. 1145–1207). New York: Wiley.

Flavell, J. H., Green, F. L., & Flavell, E. R. (1998). The mind has a mind of its own: Developing knowledge about mental uncontrollability. *Cognitive Development, 13,* 127–138.

Floyd, F. J., & Stein, T. S. (2002). Sexual orientation identity formation among gay, lesbian, and bisexual youths: Multiple patterns of milestone experiences. *Journal of Research on Adolescence, 12,* 167–191.

Fox, R. C. (1995). Bisexual identities. In A. R. D'Augelli & C. J. Patterson (Eds.), *Lesbian, gay, and bisexual identities over the lifespan* (pp. 48–86). Oxford: Oxford University Press.

Franks, B. A. (1996). Deductive reasoning in narrative contexts: Developmental trends and reading skill effects. *Genetic, Social, and General Psychology Monographs, 122,* 75–105.

Franks, B. A. (1997). Deductive reasoning with prose passages: Effects of age, inference form, prior knowledge, and reading skill. *International Journal of Behavioral Development, 21,* 501–535.

French, S. E., Seidman, E., Allen, L., & Aber, J. L. (2006). The development of ethnic identity during adolescence. *Developmental Psychology, 42,* 1–10.

Freud, S. (1960). *The ego and the id.* New York: Norton. (Original work published 1923)

Friedrich, J. (1993). Primary error detection and minimization (PEDMIN) strategies in social cognition: A reinterpretation of confirmation bias phenomena. *Psychological Review, 100,* 298–319.

Frimer, J. A., & Walker, L. J. (2009). Reconciling the self and morality: An empirical model of moral centrality development. *Developmental Psychology, 45,* 1669–1681.

Fuchs, L. S., Fuchs, D., Hamlett, C. L., & Karns, K. (1998). High-achieving students' interactions and performance on complex mathematical tasks as a function of homogeneous and hetero-geneous pairings. *American Educational Research Journal, 35,* 227–267.

Gaddy, B. B., Hall, T. W., & Marzano, R. J. (1996). *School wars: Resolving our conflicts over religion and values.* San Francisco: Jossey-Bass.

Galotti, K. M. (2002). *Making decisions that matter: How people face impor-tant life choices.* Mahwah, NJ: Lawrence Erlbaum.

Galotti, K. M. (2005). Setting goals and making plans: How children and adolescents frame their decisions. In J. E. Jacobs & P. A. Klaczynski (Eds.), *The development of judgment and decision making in children and adolescents* (pp. 303–326). Mahwah, NJ: Lawrence Erlbaum.

Garcia, L., Hart, D., & Johnson-Ray, R. (1997). What do children and adolescents think about themselves? A developmental account of self-concept. In S. Hala (Ed.), *The development of social cognition* (pp. 365–394). Hove, UK: Psychology Press.

Gelman, R., & Williams, E. M. (1998). Enabling constraints for cogni-tive development and learning: Domain specificity and epigenesis. In W. Damon & R. M. Lerner (Series Eds.) & D. Kuhn & R. Siegler (Vol. Eds.), *Handbook of child psychology: Vol. 2. Cognition, perception, and language* (5th ed., pp. 575–630). New York: Wiley.

Gergen, K. J. (2001). *Social construction in context.* London: Sage.

Gestsdottir, S., & Lerner, R. M. (2008). Positive development in ado-lescence: The development and role of intentional self-regulation. *Human Development, 51,* 202–224.

Gibbs, J. C. (2010). *Moral development and reality: Beyond the theories of Kohlberg and Hoffman* (2nd ed.). Boston: Allyn & Bacon.

Gibbs, J. C., Basinger, K. S., Grime, R. L., & Snarey, J. R. (2007). Moral judgment development across cultures: Revisiting Kohlberg's uni-versality claims. *Developmental Review, 27,* 443–500.

Gibbs, J. C., Moshman, D., Berkowitz, M. W., Basinger, K. S., & Grime, R. L. (2009). Taking development seriously: Critique of the 2008 *JME* special issue on moral functioning. *Journal of Moral Education, 38,* 271–282.

Gilligan, C. (1982). *In a different voice: Psychological theory and women's development.* Cambridge, MA: Harvard University Press.

Good, M., Grand, M. P., Newby-Clark, I. R., & Adams, G. R. (2008). The moderating effect of identity style on the relation between ado-lescent problem behavior and quality of psychological functioning. *Identity, 8,* 221–248.

Goossens, L. (2006). The many faces of adolescent autonomy: Parent-adolescent conflict, behavioral decision-making, and emotional distancing. In S. Jackson & L. Goossens (Eds.), *Handbook of adolescent development* (pp. 135–153). New York: Psychology Press.

Graham, J., Haidt, J., & Nosek, B. A. (2009). Liberals and conservatives rely on different sets of moral foundations. *Journal of Personality and Social Psychology, 96*, 1029–1046.

Graham v. Florida. 560 U.S. ___ (2010).

Graves, J. L., Jr. (2001). *The emperor's new clothes: Biological theories of race at the millennium.* New Brunswick, NJ: Rutgers University Press.

Gray, W. M. (1990). Formal operational thought. In W. F. Overton (Ed.), *Reasoning, necessity, and logic: Developmental perspectives* (pp. 227–253). Hillsdale, NJ: Lawrence Erlbaum.

Grossman, J. M., & Charmaraman, L. (2009). Race, context, and privilege: White adolescents' explanations of racial-ethnic centrality. *Journal of Youth and Adolescence, 38*, 139–152.

Grotevant, H. D. (1987). Toward of process model of identity formation. *Journal of Adolescent Research, 2*, 203–222.

Grotevant, H. D. (1993). The integrative nature of identity: Bringing the soloists to sing in the choir. In J. Kroger (Ed.), *Discussions on ego identity* (pp. 121–146). Hillsdale, NJ: Lawrence Erlbaum.

Grotevant, H. D. (1998). Adolescent development in family contexts. In W. Damon & R. M. Lerner (Series Eds.) & N. Eisenberg (Vol. Ed.), *Handbook of child psychology: Vol. 3. Social, emotional, and personality development* (5th ed., pp. 1097–1149). New York: Wiley.

Habermas, J. (1990). *Moral consciousness and communicative action.* Cambridge, MA: MIT Press.

Habermas, T., & Bluck, S. (2000). Getting a life: The emergence of the life story in adolescence. *Psychological Bulletin, 126*, 748–769.

Haidt, J. (2001). The emotional dog and its rational tail: A social intuitionist approach to moral judgment. *Psychological Review, 108*, 814–834.

Haidt, J., & Graham, J. (2007). When morality opposes justice: Conservatives have moral intuitions that liberals may not recognize. *Social Justice Research, 20*, 98–116.

Haidt, J., Koller, S. H., & Dias, M. G. (1993). Affect, culture, and morality, or is it wrong to eat your dog? *Journal of Personality and Social Psychology, 65*, 613–628.

Halford, G. S. (1989). Reflections on 25 years of Piagetian cognitive developmental psychology, 1963–1988. *Human Development, 32*, 325–357.

Hall, G. S. (1904). *Adolescence: Its psychology and its relations to physiology, anthropology, sociology, sex, crime, religion, and education.* New York: Appleton.

Hallett, D., Want, S. C., Chandler, M. J., Koopman, L. L., Flores, J. P., & Gehrke, E. C. (2008). Identity in flux: Ethnic self-identification and school attrition in Canadian Aboriginal youth. *Journal of Applied Developmental Psychology, 29*, 62–75.

Hammack, P. L. (2005). The life course development of human sexual orientation: An integrative paradigm. *Human Development, 48*, 267–290.

Hammack, P. L. (2008). Narrative and the cultural psychology of identity. *Personality and Social Psychology Review, 12,* 222–247.

Hardy, S. A., Bhattacharjee, A., Reed, A., II, & Aquino, K. (2010). Moral identity and psychological distance: The case of adolescent parental socialization. *Journal of Adolescence, 33,* 111–123.

Hardy, S. A., & Carlo, G. (2005). Identity as a source of moral motivation. *Human Development, 48,* 232–256.

Hardy, S. A., & Carlo, G. (in press). Moral identity. In S. J. Schwartz, K. Luyckx, & V. L. Vignoles (Eds.), *Handbook of identity theory and research.* New York: Springer.

Harré, R. (1998). *The singular self: An introduction to the psychology of personhood.* London: Sage.

Harris, K. R., & Alexander, P. A. (1998). Integrated, constructivist education: Challenge and reality. *Educational Psychology Review, 10,* 115–127.

Hart, D. (1998). Can prototypes inform moral developmental theory? *Developmental Psychology, 34,* 420–423.

Hart, D. (2005). The development of moral identity. In G. Carlo & C. P. Edwards (Eds.), *Moral motivation through the life span: Nebraska symposium on motivation* (Vol. 51, pp. 165–196). Lincoln: University of Nebraska Press.

Hart, D., & Fegley, S. (1995). Prosocial behavior and caring in adolescence: Relations to self-understanding and social judgment. *Child Development, 66,* 1346–1359.

Harter, S. (2006). The self. In W. Damon & R. M. Lerner (Series Eds.) & N. Eisenberg (Vol. Ed.), *Handbook of child psychology: Vol. 3. Social, emotional, and personality development* (6th ed., pp. 505–570). Hoboken, NJ: Wiley.

Hazelwood School District v. Kuhlmeier, 484 U.S. 260 (1988).

Helms, J. E. (1994). The conceptualization of racial identity and other "racial" constructs. In E. J. Trickett, R. J. Watts, & D. Birman (Eds.), *Human diversity: Perspectives on people in context* (pp. 285–311). San Francisco: Jossey-Bass.

Helwig, C. C. (1995a). Adolescents' and young adults' conceptions of civil liberties: Freedom of speech and religion. *Child Development, 66,* 152–166.

Helwig, C. C. (1995b). Social context in social cognition: Psychological harm and civil liberties. In M. Killen & D. Hart (Eds.), *Morality in everyday life: Developmental perspectives* (pp. 166–200). Cambridge, UK: Cambridge University Press.

Helwig, C. C. (1997). The role of agent and social context in judgments of freedom of speech and religion. *Child Development, 68,* 484–495.

Helwig, C. C. (1998). Children's conceptions of fair government and freedom of speech. *Child Development, 69,* 518–531.

Helwig, C. C. (2006a). Rights, civil liberties, and democracy across cultures. In M. Killen & J. Smetana (Eds.), *Handbook of moral development* (pp. 185–210). Mahwah, NJ: Lawrence Erlbaum.

Helwig, C. C. (2006b). The development of personal autonomy throughout cultures. *Cognitive Development, 21,* 458–473.

Helwig, C. C., Arnold, M. L., Tan, D., & Boyd, D. (2003). Chinese adolescents' reasoning about democratic and authority-based decision making in peer, family, and school contexts. *Child Development, 74,* 783–800.

Helwig, C. C., Arnold, M. L., Tan, D., & Boyd, D. (2007). Mainland Chinese and Canadian adolescents' judgments and reasoning about the fairness of democratic and other forms of government. *Cognitive Development, 22,* 96–109.

Helwig, C. C., Ryerson, R., & Prencipe, A. (2008). Children's, adolescents', and adults' judgments and reasoning about different methods of teaching values. *Cognitive Development, 23,* 119–135.

Helwig, C. C., Turiel, E., & Nucci, L. P. (1996). The virtues and vices of moral development theorists. *Developmental Review, 16,* 69–107.

Helwig, C. C., & Yang, S. (in press). Toward a truly democratic civics education. In H. R. Schaffer & K. Durkin (Eds.), *Blackwell handbook of developmental psychology in practice.* Oxford: Blackwell.

Helwig, C. C., Yang, S., Tan, D., Liu, C., & Shao, T. (in press). Urban and rural Chinese adolescents' judgments and reasoning about personal and group jurisdiction. *Child Development.*

Herdt, G. (2001). Social change, sexual diversity, and tolerance for bisexuality in the United States. In A. R. D'Augelli & C. J. Patterson (Eds.), *Lesbian, gay, and bisexual identities and youth: Psychological perspectives* (pp. 267–283). New York: Oxford University Press.

Hershberger, S. L. (2001). Biological factors in the development of sexual orientation. In A. R. D'Augelli & C. J. Patterson (Eds.), *Lesbian, gay, and bisexual identities and youth: Psychological perspectives* (pp. 27–51). New York: Oxford University Press.

Hershberger, S. L., Pilkington, N. W., & D'Augelli, A. R. (1997). Predictors of suicide attempts among gay, lesbian, and bisexual youth. *Journal of Adolescent Research, 12,* 477–497.

Hine, T. (1999). *The rise and fall of the American teenager.* New York: HarperCollins.

Hitlin, S., Brown, J. S., & Elder, G. H., Jr. (2006). Racial self-categorization in adolescence: Multiracial development and social pathways. *Child Development, 77,* 1298–1308.

Hofer, B. K., & Pintrich, P. R. (1997). The development of epistemological theories: Beliefs about knowledge and knowing and their relation to learning. *Review of Educational Research, 67,* 88–140.

Hofer, B. K., & Pintrich, P. R. (Eds.). (2002). *Personal epistemology: The psychology of beliefs about knowledge and knowing.* Mahwah, NJ: Lawrence Erlbaum.

Hoffman, M. L. (2000). *Empathy and moral development: Implications for caring and justice.* New York: Cambridge University Press.

Hursthouse, R. (1999). *On virtue ethics.* New York: Oxford University Press.

Hutnik, N., & Street, R. C. (2010). Profiles of British Muslim identity: Adolescent girls in Birmingham. *Journal of Adolescence, 33,* 33–42.

Hyde, J. S. (2005). The gender similarities hypothesis. *American Psychologist, 60,* 581–592.

Inhelder, B., & Piaget, J. (1958). *The growth of logical thinking from childhood to adolescence.* New York: Basic Books.

Inhelder, B., & Piaget, J. (1964). *The early growth of logic in the child: Classification and seriation.* London: Routledge.

Iordanou, K. (2010). Developing argument skills across scientific and social domains. *Journal of Cognition and Development, 11,* 293–327.

Jacobs, J. E., & Klaczynski, P. A. (Eds.). (2005). *The development of judgment and decision making in children and adolescents.* Mahwah, NJ: Lawrence Erlbaum.

Jadack, R. A., Hyde, J. S., Moore, C. F., & Keller, M. L. (1995). Moral reasoning about sexually transmitted diseases. *Child Development, 66,* 167–177.

Jaffee, S., & Hyde, J. S. (2000). Gender differences in moral orientation: A meta-analysis. *Psychological Bulletin, 126,* 703–726.

Jagose, A. (1996). *Queer theory: An introduction.* New York: New York University Press.

James, W. (1950). *The principles of psychology.* New York: Dover. (Original work published 1890)

Juujärvi, S. (2005). Care and justice in real-life moral reasoning. *Journal of Adult Development, 12,* 199–210.

Kahn, P. H., Jr., & Lourenço, O. (1999). Reinstating modernity in social science research—or—The status of Bullwinkle in a post-postmodern era. *Human Development, 42,* 92–108.

Kahneman, D. (2003). A perspective on judgment and choice: Mapping bounded rationality. *American Psychologist, 58,* 697–720.

Kakihara, F., & Tilton-Weaver, L. (2009). Adolescents' interpretations of parental control: Differentiated by domain and types of control. *Child Development, 80,* 1722–1738.

Kalakoski, V., & Nurmi, J.-E. (1998). Identity and educational transitions: Age differences in adolescent exploration and commitment related to education, occupation, and family. *Journal of Research on Adolescence, 8,* 29–47.

Kant, I. (1959). *Foundations of the metaphysics of morals.* New York: Macmillan. (Original work published 1785)

Karmiloff-Smith, A. (1992). *Beyond modularity: A developmental perspective on cognitive science.* Cambridge, MA: MIT Press.

Keating, D. P. (1980). Thinking processes in adolescence. In J. Adelson (Ed.), *Handbook of adolescent psychology* (pp. 211–246). New York: Wiley.

Keating, D. P. (1988). Byrnes' reformulation of Piaget's formal operations: Is what's left what's right? *Developmental Review, 8,* 376–384.

Keating, D. P. (1990). Structuralism, deconstruction, reconstruction: The limits of reasoning. In W. F. Overton (Ed.), *Reasoning, necessity, and logic: Developmental perspectives* (pp. 299–319). Hillsdale, NJ: Lawrence Erlbaum.

Keating, D. P., & Sasse, D. K. (1996). Cognitive socialization in adolescence: Critical period for a critical habit of mind. In G. R. Adams, R. Montemayor, & T. P. Gullotta (Eds.), *Psychosocial development during adolescence: Progress in developmental contextualism* (pp. 232–258). Thousand Oaks, CA: Sage.

Keefer, M. W. (1996). Distinguishing practical and theoretical reasoning: A critique of Deanna Kuhn's theory of informal argument. *Informal Logic, 18*, 35–55.

Kerpelman, J. L., Pittman, J. F., & Lamke, L. K. (1997). Toward a microprocess perspective on adolescent identity development: An identity control theory approach. *Journal of Adolescent Research, 12*, 325–346.

Killen, M. (1991). Social and moral development in early childhood. In W. M. Kurtines & J. L. Gewirtz (Eds.), *Handbook of moral behavior and development* (Vol. 2, pp. 115–138). Hillsdale, NJ: Lawrence Erlbaum.

Killen, M., Margie, N. G., & Sinno, S. (2006). Morality in the context of intergroup relations. In M. Killen & J. Smetana (Eds.), *Handbook of moral development* (pp. 155–183). Mahwah, NJ: Lawrence Erlbaum.

Killen, M., & Wainryb, C. (2000). Independence and interdependence in diverse cultural contexts. In S. Harkness & C. Raeff (Eds.), *Individualism and collectivism as cultural contexts for development* (pp. 5–21). San Francisco: Jossey-Bass.

Kim, M., & Sankey, D. (2009). Towards a dynamic systems approach to moral development and moral education: A response to the *JME* special issue, September 2008. *Journal of Moral Education, 38*, 283–298.

King, P. M., & Kitchener, K. S. (1994). *Developing reflective judgment: Understanding and promoting intellectual growth and critical thinking in adolescents and adults.* San Francisco: Jossey-Bass.

King, P. M., & Kitchener, K. S. (2002). The reflective judgment model: Twenty years of research on epistemic cognition. In B. K. Hofer & P. R. Pintrich (Eds.), *Personal epistemology: The psychology of beliefs about knowledge and knowing* (pp. 37–61). Mahwah, NJ: Lawrence Erlbaum.

Kitchener, K. S. (2002). Skills, tasks, and definitions: Discrepancies in the understanding and data on the development of folk epistemology. *New Ideas in Psychology, 20*, 309–328.

Klaczynski, P. A. (1997). Bias in adolescents' everyday reasoning and its relationship with intellectual ability, personal theories, and self-serving motivation. *Developmental Psychology, 33*, 273–283.

Klaczynski, P. A. (2000). Motivated scientific reasoning biases, epistemological beliefs, and theory polarization: A two-process approach to adolescent cognition. *Child Development, 71*, 1347–1366.

Klaczynski, P. A. (2001). Analytic and heuristic processing influences on adolescent reasoning and decision-making. *Child Development, 72*, 844–861.

Klaczynski, P. A. (2004). A dual-process model of adolescent development: Implications for decision making, reasoning, and identity. In R. V. Kail (Ed.), *Advances in child development and behavior* (Vol. 31, pp. 73–123). San Diego, CA: Academic Press.

Klaczynski, P. A. (2005). Metacognition and cognitive variability: A dual-process model of decision making and its development. In J. E. Jacobs & P. A. Klaczynski (Eds.), *The development of judgment and decision making in children and adolescents* (pp. 39–76). Mahwah, NJ: Lawrence Erlbaum.

Klaczynski, P. A. (2009). Cognitive and social cognitive development: Dual-process research and theory. In J. St. B. T. Evans & K. Frankish (Eds.), *In two minds: Psychological and philosophical theories of dual processing* (pp. 265–292). Oxford: Oxford University Press.

Klaczynski, P. A., Byrnes, J. P., & Jacobs, J. E. (2001). Introduction to the special issue: The development of decision making. *Journal of Applied Development Psychology, 22*, 225–236.

Klaczynski, P. A., & Fauth, J. (1997). Developmental differences in memory-based intrusions and self-serving statistical reasoning biases. *Merrill-Palmer Quarterly, 43*, 539–566.

Klaczynski, P. A., & Gordon, D. H. (1996a). Everyday statistical reasoning during adolescence and young adulthood: Motivational, general ability, and developmental influences. *Child Development, 67*, 2873–2891.

Klaczynski, P. A., & Gordon, D. H. (1996b). Self-serving influences on adolescents' evaluations of belief-relevant evidence. *Journal of Experimental Child Psychology, 62*, 317–339.

Klaczynski, P. A., & Narasimham, G. (1998). Development of scientific reasoning biases: Cognitive versus ego-protective explanations. *Developmental Psychology, 34*, 175–187.

Klaczynski, P. A., Schuneman, M. J., & Daniel, D. B. (2004). Theories of conditional reasoning: A developmental examination of competing hypotheses. *Developmental Psychology, 40*, 559–571.

Klahr, D. (2000). *Exploring science: The cognition and development of discovery processes.* Cambridge, MA: MIT Press.

Klayman, J., & Ha, Y.-W. (1987). Confirmation, disconfirmation, and information in hypothesis testing. *Psychological Review, 94*, 211–228.

Kohlberg, L. (1970). Education for justice: A modern statement of the Platonic view. In N. F. Sizer & T. R. Sizer (Eds.), *Five lectures on moral education.* Cambridge, MA: Harvard University Press.

Kohlberg, L. (1981). *The philosophy of moral development.* San Francisco: Harper & Row.

Kohlberg, L. (1984). *The psychology of moral development.* San Francisco: Harper & Row.

Kohlberg, L., Boyd, D. R., & Levine, C. (1990). The return of Stage 6: Its principle and moral point of view. In T. E. Wren (Ed.), *The moral domain* (pp. 151–181). Cambridge, MA: MIT Press.

Koslowski, B. (1996). *Theory and evidence: The development of scientific reasoning.* Cambridge, MA: MIT Press.

Koslowski, B., Marasia, J., Chelenza, M., & Dublin, R. (2008). Information becomes evidence when an explanation can incorporate it into a causal framework. *Cognitive Development, 23,* 472–487.

Krebs, D. L., & Denton, K. (2005). Toward a more pragmatic approach to morality: A critical evaluation of Kohlberg's model. *Psychological Review, 112,* 629–649.

Krettenauer, T. (2004). Metaethical cognition and epistemic reasoning development in adolescence. *International Journal of Behavioral Development, 28,* 461–470.

Krettenauer, T. (2005). The role of epistemic cognition in adolescent identity formation: Further evidence. *Journal of Youth and Adolescence, 34,* 185–198.

Kristjánsson, K. (2009). Putting emotion into the self: A response to the 2008 *Journal of Moral Education* special issue on moral functioning. *Journal of Moral Education, 38,* 255–270.

Kroger, J. (1993). Ego identity: An overview. In J. Kroger (Ed.), *Discussions on ego identity* (pp. 1–20). Hillsdale, NJ: Lawrence Erlbaum.

Kroger, J. (1995). The differentiation of "firm" and "developmental" foreclosure identity statuses: A longitudinal study. *Journal of Adolescent Research, 10,* 317–337.

Kroger, J. (2003). What transits in an identity status transition? *Identity, 3,* 197–220.

Kroger, J., & Marcia, J. (in press). The identity statuses: Origins, meanings, and interpretations. In S. J. Schwartz, K. Luyckx, & V. L. Vignoles (Eds.), *Handbook of identity theory and research.* New York: Springer.

Kruger, A. C. (1992). The effect of peer and adult-child transactive discussions on moral reasoning. *Merrill-Palmer Quarterly, 38,* 191–211.

Kruger, A. C. (1993). Peer collaboration: Conflict, cooperation, or both? *Social Development, 2,* 165–182.

Kuhn, D. (1989). Children and adults as intuitive scientists. *Psychological Review, 96,* 674–689.

Kuhn, D. (1991). *The skills of argument.* Cambridge, UK: Cambridge University Press.

Kuhn, D. (1999). Metacognitive development. In L. Balter & C. Tamis-LeMonda (Eds.), *Child psychology: A handbook of contemporary issues* (pp. 259–286). Philadelphia: Psychology Press.

Kuhn, D. (2000). Theory of mind, metacognition, and reasoning: A life-span perspective. In P. Mitchell & K. J. Riggs (Eds.), *Children's reasoning and the mind* (pp. 301–326). Hove, UK: Psychology Press.

Kuhn, D. (2005). *Education for thinking.* Cambridge, MA: Harvard University Press.

Kuhn, D. (2006). Do cognitive changes accompany developments in the adolescent brain? *Perspectives on Psychological Science, 1,* 59–67.

Kuhn, D. (2008). Formal operations from a twenty-first century perspective. *Human Development, 51,* 48–55.

Kuhn, D. (2009). Adolescent thinking. In R. M. Lerner & L. Steinberg (Eds.), *Handbook of adolescent psychology* (3rd ed., Vol. 1, pp. 152–186). Hoboken, NJ: Wiley.

Kuhn, D., Amsel, E., & O'Loughlin, M. (1988). *The development of scientific thinking skills.* San Diego, CA: Academic Press.

Kuhn, D., Cheney, R., & Weinstock, M. (2000). The development of epistemological understanding. *Cognitive Development, 15,* 309–328.

Kuhn, D., & Franklin, S. (2006). The second decade: What develops (and how)? In W. Damon & R. M. Lerner (Series Eds.) & D. Kuhn & R. Siegler (Vol. Eds.), *Handbook of child psychology, Vol. 2: Cognition, perception, and language* (6th ed., pp. 953–993). Hoboken, NJ: Wiley.

Kuhn, D., Garcia-Mila, M., Zohar, A., & Andersen, C. (1995). Strategies of knowledge acquisition. *Monographs of the Society for Research in Child Development, 60,* Serial No. 245.

Kuhn, D., Goh, W., Iordanou, K., & Shaenfield, D. (2008). Arguing on the computer: A microgenetic study of developing argument skills in a computer-supported environment. *Child Development, 79,* 1310–1328.

Kuhn, D., Iordanou, K., Pease, M., & Wirkala, C. (2008). Beyond control of variables: What needs to develop to achieve skilled scientific thinking? *Cognitive Development, 23,* 435–451.

Kuhn, D., & Lao, J. (1998). Contemplation and conceptual change: Integrating perspectives from social and cognitive psychology. *Developmental Review, 18,* 125–154.

Kuhn, D., & Pearsall, S. (1998). Relations between metastrategic knowledge and strategic performance. *Cognitive Development, 13,* 227–247.

Kuhn, D., Shaw, V., & Felton, M. (1997). Effects of dyadic interaction on argumentive reasoning. *Cognition and Instruction, 15,* 287–315.

Kuhn, D., & Udell, W. (2003). The development of argument skills. *Child Development, 74,* 1245–1260.

Kuhn, D., & Weinstock, M. (2002). What is epistemological thinking and why does it matter? In B. K. Hofer & P. R. Pintrich (Eds.), *Personal epistemology: The psychology of beliefs about knowledge and knowing* (pp. 121–144). Mahwah, NJ: Lawrence Erlbaum.

Kunnen, E. S. (2006). Are conflicts the motor in identity change? *Identity*, *6*, 169–186.

Kunnen, E. S., & Bosma, H. A. (2003). Fischer's skill theory applied to identity development: A response to Kroger. *Identity*, *3*, 247–270.

Kunnen, E. S., Bosma, H. A., & van Geert, P. L. C. (2001). A dynamic systems approach to identity formation: Theoretical background and methodological possibilities. In J.-E. Nurmi (Ed.), *Navigating through adolescence: European perspectives* (pp. 251–278). New York: Routledge Falmer.

Lahat, A., Helwig, C. C., Yang, S., Tan, D., & Liu, C. (2009). Mainland Chinese adolescents' judgments and reasoning about self-determination and nurturance rights. *Social Development*, *18*, 690–710.

Lalonde, C. E., & Chandler, M. J. (2002). Children's understanding of interpretation. *New Ideas in Psychology*, *20*, 163–198.

Lalonde, C. E., & Chandler, M. J. (2004). Culture, selves, and time: Theories of personal persistence in Native and non-Native youth. In C. Lightfoot, C. Lalonde, & M. Chandler (Eds.), *Changing conceptions of psychological life* (pp. 207–229). Mahwah, NJ: Lawrence Erlbaum.

Langer, J. (1980). *The origins of logic: From six to twelve months.* San Francisco: Academic Press.

Langer, J. (1986). *The origins of logic: One to two years.* Orlando, FL: Academic Press.

Lapsley, D. K. (1996). *Moral psychology.* Boulder, CO: Westview.

LaVoie, J. C. (1994). Identity in adolescence: Issues of theory, structure and transition. *Journal of Adolescence*, *17*, 17–28.

Leak, G. K. (2009). An assessment of the relationship between identity development, faith development, and religious commitment. *Identity*, *9*, 201–218.

Lehrer, K. (1990). *Metamind.* Oxford: Oxford University Press.

Leiser, D. (1982). Piaget's logical formalism for formal operations: An interpretation in context. *Developmental Review*, *2*, 87–99.

Leitao, S. (2000). The potential of argument in knowledge building. *Human Development*, *43*, 332–360.

Lent, R. C., & Pipkin, G. (Eds.). (2003). *Silent no more: Voices of courage in American schools.* Portsmouth, NH: Heinemann.

Lerner, R. M., Freund, A. M., De Stefanis, I., & Habermas, T. (2001). Understanding developmental regulation in adolescence: The use of the selection, optimization, and compensation model. *Human Development*, *44*, 29–50.

Lerner, R. M., & Steinberg, L. (Eds.). (2009). *Handbook of adolescent psychology, 3rd edition.* Hoboken, NJ: Wiley.

Levesque, R. J. R. (2000). *Adolescents, sex, and the law: Preparing adolescents for responsible citizenship.* Washington, DC: American Psychological Association.

Levesque, R. J. R. (2007). *Adolescents, media, and the law: What developmental science reveals and free speech requires*. New York: Oxford University Press.

Li, J. (2006). Self in learning: Chinese adolescents' goals and sense of agency. *Child Development, 77*, 482–501.

Lipman, M. (1991). *Thinking in education*. Cambridge, UK: Cambridge University Press.

Lourenço, O. (1996). Reflections on narrative approaches to moral development. *Human Development, 39*, 83–99.

Loving v. Virginia, 388 U.S. 1 (1967).

Luciana, M. (2010). Adolescent brain development: Current themes and future directions. *Brain and Cognition, 72*, 1–5.

Luyckx, K., Goossens, L., & Soenens, B. (2006). A developmental contextual perspective on identity construction in emerging adulthood: Change dynamics in commitment formation and commitment evaluation. *Developmental Psychology, 42*, 366–380.

Luyckx, K., Goossens, L., Soenens, B., Beyers, W., & Vansteenkiste, M. (2005). Identity statuses based on 4 rather than 2 identity dimensions: Extending and refining Marcia's paradigm. *Journal of Youth and Adolescence, 34*, 605–618.

Luyckx, K., Schwartz, S. J., & Goossens, L. (in press). Personal identity in the making: A process-oriented model of identity formation and evaluation. In S. J. Schwartz, K. Luyckx, & V. L. Vignoles (Eds.), *Handbook of identity theory and research*. New York: Springer.

Lynch, M. P. (1998). *Truth in context: An essay on pluralism and objectivity*. Cambridge, MA: MIT Press.

Lysne, M., & Levy, G. D. (1997). Differences in ethnic identity in Native American adolescents as a function of school context. *Journal of Adolescent Research, 12*, 372–388.

Maalouf, A. (2001). *In the name of identity: Violence and the need to belong*. New York: Arcade.

Males, M. (2009). Does the adolescent brain make risk taking inevitable? A skeptical appraisal. *Journal of Adolescent Research, 24*, 3–20.

Males, M. A. (2010). Is jumping off the roof *always* a bad idea? A rejoinder on risk taking and the adolescent brain. *Journal of Adolescent Research, 25*, 48–63.

Mansfield, A. F., & Clinchy, B. M. (2002). Toward the integration of objectivity and subjectivity: Epistemological development from 10 to 16. *New Ideas in Psychology, 20*, 225–262.

Marcia, J. E. (1966). Development and validation of ego identity status. *Journal of Personality and Social Psychology, 3*, 551–558.

Marcia, J. E., Waterman, A. S., Matteson, D. R., Archer, S. L., & Orlofsky, J. L. (Eds.). (1993). *Ego identity: A handbook for psychosocial research*. New York: Springer-Verlag.

Markovits, H. (2006). Making conditional inferences: The interplay between knowledge and logic. In L. Smith & J. Vonèche (Eds.),

Norms in human development (pp. 237–252). New York: Cambridge University Press.

Markovits, H., & Barrouillet, P. (2002). The development of conditional reasoning: A mental model account. *Developmental Review, 22,* 5–36.

Markovits, H., & Bouffard-Bouchard, T. (1992). The belief-bias effect in reasoning: The development and activation of competence. *British Journal of Developmental Psychology, 10,* 269–284.

Markovits, H., & Nantel, G. (1989). The belief-bias effect in the production and evaluation of logical conclusions. *Memory and Cognition, 17,* 11–17.

Markovits, H., & Vachon, R. (1989). Reasoning with contrary-to-fact propositions. *Journal of Experimental Child Psychology, 47,* 398–412.

Markus, H. R., & Kitayama, S. (1991). Culture and the self: Implications for cognition, emotion, and motivation. *Psychological Review, 98,* 224–253.

Marshall, H. H. (1996). Implications of differentiating and understanding constructivist approaches. *Educational Psychologist, 31,* 235–240.

Marshall, S. K., Young, R. A., Domene, J. F., & Zaidman-Zait, A. (2008). Adolescent possible selves as jointly constructed in parent-adolescent career conversations and related activities. *Identity, 8,* 185–204.

Martin, J., Sokol, B. W., & Elfers, T. (2008). Taking and coordinating perspectives: From prereflective interactivity, through reflective intersubjectivity, to metareflective sociality. *Human Development, 51,* 294–317.

McAdams, D. (in press). Narrative identity. In S. J. Schwartz, K. Luyckx, & V. L. Vignoles (Eds.), *Handbook of identity theory and research.* New York: Springer.

McConnell, J. H. (1994). Lesbian and gay male identities as paradigms. In S. L. Archer (Ed.), *Interventions for adolescent identity development* (pp. 103–118). Thousand Oaks, CA: Sage.

McLean, K. C., Breen, A. V., & Fournier, M. A. (2010). Constructing the self in early, middle, and late adolescent boys: Narrative identity, individuation, and well-being. *Journal of Research on Adolescence, 20,* 166–187.

Meeus, W., Iedema, J., Helsen, M., & Vollebergh, W. (1999). Patterns of adolescent identity development: Review of literature and longitudinal analysis. *Developmental Review, 19,* 419–461.

Michels, T. M., Kropp, R. Y., Eyre, S. L., & Halpern-Felsher, B. L. (2005). Initiating sexual experiences: How do young adolescents make decisions regarding early sexual activity? *Journal of Research on Adolescence, 15,* 583–607.

Miller, S. A., Custer, W. L., & Nassau, G. (2000). Children's understanding of the necessity of logically necessary truths. *Cognitive Development, 15,* 383–403.

Millstein, S. G., & Halpern-Felsher, B. L. (2002). Judgments about risk and perceived invulnerability in adolescents and young adults. *Journal of Research on Adolescence, 12,* 399–422.

Mitchell, P., & Riggs, K. J. (Eds.). (2000). *Children's reasoning and the mind.* Hove, UK: Psychology Press.

Moilanen, K. L., Crockett, L. J., Raffaelli, M., & Jones, B. L. (2010). Trajectories of sexual risk from middle adolescence to early adulthood. *Journal of Research on Adolescence, 20,* 114–139.

Moors, A., & De Houwer, J. (2006). Automaticity: A theoretical and conceptual analysis. *Psychological Bulletin, 132,* 297–326.

Morris, A. K. (2000). Development of logical reasoning: Children's ability to verbally explain the nature of the distinction between logical and nonlogical forms of argument. *Developmental Psychology, 36,* 741–758.

Morsink, J. (2009). *Inherent human rights: Philosophical roots of the Universal Declaration.* Philadelphia: University of Pennsylvania Press.

Moshman, D. (1979). The stage beyond. *Worm Runner's Digest, 21,* 107–108.

Moshman, D. (1989). *Children, education, and the First Amendment: A psycholegal analysis.* Lincoln: University of Nebraska Press.

Moshman, D. (1990a). The development of metalogical understanding. In W. F. Overton (Ed.), *Reasoning, necessity, and logic: Developmental perspectives* (pp. 205–225). Hillsdale, NJ: Lawrence Erlbaum.

Moshman, D. (1990b). Rationality as a goal of education. *Educational Psychology Review, 2,* 335–364.

Moshman, D. (1993). Adolescent reasoning and adolescent rights. *Human Development, 36,* 27–40.

Moshman, D. (1994). Reason, reasons, and reasoning: A constructivist account of human rationality. *Theory and Psychology, 4,* 245–260.

Moshman, D. (1995a). Reasoning as self-constrained thinking. *Human Development, 38,* 53–64.

Moshman, D. (1995b). The construction of moral rationality. *Human Development, 38,* 265–281.

Moshman, D. (1998). Cognitive development beyond childhood. In W. Damon & R. M. Lerner (Series Eds.) & D. Kuhn & R. Siegler (Vol. Eds.), *Handbook of child psychology: Vol. 2. Cognition, perception, and language* (5th ed., pp. 947–978). New York: Wiley.

Moshman, D. (2003). Developmental change in adulthood. In J. Demick & C. Andreoletti (Eds.), *Handbook of adult development* (pp. 43–61). New York: Kluwer Academic/Plenum.

Moshman, D. (2004a). False moral identity: Self-serving denial in the maintenance of moral self-conceptions. In D. K. Lapsley & D. Narvaez (Eds.), *Moral development, self, and identity* (pp. 83–109). Mahwah, NJ: Lawrence Erlbaum.

Moshman, D. (2004b). From inference to reasoning: The construction of rationality. *Thinking and Reasoning, 10,* 221–239.

Moshman, D. (2004c). Theories of self and theories as selves: Identity in Rwanda. In C. Lightfoot, C. Lalonde, & M. Chandler (Eds.), *Changing conceptions of psychological life* (pp. 183–206). Mahwah, NJ: Lawrence Erlbaum.

Moshman, D. (2005). Advanced moral development. In W. van Haaften, T. Wren, & A. Tellings (Eds.), *Moral sensibilities and education III: The adolescent* (pp. 13–31). Bemmel, the Netherlands: Concorde.

Moshman, D. (2007). Us and them: Identity and genocide. *Identity, 7*, 115–135.

Moshman, D. (2008). Epistemic development and the perils of Pluto. In M. F. Shaughnessy, M. V. J. Veenman, & C. Kleyn-Kennedy (Eds.), *Meta-cognition: A recent review of research, theory and perspectives* (pp. 161–174). New York: Nova Science.

Moshman, D. (2009a). Adolescence. In U. Müller, J. I. M. Carpendale, & L. Smith (Eds.), *Cambridge companion to Piaget* (pp. 255–269). Cambridge, UK: Cambridge University Press.

Moshman, D. (2009b). *Liberty and learning: Academic freedom for teachers and students.* Portsmouth, NH: Heinemann.

Moshman, D. (2009c). The development of rationality. In H. Siegel (Ed.), *Oxford handbook of philosophy of education* (pp. 145–161). Oxford: Oxford University Press.

Moshman, D. (in press-a). Epistemic cognition. In R. J. R. Levesque (Ed.), *Encyclopedia of adolescence.* New York: Springer.

Moshman, D. (in press-b). Identity, genocide, and group violence. In S. J. Schwartz, K. Luyckx, & V. L. Vignoles (Eds.), *Handbook of identity theory and research.* New York: Springer.

Moshman, D., & Franks, B. A. (1986). Development of the concept of inferential validity. *Child Development, 57*, 153–165.

Moshman, D., & Geil, M. (1998). Collaborative reasoning: Evidence for collective rationality. *Thinking and Reasoning, 4*, 231–248.

Müller, U. (1999). Structure and content of formal operational thought: An interpretation in context. *Archives de Psychologie, 67*, 21–35.

Müller, U., Carpendale, J. I. M., & Smith, L. (Eds.). (2009). *The Cambridge companion to Piaget.* New York: Cambridge University Press.

Müller, U., Overton, W. F., & Reene, K. (2001). Development of conditional reasoning: A longitudinal study. *Journal of Cognition and Development, 2*, 27–49.

Mustakova-Possardt, E. (1998). Critical consciousness: An alternative pathway for positive personal and social development. *Journal of Adult Development, 5*, 13–30.

Nagel, T. (1986). *The view from nowhere.* New York: Oxford University Press.

Narvaez, D. (1998). The influence of moral schemas on the reconstruction of moral narratives in eighth graders and college students. *Journal of Educational Psychology, 90*, 13–24.

Narvaez, D. (2010). Moral complexity: The fatal attraction of truthiness and the importance of mature moral functioning. *Perspectives on Psychological Science, 5,* 163–181.

Neff, K. D., & Helwig, C. C. (2002). A constructivist approach to understanding the development of reasoning about rights and authority within cultural contexts. *Cognitive Development, 17,* 1429–1450.

Neimark, E. D. (1975). Intellectual development during adolescence. In F. D. Horowitz (Ed.), *Review of child development research* (Vol. 4, pp. 541–594). Chicago: University of Chicago Press.

Neisser, U. (2008). Self-narratives: True and false. In U. Neisser & R. Fivush (Eds.), *The remembering self: Construction and accuracy in the self-narrative* (pp. 1–18). New York: Cambridge University Press. (Original work published 1994)

Nichols, S. L., & Good, T. L. (2004). *America's teenagers—Myths and realities: Media images, schooling, and the social costs of careless indifference.* Mahwah, NJ: Lawrence Erlbaum.

Nisbett, R. E., Peng, K., Choi, I., & Norenzayan, A. (2001). Culture and systems of thought: Holistic versus analytic cognition. *Psychological Review, 108,* 291–310.

Norenzayan, A., & Heine, S. J. (2005). Psychological universals: What are they and how can we know? *Psychological Bulletin, 131,* 763–784.

Nozick, R. (1993). *The nature of rationality.* Princeton, NJ: Princeton University Press.

Nucci, L. P. (1996). Morality and the personal sphere of actions. In E. S. Reed, E. Turiel, & T. Brown (Eds.), *Values and knowledge* (pp. 41–60). Mahwah, NJ: Lawrence Erlbaum.

Nucci, L. P. (2001). *Education in the moral domain.* Cambridge, UK: Cambridge University Press.

Nucci, L. P. (2004). Reflections on the moral self construct. In D. K. Lapsley & D. Narvaez (Eds.), *Moral development, self, and identity* (pp. 111–132). Mahwah, NJ: Lawrence Erlbaum.

Nucci, L. (2009). *Nice is not enough: Facilitating moral development.* Upper Saddle River, NJ: Merrill Prentice Hall.

Nussbaum, M. (2008). In defense of universal values. In C. Wainryb, J. G. Smetana, & E. Turiel (Eds.), *Social development, social inequalities, and social justice* (pp. 209–233). New York: Lawrence Erlbaum.

Ogbu, J. U. (1993). Differences in cultural frame of reference. *International Journal of Behavioral Development, 16,* 483–506.

O'Neill, O. (2004). Kant: Rationality as practical reason. In A. R. Mele & P. Rawling (Eds.), *The Oxford handbook of rationality* (pp. 93–109). Oxford: Oxford University Press.

Ong, A. D., Fuller-Rowell, T. E., & Phinney, J. S. (2010). Measurement of ethnic identity: Recurrent and emergent issues. *Identity, 10,* 39–49.

Overton, W. F. (1990). Competence and procedures: Constraints on the development of logical reasoning. In W. F. Overton (Ed.), *Reasoning, necessity, and logic: Developmental perspectives* (pp. 1–32). Hillsdale, NJ: Lawrence Erlbaum.

Overton, W. F. (2006). Developmental psychology: Philosophy, concepts, and methodology. In W. Damon & R. M. Lerner (Series Eds.) & R. M. Lerner (Vol. Ed.), *Handbook of child psychology: Vol. 1. Theoretical models of human development* (6th ed., pp. 18–88). Hoboken, NJ: Wiley.

Oyserman, D., Coon, H. M., & Kemmelmeier, M. (2002). Rethinking individualism and collectivism: Evaluation of theoretical assumptions and meta-analyses. *Psychological Bulletin, 128*, 3–72.

Packer, G. (2002). Justice on a hill. In N. Mills & K. Brunner (Eds.), *The new killing fields: Massacre and the politics of intervention* (pp. 129–153). New York: Basic Books.

Paley, G. (1984). Introduction. In *The Shalom Seders: Three Haggadahs.* New York: Adama Books.

Pasupathi, M., Mansour, E., & Brubaker, J. R. (2007). Developing a life story: Constructing relations between self and experience in autobiographical narratives. *Human Development, 50*, 85–110.

Patterson, S. J., Sochting, I., & Marcia, J. E. (1992). The inner space and beyond: Women and identity. In G. R. Adams, T. P. Gullotta, & R. Montemayor (Eds.), *Adolescent identity formation* (pp. 9–24). Newbury Park, CA: Sage.

Paul, R. (1990). *Critical thinking.* Rohnert Park, CA: Center for Critical Thinking and Moral Critique, Sonoma State University.

Paus, T. (2009). Brain development. In R. M. Lerner & L. Steinberg (Eds.), *Handbook of adolescent psychology* (3rd ed., Vol. 1, pp. 95–115). Hoboken, NJ: Wiley.

Peng, K., & Nisbett, R. E. (1999). Culture, dialectics, and reasoning about contradiction. *American Psychologist, 54*, 741–754.

Penuel, W. R., & Wertsch, J. V. (1995). Vygotsky and identity formation: A sociocultural approach. *Educational Psychologist, 30*, 83–92.

Peplau, L. A., Garnets, L. D., Spalding, L. R., Conley, T. D., & Veniegas, R. C. (1998). A critique of Bem's "Exotic Becomes Erotic" theory of sexual orientation. *Psychological Review, 105*, 387–394.

Perry, M. J. (1997). Are human rights universal? The relativist challenge and related matters. *Human Rights Quarterly, 19*, 461–509.

Perry, W. G. (1970). *Forms of intellectual and ethical development in the college years: A scheme.* New York: Holt, Rinehart, and Winston.

Peterson, D. M., Marcia, J. E., & Carpendale, J. I. M. (2004). Identity: Does thinking make it so? In C. Lightfoot, C. Lalonde, & M. Chandler (Eds.), *Changing conceptions of psychological life* (pp. 113–126). Mahwah, NJ: Lawrence Erlbaum.

Phillips, D. C. (1997). How, why, what, when, and where: Perspectives on constructivism in psychology and education. *Issues in Education: Contributions From Educational Psychology, 3,* 151–194.

Phinney, J. S. (1996). When we talk about American ethnic groups, what do we mean? *American Psychologist, 51,* 918–927.

Phinney, J. S., & Alipuria, L. L. (1996). At the interface of cultures: Multiethnic/multiracial high school and college students. *Journal of Social Psychology, 136,* 139–158.

Phinney, J. S., Cantu, C. L., & Kurtz, D. A. (1997). Ethnic and American identity as predictors of self-esteem among African American, Latino, and White adolescents. *Journal of Youth and Adolescence, 26,* 165–185.

Phinney, J. S., & Devich-Navarro, M. (1997). Variations in bicultural identification among African American and Mexican American adolescents. *Journal of Research on Adolescence, 7,* 3–32.

Phinney, J. S., Ferguson, D. L., & Tate, J. D. (1997). Intergroup attitudes among ethnic minority adolescents: A causal model. *Child Development, 68,* 955–969.

Phinney, J. S., Jacoby, B., & Silva, C. (2007). Positive intergroup attitudes: The role of ethnic identity. *International Journal of Behavioral Development, 31,* 478–490.

Phinney, J. S., & Rosenthal, D. A. (1992). Ethnic identity in adolescence: Process, context, and outcome. In G. R. Adams, T. P. Gullotta, & R. Montemayor (Eds.), *Adolescent identity formation* (pp. 145–172). Newbury Park, CA: Sage.

Piaget, J. (1965). *The moral judgment of the child.* New York: Free Press. (Original work published 1932)

Piaget, J. (1972a). Intellectual evolution from adolescence to adulthood. *Human Development, 15,* 1–12.

Piaget, J. (1972b). *Judgment and reasoning in the child.* Totowa, NJ: Littlefield, Adams. (Original work published 1928)

Piaget, J. (1985). *The equilibration of cognitive structures.* Chicago: University of Chicago Press.

Piaget, J. (1987). *Possibility and necessity.* Minneapolis: University of Minnesota Press.

Piaget, J. (1995). *Sociological studies.* London: Routledge.

Piaget, J. (2001). *Studies in reflecting abstraction.* Philadelphia: Psychology Press.

Piaget, J. (2006). Reason. *New Ideas in Psychology, 24,* 1–29.

Piéraut-Le Bonniec, G. (1980). *The development of modal reasoning: Genesis of necessity and possibility notions.* New York: Academic Press.

Pillow, B. H. (1999). Children's understanding of inferential knowledge. *Journal of Genetic Psychology, 160,* 419–428.

Pillow, B. H. (2002). Children's and adults' evaluation of the certainty of deductive inferences, inductive inferences, and guesses. *Child Development, 73,* 779–792.

Pillow, B. H., & Anderson, K. L. (2006). Children's awareness of their own certainty and understanding of deduction and guessing. *British Journal of Developmental Psychology*, *24*, 823–849.

Pillow, B. H., Hill, V., Boyce, A., & Stein, C. (2000). Understanding inference as a source of knowledge: Children's ability to evaluate the certainty of deduction, perception, and guessing. *Developmental Psychology*, *36*, 169–179.

Pink Floyd. (1973). Brain Damage. *The dark side of the moon* [vinyl album]. Hollywood, CA: Capitol Records.

Pipkin, G., & Lent, R. C. (2002). *At the schoolhouse gate: Lessons in intellectual freedom.* Portsmouth, NH: Heinemann.

Pizarro, D. A., & Bloom, P. (2003). The intelligence of the moral intuitions: Comment on Haidt (2001). *Psychological Review*, *110*, 193–196.

Postmes, T., & Jetten, J. (Eds.). (2006). *Individuality and the group: Advances in social identity.* London: Sage.

Pratt, M. W., Skoe, E. E., & Arnold, M. L. (2004). Care reasoning development and family socialisation patterns in later adolescence: A longitudinal analysis. *International Journal of Behavioral Development*, *28*, 139–147.

Prawat, R. S. (1996). Constructivisms, modern and postmodern. *Educational Psychologist*, *31*, 215–225.

Proulx, T., & Chandler, M. J. (2009). Jekyll and Hyde and me: Age-graded differences in conceptions of self-unity. *Human Development*, *52*, 261–286.

Quadrel, M. J., Fischhoff, B., & Davis, W. (1993). Adolescent (in)vulnerability. *American Psychologist*, *48*, 102–116.

Raeff, C. (2006). Multiple and inseparable: Conceptualizing the development of independence and interdependence. *Human Development*, *49*, 96–121.

Rai, R., & Mitchell, P. (2006). Children's ability to impute inferentially based knowledge. *Child Development*, *77*, 1081–1093.

Rawls, J. (1971). *A theory of justice.* Cambridge, MA: Harvard University Press.

Rawls, J. (2001). *Justice as fairness: A restatement.* Cambridge, MA: Harvard University Press.

Reed, D. C. (2009). A multi-level model of moral functioning revisited. *Journal of Moral Education*, *38*, 299–313.

Rescher, N. (1988). *Rationality.* New York: Oxford University Press.

Rest, J. R. (1983). Morality. In J. H. Flavell & E. M. Markman (Eds.) & P. H. Mussen (Series Ed.), *Handbook of child psychology: Vol. 3. Cognitive development* (pp. 556–629). New York: Wiley.

Rest, J. R. (1984). The major components of morality. In W. M. Kurtines & J. L. Gewirtz (Eds.), *Morality, moral behavior and moral development* (pp. 24–38). New York: Wiley.

Rest, J., Narvaez, D., Bebeau, M. J., & Thoma, S. J. (1999). *Postconventional moral thinking: A neo-Kohlbergian approach.* Mahwah, NJ: Lawrence Erlbaum.

Reyna, V. F., Adam, M. B., Poirier, K. M., LeCroy, C. W., & Brainerd, C. J. (2005). Risky decision making in childhood and adolescence: A fuzzy-trace theory approach. In J. E. Jacobs & P. A. Klaczynski (Eds.), *The development of judgment and decision making in children and adolescents* (pp. 77–106). Mahwah, NJ: Lawrence Erlbaum.

Reyna, V. F., & Farley, F. (2006). Risk and rationality in adolescent decision making: Implications for theory, practice, and public policy. *Psychological Science in the Public Interest, 7*, 1–43.

Ricco, R. B. (1993). Revising the logic of operations as a relevance logic: From hypothesis testing to explanation. *Human Development, 36*, 125–146.

Ricco, R. B. (2010). Development of deductive reasoning across the lifespan. In R. M. Lerner (Ed.) and W. F. Overton (Vol. Ed.), *Handbook of lifespan development, Vol. 1: Cognition, biology, and methods across the lifespan* (pp. 391–430). Hoboken, NJ: Wiley.

Riegel, K. F. (1973). Dialectic operations: The final period of cognitive development. *Human Development, 16*, 346–370.

Rivers, I., & D'Augelli, A. R. (2001). The victimization of lesbian, gay, and bisexual youths. In A. R. D'Augelli & C. J. Patterson (Eds.), *Lesbian, gay, and bisexual identities and youth: Psychological perspectives* (pp. 199–223). New York: Oxford University Press.

Rogoff, B. (1998). Cognition as a collaborative process. In W. Damon & R. M. Lerner (Series Eds.) & D. Kuhn & R. Siegler (Vol. Eds.), *Handbook of child psychology: Vol. 2. Cognition, perception, and language* (5th ed., pp. 679–744). New York: Wiley.

Rotheram-Borus, M. J., & Wyche, K. F. (1994). Ethnic differences in identity development in the United States. In S. L. Archer (Ed.), *Interventions for adolescent identity development* (pp. 62–83). Thousand Oaks, CA: Sage.

Rovane, C. (2004). Rationality and persons. In A. R. Mele & P. Rawling (Eds.), *The Oxford handbook of rationality* (pp. 320–342). Oxford: Oxford University Press.

Ruck, M. D., Abramovitch, R., & Keating, D. P. (1998). Children's and adolescents' understanding of rights: Balancing nurturance and self-determination. *Child Development, 64*, 404–417.

Ruffman, T. (1999). Children's understanding of logical inconsistency. *Child Development, 70*, 872–886.

Russell, S. T., Clarke, T. J., & Clary, J. (2009). Are teens "post-gay"? Contemporary adolescents' sexual identity labels. *Journal of Youth and Adolescence, 38*, 884–890.

Saltzstein, H. D. (Ed.). (1997). *Culture as a context for moral development: New perspectives on the particular and the universal.* San Francisco: Jossey-Bass.

Sandel, M. J. (2009). *Justice: What's the right thing to do?* New York: Farrar, Straus, & Giroux.

Sarbin, T. R. (1997). The poetics of identity. *Theory and Psychology, 7,* 67–82.

Sarroub, L. K. (2005). *All American Yemeni girls: Being Muslim in a public school.* Philadelphia: University of Pennsylvania Press.

Savin-Williams, R. C. (1995). Lesbian, gay male, and bisexual adolescents. In A. R. D'Augelli & C. J. Patterson (Eds.), *Lesbian, gay, and bisexual identities over the lifespan* (pp. 165–189). Oxford: Oxford University Press.

Savin-Williams, R. C. (1998). The disclosure to families of same-sex attractions by lesbian, gay, and bisexual youths. *Journal of Research on Adolescence, 8,* 49–68.

Savin-Williams, R. C. (2005). *The new gay teenager.* Cambridge, MA: Harvard University Press.

Schachter, E. P. (2002). Identity constraints: The perceived structural requirements of a "good" identity. *Human Development, 45,* 416–433.

Schachter, E. P., & Ventura, J. J. (2008). Identity agents: Parents as active and reflective participants in their children's identity formation. *Journal of Research on Adolescence, 18,* 449–476.

Schauble, L. (1996). The development of scientific reasoning in knowledge-rich contexts. *Developmental Psychology, 32,* 102–119.

Scheffler, I. (1997). Moral education and the democratic ideal. *Inquiry: Critical Thinking Across the Disciplines, 16,* 27–34.

Schneider, M. S. (2001). Toward a reconceptualization of the coming-out process for adolescent females. In A. R. D'Augelli & C. J. Patterson (Eds.), *Lesbian, gay, and bisexual identities and youth: Psychological perspectives* (pp. 71–96). New York: Oxford University Press.

Scholnick, E. K., & Friedman, S. L. (1993). Planning in context: Developmental and situational considerations. *International Journal of Behavioral Development, 16,* 145–167.

Scholnick, E. K., & Wing, C. S. (1995). Logic in conversation: Comparative studies of deduction in children and adults. *Cognitive Development, 10,* 319–345.

Schraw, G. (1997). On the development of adult metacognition. In C. Smith & T. Pourchot (Eds.), *Adult development: Perspectives from educational psychology* (pp. 89–106). Mahwah, NJ: Lawrence Erlbaum.

Schraw, G., & Moshman, D. (1995). Metacognitive theories. *Educational Psychology Review, 7,* 351–371.

Schwartz, S. J. (2001). The evolution of Eriksonian and neo-Eriksonian identity theory and research: A review and integration. *Identity, 1,* 7–58.

Schwartz, S. J. (2002). In search of mechanisms of change in identity development: Integrating the constructivist and discovery perspectives on identity. *Identity, 2,* 317–339.

Schwartz, S. J., Mullis, R. L., Waterman, A. S., & Dunham, R. M. (2000). Ego identity status, identity style, and personal expressiveness: An empirical investigation of three convergent constructs. *Journal of Adolescent Research, 15*, 504–521.

Schwartz, S. J., Zamboanga, B. L., Weisskirch, R. S., & Rodriguez, L. (2009). The relationships of personal and ethnic identity exploration to indices of adaptive and maladaptive psychosocial functioning. *International Journal of Behavioral Development, 33*, 131–144.

Searle, J. R. (2001). *Rationality in action.* Cambridge, MA: MIT Press.

Seaton, C. L., & Beaumont, S. L. (2008). Individual differences in identity styles predict proactive forms of positive adjustment. *Identity, 8*, 249–268.

Seaton, E. K., Scottham, K. M., & Sellers, R. M. (2006). The status model of racial identity development in African American adolescents: Evidence of structure, trajectories, and well-being. *Child Development, 77*, 1416–1426.

Selman, R. L. (1980). *The growth of interpersonal understanding: Developmental and clinical analyses.* New York: Academic Press.

Sen, A. (1999). *Development as freedom.* New York: Knopf.

Sen, A. (2002). *Rationality and freedom.* Cambridge, MA: Harvard University Press.

Sen, A. (2006). *Identity and violence: The illusion of destiny.* New York: Norton.

Sen, A. (2009). *The idea of justice.* Cambridge, MA: Harvard University Press.

Sercombe, H. (2010). The gift and the trap: Working the "teen brain" into our concept of youth. *Journal of Adolescent Research, 25*, 31–47.

Shestack, J. J. (1998). The philosophic foundations of human rights. *Human Rights Quarterly, 20*, 201–234.

Shih, M., & Sanchez, D. T. (2005). Perspectives and research on the positive and negative implications of having multiple racial identities. *Psychological Bulletin, 131*, 569–591.

Shimizu, H. (2000). Beyond individualism and sociocentrism: An ontological analysis of the opposing elements in personal experiences of Japanese adolescents. *Human Development, 43*, 195–211.

Shweder, R. A., Goodnow, J., Hatano, G., LeVine, R. A., Markus, H., & Miller, P. (2006). The cultural psychology of development: One mind, many mentalities. In W. Damon & R. M. Lerner (Series Eds.) & R. M. Lerner (Vol. Ed.), *Handbook of child psychology: Vol. 1. Theoretical models of human development* (6th ed., pp. 716–792). Hoboken, NJ: Wiley.

Shweder, R. A., Mahapatra, M., & Miller, J. G. (1987). Culture and moral development. In J. Kagan & S. Lamb (Eds.), *The emergence of morality in young children* (pp. 1–83). Chicago: University of Chicago Press.

Siegel, H. (1987). *Relativism refuted: A critique of contemporary epistemological relativism.* Dordrecht, Holland: Reidel.

Siegel, H. (1988). *Educating reason: Rationality, critical thinking, and education*. London: Routledge.

Siegel, H. (1997). *Rationality redeemed? Further dialogues on an educational ideal*. London: Routledge.

Siegel, H. (2004). Relativism. In I. Niiniluoto, M. Sintonen, & J. Wolenski (Eds.), *Handbook of epistemology* (pp. 747–780). Norwell, MA: Kluwer.

Siegler, R. S. (1996). *Emerging minds: The process of change in children's thinking*. Oxford: Oxford University Press.

Silverberg, S. B., & Gondoli, D. M. (1996). Autonomy in adolescence: A contextualized perspective. In G. R. Adams, R. Montemayor, & T. P. Gullotta (Eds.), *Psychosocial development during adolescence: Progress in developmental contextualism* (pp. 12–61). Thousand Oaks, CA: Sage.

Simoneau, M., & Markovits, H. (2003). Reasoning with premises that are not empirically true: Evidence for the role of inhibition and retrieval. *Developmental Psychology, 39*, 964–975.

Singer-Freeman, K. E. (2005). Analogical reasoning in 2-year-olds: The development of access and relational inference. *Cognitive Development, 20*, 214–234.

Singer-Freeman, K. E., & Bauer, P. J. (2008). The ABCs of analogical abilities: Evidence for formal analogical reasoning abilities in 24-month-olds. *British Journal of Developmental Psychology, 26*, 317–335.

Sinnott, J. D. (2003). Postformal thought and adult development: Living in balance. In J. Demick & C. Andreoletti (Eds.), *Handbook of adult development* (pp. 221–238). New York: Kluwer Academic/Plenum.

Slack, A. T. (1988). Female circumcision: A critical appraisal. *Human Rights Quarterly, 10*, 437–486.

Slade, C. (1995). Reflective reasoning in groups. *Informal Logic, 17*, 223–234.

Smetana, J. G. (2006). Social-cognitive domain theory: Consistencies and variations in children's moral and social judgments. In M. Killen & J. G. Smetana (Eds.), *Handbook of moral development* (pp. 119–153). Mahwah, NJ: Lawrence Erlbaum.

Smetana, J. G., & Bitz, B. (1996). Adolescents' conceptions of teachers' authority and their relations to rule violations in school. *Child Development, 67*, 1153–1172.

Smetana, J. G., & Killen, M. (2008). Moral cognition, emotions, and neuroscience: An integrative developmental view. *European Journal of Developmental Science, 2*, 324–339.

Smetana, J. G., Killen, M., & Turiel, E. (1991). Children's reasoning about interpersonal and moral conflicts. *Child Development, 62*, 629–644.

Smetana, J. G., & Villalobos, M. (2009). Social cognitive development in adolescence. In R. M. Lerner & L. Steinberg (Eds.), *Handbook of adolescent psychology* (3rd ed., Vol. 1, pp. 187–228). Hoboken, NJ: Wiley.

Smith, L. (1987). A constructivist interpretation of formal operations. *Human Development*, *30*, 341–354.

Smith, L. (1993). *Necessary knowledge: Piagetian perspectives on constructivism*. Hillsdale, NJ: Lawrence Erlbaum.

Smith, L. (2009). Piaget's developmental epistemology. In U. Müller, J. I. M. Carpendale, & L. Smith (Eds.), *The Cambridge companion to Piaget* (pp. 64–93). New York: Cambridge University Press.

Smith, L., & Vonèche, J. (Eds.). (2006). *Norms in human development*. New York: Cambridge University Press.

Snarey, J. (1985). Cross-cultural universality of social-moral development: A critical review of Kohlbergian research. *Psychological Bulletin*, *97*, 202–232.

Sodian, B., & Wimmer, H. (1987). Children's understanding of inference as a source of knowledge. *Child Development*, *58*, 424–433.

Somerville, S. C., Hadkinson, B. A., & Greenberg, C. (1979). Two levels of inferential behavior in young children. *Child Development*, *50*, 119–131.

Spear, L. (2010). *The behavioral neuroscience of adolescence*. New York: Norton.

Spelke, E. S., & Newport, E. L. (1998). Nativism, empiricism, and the development of knowledge. In W. Damon & R. M. Lerner (Series Eds.) & R. M. Lerner (Vol. Ed.), *Handbook of child psychology: Vol. 1. Theoretical models of human development* (5th ed., pp. 275–340). New York: Wiley.

Spiro, M. (1993). Is the Western conception of the self "peculiar" within the context of the world cultures? *Ethos*, *21*, 107–153.

Stams, G. J., Brugman, D., Dekovic, M., van Rosmalen, L., van der Laan, P., & Gibbs, J. C. (2006). The moral judgment of juvenile delinquents: A meta-analysis. *Journal of Abnormal Child Psychology*, *34*, 697–713.

Stanovich, K. E. (1999). *Who is rational? Studies of individual differences in reasoning*. Mahwah, NJ: Lawrence Erlbaum.

Stanovich, K. E. (2001). The rationality of educating for wisdom. *Educational Psychologist*, *36*, 247–251.

Stanovich, K. E. (2008). Higher-order preferences and the master rationality motive. *Thinking and Reasoning*, *14*, 111–127.

Stanovich, K. E., & West, R. F. (1997). Reasoning independently of prior belief and individual differences in actively open-minded thinking. *Journal of Educational Psychology*, *89*, 342–357.

Stanovich, K. E., & West, R. F. (2000). Individual differences in reasoning: Implications for the rationality debate? *Behavioral and Brain Sciences*, *23*, 645–665.

Steinberg, L. (2007). Risk taking in adolescence: New perspectives from brain and behavioral science. *Current Directions in Psychological Science*, *16*, 55–59.

Steinberg, L. (2009). Should the science of adolescent brain development inform public policy? *American Psychologist*, *64*, 739–750.

Steinberg, L. (2010). A behavioral scientist looks at the science of adolescent brain development. *Brain and Cognition, 72*, 160–164.

Steinberg, L., Cauffman, E., Woolard, J., Graham, S., & Banich, M. (2009). Are adolescents less mature than adults? Minors' access to abortion, the juvenile death penalty, and the alleged APA "flip-flop." *American Psychologist, 64*, 583–594.

Steinberg, L., Graham, S., O'Brien, L., Woolard, J., Cauffman, E., & Banich, M. (2009). Age differences in future orientation and delay discounting. *Child Development, 80*, 28–44.

Steinberg, L., & Morris, A. S. (2001). Adolescent development. *Annual Review of Psychology, 52*, 83–110.

Steinberg, L., & Scott, E. S. (2003). Less guilty by reason of adolescence: Developmental immaturity, diminished responsibility, and the juvenile death penalty. *American Psychologist, 58*, 1009–1018.

Sternberg, R. J. (2001). Why schools should teach for wisdom: The balance theory of wisdom in educational settings. *Educational Psychologist, 36*, 227–245.

Stiles, J. (2009). On genes, brains, and behavior: Why should developmental psychologists care about brain development? *Child Development Perspectives, 3*, 196–202.

Strike, K. A. (1999). Justice, caring, and universality: In defense of moral pluralism. In M. S. Katz, N. Noddings, & K. A. Strike (Eds.), *Justice and caring: The search for common ground in education*. New York: Teachers College Press.

Tappan, M. B. (1997). Language, culture, and moral development: A Vygotskian perspective. *Developmental Review, 17*, 78–100.

Tappan, M. B. (2006). Mediated moralities: Sociocultural approaches to moral development. In M. Killen & J. Smetana (Eds.), *Handbook of moral development* (pp. 351–374). Mahwah, NJ: Lawrence Erlbaum.

Tarricone, P. (in press). *A taxonomy of metacognition*. New York: Psychology Press.

Thoma, S. J. (2006). Research on the defining issues test. In M. Killen & J. Smetana (Eds.), *Handbook of moral development* (pp. 67–91). Mahwah, NJ: Lawrence Erlbaum.

Thompson, E. M., & Morgan, E. M. (2008). "Mostly straight" young women: Variations in sexual behavior and identity development. *Developmental Psychology, 44*, 15–21.

Tilley, J. J. (2000). Cultural relativism. *Human Rights Quarterly, 22*, 501–547.

Tinker v. Des Moines Independent Community School District, 393 U.S. 503 (1969).

Turiel, E. (1996). Equality and hierarchy: Conflict in values. In E. S. Reed, E. Turiel, & T. Brown (Eds.), *Values and knowledge* (pp. 75–101). Mahwah, NJ: Lawrence Erlbaum.

Turiel, E. (2002). *The culture of morality: Social development, context, and conflict*. Cambridge, UK: Cambridge University Press.

Turiel, E. (2006a). The development of morality. In W. Damon & R. M. Lerner (Series Eds.) & N. Eisenberg (Vol. Ed.), *Handbook of child psychology: Vol. 3. Social, emotional, and personality development* (6th ed., pp. 789–857). Hoboken, NJ: Wiley.

Turiel, E. (2006b). Thought, emotions, and social interactional processes in moral development. In M. Killen & J. Smetana (Eds.), *Handbook of moral development* (pp. 7–35). Mahwah, NJ: Lawrence Erlbaum.

Turiel, E. (2008). The development of children's orientations toward moral, social, and personal orders: More than a sequence in development. *Human Development*, *51*, 21–39.

Turiel, E., Hildebrandt, C., & Wainryb, C. (1991). Judging social issues. *Monographs of the Society for Research in Child Development*, *56*, Serial No. 224.

Turiel, E., Killen, M., & Helwig, C. C. (1987). Morality: Its structure, functions, and vagaries. In J. Kagan & S. Lamb (Eds.), *The emergence of morality in young children* (pp. 155–243). Chicago: University of Chicago Press.

Udell, W. (2007). Enhancing adolescent girls' argument skills in reasoning about personal and non-personal decisions. *Cognitive Development*, *22*, 341–352.

Uhlmann, E. L., Pizarro, D. A., Tannenbaum, D., & Ditto, P. H. (2009). The motivated use of moral principles. *Judgment and Decision Making*, *4*, 479–491.

Umaña-Taylor, A. J., Gonzales-Backen, M. A., & Guimond, A. B. (2009). Latino adolescents' ethnic identity: Is there a developmental progression and does growth in ethnic identity predict growth in self-esteem? *Child Development*, *80*, 391–405.

Umeh, K. (2009). *Understanding adolescent health behaviour: A decision making perspective*. New York: Cambridge University Press.

Valde, G. A. (1996). Identity closure: A fifth identity status. *Journal of Genetic Psychology*, *157*, 245–254.

Valsiner, J. (1998). The development of the concept of development: Historical and epistemological perspectives. In W. Damon & R. M. Lerner (Series Eds.) & R. M. Lerner (Vol. Ed.), *Handbook of child psychology: Vol. 1. Theoretical models of human development* (5th ed., pp. 189–232). New York: Wiley.

Van Haaften, W. (1998). Preliminaries to a logic of development. *Theory and Psychology*, *8*, 399–422.

Van Haaften, W. (2001). Ideational movements: Developmental patterns. *Developmental Review*, *21*, 67–92.

Van Hoof, A. (1999a). The identity status approach: In need of fundamental revision and qualitative change. *Developmental Review*, *19*, 622–647.

Van Hoof, A. (1999b). The identity status field re-reviewed: An update of unresolved and neglected issues with a view on some alternative approaches. *Developmental Review*, *19*, 497–556.

Van Leijenhorst, L., & Crone, E. A. (2010). Paradoxes in adolescent risk taking. In P. D. Zelazo, M. Chandler, & E. Crone (Eds.), *Developmental social cognitive neuroscience* (pp. 209–225). New York: Psychology Press.

Venet, M., & Markovits, H. (2001). Understanding uncertainty with abstract conditional premises. *Merrill-Palmer Quarterly*, *47*, 74–99.

Verkuyten, M., & Slooter, L. (2008). Muslim and non-Muslim adolescents' reasoning about freedom of speech and minority rights. *Child Development*, *79*, 514–528.

Wainryb, C. (1995). Reasoning about social conflicts in different cultures: Druze and Jewish children in Israel. *Child Development*, *66*, 390–401.

Wainryb, C. (2006). Moral development in culture: Diversity, tolerance, and justice. In M. Killen & J. Smetana (Eds.), *Handbook of moral development* (pp. 211–240). Mahwah, NJ: Lawrence Erlbaum.

Wainryb, C., Shaw, L. A., Laupa, M., & Smith, K. R. (2001). Children's, adolescents', and young adults' thinking about different types of disagreements. *Developmental Psychology*, *37*, 373–386.

Wainryb, C., Shaw, L. A., & Maianu, C. (1998). Tolerance and intolerance: Children's and adolescents' judgments of dissenting beliefs, speech, persons, and conduct. *Child Development*, *69*, 1541–1555.

Wainryb, C., & Turiel, E. (1995). Diversity in social development: Between or within cultures? In M. Killen & D. Hart (Eds.), *Morality in everyday life: Developmental perspectives* (pp. 283–313). Cambridge, UK: Cambridge University Press.

Walker, J. S. (2000). Choosing biases, using power and practicing resistance: Moral development in a world without certainty. *Human Development*, *43*, 135–156.

Walker, L. J. (1982). The sequentiality of Kohlberg's stages of moral development. *Child Development*, *53*, 1330–1336.

Walker, L. J. (1984). Sex differences in the development of moral reasoning: A critical review. *Child Development*, *55*, 677–691.

Walker, L. J. (1989). A longitudinal study of moral reasoning. *Child Development*, *60*, 157–166.

Walker, L. J. (1991). Sex differences in moral reasoning. In W. M. Kurtines & J. L. Gewirtz (Eds.), *Handbook of moral behavior and development* (Vol. 2, pp. 333–364). Hillsdale, NJ: Lawrence Erlbaum.

Walker, L. J. (2006). Gender and morality. In M. Killen & J. Smetana (Eds.), *Handbook of moral development* (pp. 93–115). Mahwah, NJ: Lawrence Erlbaum.

Walker, L. J., Gustafson, P., & Hennig, K. H. (2001). The consolidation/transition model in moral reasoning development. *Developmental Psychology*, *37*, 187–197.

Walker, L. J., & Hennig, K. H. (1997). Moral development in the broader context of personality. In S. Hala (Ed.), *The development of social cognition* (pp. 297–327). Hove, UK: Psychology Press.

Walker, L. J., Hennig, K. H., & Krettenauer, T. (2000). Parent and peer contexts for children's moral reasoning development. *Child Development*, *71*, 1033–1048.

Walker, L. J., & Pitts, R. C. (1998). Naturalistic conceptions of moral maturity. *Developmental Psychology*, *34*, 403–419.

Wark, G. R., & Krebs, D. L. (1996). Gender and dilemma differences in real-life moral judgment. *Developmental Psychology*, *32*, 220–230.

Wark, G. R., & Krebs, D. L. (1997). Sources of variation in moral judgment: Toward a model of real-life morality. *Journal of Adult Development*, *4*, 163–178.

Warren, J., Kuhn, D., & Weinstock, M. (2010). How do jurors argue with one another? *Judgment and Decision Making*, *5*, 64–71.

Wason, P. C. (1968). Reasoning about a rule. *Quarterly Journal of Experimental Psychology*, *20*, 273–281.

Wason, P. C., & Johnson-Laird, P. N. (1972). *Psychology of reasoning: Structure and content*. Cambridge, MA: Harvard University Press.

Waterman, A. S. (1992). Identity as an aspect of optimal psychological functioning. In G. R. Adams, T. P. Gullotta, & R. Montemayor (Eds.), *Adolescent identity formation* (pp. 50–72). Newbury Park, CA: Sage.

Waterman, A. S. (1999). Identity, the identity statuses, and identity status development: A contemporary statement. *Developmental Review*, *19*, 591–621.

Waterman, A. S. (2004). Finding someone to be: Studies on the role of intrinsic motivation in identity formation. *Identity*, *4*, 209–228.

Waterman, A. (in press). Eudaimonistic identity theory: Identity as self-discovery. In S. J. Schwartz, K. Luyckx, & V. L. Vignoles (Eds.), *Handbook of identity theory and research*. New York: Springer.

Weithorn, L. A., & Campbell, S. B. (1982). The competency of children and adolescents to make informed treatment decisions. *Child Development*, *53*, 1589–1598.

Wellman, H. M., Cross, D., & Watson, J. (2001). Meta-analysis of theory-of-mind development: The truth about false belief. *Child Development*, *72*, 655–684.

Wellman, H. M., & Gelman, S. A. (1998). Knowledge acquisition in foundational domains. In W. Damon & R. M. Lerner (Series Eds.) & D. Kuhn & R. Siegler (Vol. Eds.), *Handbook of child psychology: Vol. 2. Cognition, perception, and language* (5th ed., pp. 523–573). New York: Wiley.

Werner, H. (1957). The concept of development from a comparative and organismic point of view. In D. B. Harris (Ed.), *The concept of development* (pp. 125–147). Minneapolis: University of Minnesota Press.

West Virginia State Board of Education v. Barnette, 319 U.S. 624 (1943).

Whitbourne, S. K., & VanManen, K.-J. W. (1996). Age differences in and correlates of identity status from college through middle adulthood. *Journal of Adult Development, 3,* 59–70.

Whitehead, K. A., Ainsworth, A. T., Wittig, M. A., & Gadino, B. (2009). Implications of ethnic identity exploration and ethnic identity affirmation and belonging for intergroup attitudes among adolescents. *Journal of Research on Adolescence, 19,* 123–135.

Wikan, U. (2008). Honor, truth, and justice. In C. Wainryb, J. G. Smetana, & E. Turiel (Eds.), *Social development, social inequalities, and social justice* (pp. 185–208). New York: Lawrence Erlbaum.

Yates, M., & Youniss, J. (1998). Community service and political identity development in adolescence. *Journal of Social Issues, 54,* 495–512.

Youniss, J., & Damon, W. (1992). Social construction in Piaget's theory. In H. Beilin & P. B. Pufall (Eds.), *Piaget's theory: Prospects and possibilities* (pp. 267–286). Hillsdale, NJ: Lawrence Erlbaum.

Zimmerman, C. (2000). The development of scientific reasoning skills. *Developmental Review, 20,* 99–149.

Author Index

Subject Index